JAVA PAGEANT

BALADEWA AND SOEBADRA

TWO OF THE MOST FAMILIAR CHARACTERS IN THE JAVANESE *Wayang* OR MYTHOLOGICAL PLAYS.

JAVA PAGEANT

Impressions from the 1930s

H. W. PONDER

SINGAPORE
OXFORD UNIVERSITY PRESS
OXFORD NEW YORK
1988

Oxford University Press

Oxford   New York   Toronto
Delhi   Bombay   Calcutta   Madras   Karachi
Petaling Jaya   Singapore   Hong Kong   Tokyo
Nairobi   Dar es Salaam   Cape Town
Melbourne   Auckland
and associated companies in
Berlin   Ibadan

Oxford is a trade mark of Oxford University Press

Originally published as Java Pageant by
Seeley Service & Co. Ltd., London, 1934

First issued as an Oxford University Press paperback 1988

ISBN 0 19 588909 6

Printed in Malaysia by Peter Chong Printers Sdn. Bhd.
Published by Oxford University Press Pte. Ltd.,
Unit 221, Ubi Avenue 4, Singapore 1440

PREFACE

WHEN I first went to Java, a good many years ago now, I fell in love with the place as a matter of course. It was inevitable; for Java is irresistible. But love soon aroused curiosity. I wanted to know much more about this intriguing Eastern charmer than appeared on the surface. What was her history? Why was Java so different from all the adjacent islands? When? . . . Why? . . . A thousand "Why's" and "When's" . . . until I became a mere walking interrogation-mark, and, I have not the slightest doubt, an unutterable bore.

The trouble was that there seemed to be no means of satisfying that ardent curiosity. No volume of general information was to be had at any of the otherwise admirably stocked bookshops, though I certainly learned that Java was remarkable for the discovery of a human "missing link" in the shape of the Trinil skull. The guide-books, somehow, did not quite meet the case. They told me how to reserve a bedroom by telegram, a thing I never do, and warned me not to linger in the craters of volcanoes for fear of poisonous vapours, which surely no sane person would ever dream of doing. They sent me on all manner of pleasant excursions; but having directed me to Boroboedoer, they left me there in an inextricable tangle with Buddha and the Hindus. Or they hinted tantalizingly at romance behind the mock-royalty of the Sultans; and then clean forgot to tell me the story.

It seemed as though there was nothing for it but to try and manufacture the kind of book I was seeking, myself, presumptuous though it might appear on the part of an English resident. So, little by little, as time drifted on,

9

Preface

while I lived in Java in daily contact with its people, I unravelled some of the tangles that had baffled me, and discovered the answers to some of my own innumerable questions. And I have set them down here in the hope that there may be others who share my curiosity regarding this romantic and entrancingly lovely island.

CONTENTS

11

LIST OF ILLUSTRATIONS

List of Illustrations

INDIA

CEYLON

COCHIN CHINA

CHINA SE

MALAY PENIN

Equator

SUMATRA

BORN

I N D I A N

JAVA

O C E A N

Cocos or
Keeling Is.

SUMATRA

JAVA

Sunda Straits

Thousand
Is.

Bantam

Tangerang

Chillinching

Indramayu

Serang

Labuan

Pandglang

BATAVIA

Meres

Princes I.
Java Hd

BANTAM

BUITENZORG

Mt SALAK

Mt
GEDEH

Mt
CHEREMAI

Cheribon

PREANGER

TANGKUBAN
Bandung PRAHU

DIENG
Plateau

Garut

Telaga
-Bodas

Mt SINDORO

Mt
PAPANDAYAN

Boro

I N D I A N

Kambangan

O C E A N

JAVA

0   25   50   75   100   125   150   175   200 Miles.

PHILIPPINE
ISLANDS

Caroline Islands

EAST INDIES

The Moluccas

NEW GUINEA

NEW BRITAIN
ARCHIP.

AUSTRALIA

Karimon
java Is.

S E A

aparag
malon-
gan
Demak
arang
Grisee
SURABAYA
MADURA
Mt Ungaran
Salatiga
Mt MERBABU
Mojokerto
Madura
rapu
Surakarta
Mt Lawu
Boyolali
Pasuruan
Probolinggo
chandi
Klaten
Mendut
Brembanan
Mt ARJUNA
OJOCJAKARTA
Mt WILIS
Kediri
Mt KAWI
Mt BROMO
Tennger Mts.
Banjuwangi
Mt KLUT
Mt BUTAK
Mt SEMIRO

Straits
Bali

BALI

AUTHOR'S NOTE

THE author gratefully acknowledges the courtesy of the Lands, Irrigation, Public Works, and Agricultural Departments of the Government of Java, in supplying information and in permitting the use of their libraries; as well as the assistance and information given by many Dutch friends.

Acknowledgment is also made of historical and other facts derived from the following sources: Journals of the Royal Asiatic Society (H. Muller and others); *Indian Records* (Birdwood); *Indian Records* (Danvers); *Malay Papers* (Wilkinson); *Early English Adventurers in the East* (H. Wright); *Annesley of Surat and his Times* (Wright); *English Factories* (Foster); *Court Minutes of the East India Company* (Sainsbury), and its Introduction by Foster; *Cambridge Modern History* (P. E. Roberts); *History of Java* (Raffles); *Possessions Néerlandaises* (Temminck); *Life of Raffles* (Egerton); *Memoirs of a Malayan Family* (Marsden); *The Indian Archipelago* (Crawford); *Sarawak* (Baring-Gould and Bampfylde); *British Malaya* (Swettenham); *Hikayat Abdullah* (translated by T. Braddell); *Tropical Agriculture* (Nicholls and Holland); *Inter-Ocean*; and the Journals of the Indian Archipelago.

way that a confectioner ices a cake. The cloth is then placed in a large shallow vat, usually made of cement, a few inches deep, filled with dye of the required colour. After soaking, it is taken out and hung up to dry, the dye having affected only the portions unprotected by the wax.

The wax is next dissolved with acid and the cloth hung up to dry once more; the dyed part is protected with more wax, and a second pattern drawn in. Again the cloth is laid in the dye, this time of a different colour; and the process is repeated as often as the designer wishes.

In "Batik chap" the desired pattern is cut out in leather, dipped in wax, and pressed on the cloth in the manner of an office rubber stamp. It is much cheaper than the "Batik toelis," and the too great regularity of the pattern betrays it to the sophisticated native, who will have nothing to do with it if he has a few coins to buy a better one.

Some of the results of this primitive dye-work are really beautiful, and all are more or less decorative. The designs are amazing in their variety, for, naturally, no two can ever be exactly alike. The colour combinations vary in different parts of the island; those made in the districts round Soerakarta and Djokjakarta, in warm mellow browns and rich blues, are especially delightful.

All the colours are produced with forest dyes, made by old native recipes from various fruits and bark originally found in the jungle, and now cultivated in native gardens.

The sarong is worn in many ways, and has many uses. The correct conventional mode for both men and women is to wear it as a skirt, wrapped over and tucked in at the waist. The women wear with it little tight-fitting coats called "badjoes," made of gay-coloured muslin, the brighter the better, over an under-bodice of white embroidery. But when hard at work in the fields, or when washing or sweeping, they discard the upper garments and fix the sarong round the body under the armpits instead of round the waist, leaving their arms and ankles free. And very charming they look, with their smooth, shapely, golden-brown arms and shoulders—for they are blessed with perfect skins—emerging from the brightly coloured sarong sheath.

Javanese women go bareheaded, with their dark hair, always immaculately neat, brushed smoothly back and gathered into a big knot at the nape of the neck. And when they are going to market they complete their toilet with a long Batik scarf called a "kain panjang" or a "selendang," in which their purchases, and the baby if they happen to have one, can all be securely tucked, leaving the wearer free to walk at her ease, shading her head with a "payong," or wide Chinese umbrella, as flowerlike as her garments.

The Javanese countryman is quite indifferent whether he wears shirt or vest with his shorts and sarong, or goes bare to the waist. He may wear his sarong round him like a sash, or over his shoulders in a shower of rain. He may use it as a sack, at a pinch, or even as a fishing-net. But he would rather die a thousand deaths than remove his head-dress. You will never under any circumstances see him bareheaded, for this is a matter of religion to him, and very deeply ingrained. From childhood he wears a "kain kepala," or head-cloth—a square of Batik folded into a small turban—and a most attractive head-dress it is. It varies in shape and style in every village and district, and according to the rank and status of the wearer. Some have corners sticking out like a kitten's ears, giving the wearer a somewhat rakish air; others are all little ridges and valleys; and some swathed sedately across the forehead, fitting closely as a smart woman's "cloche." To twist one up in a few minutes is an easy matter to any Javanese, but I have never yet met a European who had mastered the trick of this primitive millinery.

In the towns, especially among the younger generation —more susceptible to outside influences—there is a considerable sprinkling of another mode: the flat black, brown, or crimson velvet Mohammedan cap as worn by the Malays in the Peninsula. It, too, is a most becoming head-dress, especially when compared to our Western atrocities, but less so than the true Javanese style. So it is pleasant to see that there seems little indication among the rank and file of Java's millions of a change in the accepted modes for men.

The Javanese is almost as hard to separate from his sarong as from his kain kepala—but not quite; for in this matter he is susceptible to influence to some degree. As house-boy in European households he will consent to wear white drill jacket and trousers of Western cut. But his sarong is almost always twisted up round his middle under his jacket; and the moment he is sent out in the streets on an errand, or goes off duty, down it comes, hiding his Western garb, and altering in some subtle way his personality. In a moment he is transformed from your well-trained servant, waiting on you at table, cleaning the silver, making your bed, dusting the piano, or going deftly about any other of his household duties, and becomes a different being—a member of an ancient race, a believer in witch-doctors and magic and the like; and for all his proven devotion to you, and your sincere affection for him, you feel that, after all, he is a stranger whom you can never really quite understand.

The traffic in the streets of Java's larger towns is infinite in its variety, and can be guaranteed to cure even the most bored and blasé of motorists of ennui.

Among the kaleidoscopic medley that composes it, pride of place by virtue of numbers must certainly go to the "sadoes," small two-wheeled pony carriages, drawn by diminutive locally bred ponies, whose harness glitters with nickel-plate and jingles with bells as the tiny hoofs patter along. The driver sits cross-legged, clanging an outsize bicycle bell every now and then with his bare toe, and cracking a long whip. He has a peculiar weakness for the very middle of the road, and an incurable aversion to his proper side. The ponies are well fed and groomed, and extremely lively; and small as most of them are, they are very strong, and are able, apparently with ease, to pull enormous loads in big square carts known as "grobaks."

Then there are bullock carts, with bigger loads still, creaking along quite regardless of faster traffic. And, most characteristic of all, there are "push bikes," not in tens or even hundreds, but in thousands. Every one who has been to Holland knows how popular the bicycle is with the Dutch, and they have taken the taste with them to the East, where fathers, mothers, and children in every household all make use of this handy means of locomotion.

The business man pedals solemnly to his office, with his handle-bars set rather high (so that he sits very square and upright), and his black leather portfolio strapped on in front. Stout mevrouws, active and full of energy despite their buxom proportions, bicycle to town to do their shopping; and so do the smart young mothers, with a baby, or perhaps a jolly curly-headed youngster of four or five, sitting in a "rotan" basket securely fixed above the back mudguard.

Boys and girls of all ages ride their bikes to and from school, and though the traffic regulations are very severe in other respects, nobody seems to object to these youngsters riding three or four abreast, with hands on each other's shoulders, all over the road.

The Chinese and Eurasians, and the better-off natives in the towns, have all taken equally kindly to the "bike." Every clerk and every house-boy buys one, for ten guilders down, and the rest in monthly payments. And as there are about two million bicycles in use in Java, and every owner pays one guilder a year for his licence, the tax, modest as it is, brings in quite a useful addition to the revenue.

There are plenty of motor-cars, of course—one big American firm has a large factory at Tandjong Priok, the port of Batavia—and the Javanese native, who displays considerable "abandon" as a chauffeur, contributes his full share to the fun of the streets. But, strangely enough, he very seldom comes to grief.

There are handcarts almost as big as lorries, loaded twenty feet high, pushed and dragged by teams of cheery native coolies, singing as they go. There are peddlers innumerable, and there is the swarming miscellany of other foot traffic: crowds of busy, gaily dressed people, all just as intent upon their various affairs as the crowds in London or Birmingham, but looking so infinitely more cheerful about it! There seems, in fact, to be only one item lacking in the street traffic of Java, and that is the rickshaw.

In Batavia the crowning touch is added by the "steam trams," and why they should be so called is a mystery, for they consist of an engine and a long train of carriages of different classes. They run on a double set of rails which cross from one side of the street to the other with airy inconsequence, so that you are never sure whether you are likely to be attacked in the front or in the rear; a most disturbing state of things to the stranger who is unaccustomed to meeting a train wandering across the road, puffing up unexpectedly behind him, or popping suddenly round a corner with complete disregard for its right or wrong side. And when these "trams" get up steam, and gallop off at headlong speed, with whistle screaming and bell clanging, round the wide curve at the head of the Molenvliet canal, it is calculated to strike terror into the heart of the bravest.

And all this, as I said before, only two or three days' sail from matter-of-fact "White Australia."

Some Town & Country Scenes

THE European towns of Java are very pleasant places. The Dutch have always been good architects, and the "Colonial" style they introduced into their Eastern colony at the beginning of the last century is as delightful to the eye as it is perfectly adapted to the climate.

The houses are one-storied, spacious, and dignified, with big lofty rooms and wide verandas. Many of them, happily, still remain, though some have been overtaken by the march of progress and transformed into shops, which gives a very unusual character to part of the European shopping quarter in Batavia and Soerabaya. For, as often as not, when you visit the florist, the watchmaker, the grocer, or whoever it may be, you go up a sweeping driveway through a front garden with velvet lawns and flowering shrubs, enter a high pillared porch giving on to a cool, dim hall, and transact your business where, perhaps, a prosperous early colonial and his family once sat down to dine. Others of these fine old houses have been turned into hotels and boarding-houses, and very comfortable ones they make; but happily some are still occupied by well-to-do residents, and so preserve the picture of how they must have looked a hundred years ago.

Old Batavia, the "Benedenstad," or Lower Town, as they call it, which dates from 1619, is now entirely a business centre. Built on reclaimed land, with narrow streets and many canals, it was formerly swampy and unhealthy, and at the beginning of the nineteenth century the European population moved a few miles inland and built a new residential town, which they named Welte-vreden, which means the "Well Content." The two towns are connected by about two miles of river and canal, along the side of which there runs a wide, shady road.

But nowadays, having grown into a town just as big and as busy as Old Batavia, Weltevreden has to pay the penalty of success. Only a year or two ago it was officially deprived of its delightful and well-deserved name, and rechristened by the uninspiring one of "Batavia Centrum." Yet I think and hope the old name will be a long time a-dying, and that not even the ugly official label will ever make Weltevreden less "well contented."

There is one street in this Weltevreden, known as the Pasar Baroe (New Bazaar), than which there can surely be few more entertaining shopping centres in the world, nor a better index to the commercial ingenuity of the Chinese.

It is usually the first place to be visited by strangers, who, lured by descriptions of it as the "Chinese shopping quarter," expect to find it a glorious vista of perpendicular ideographic signs something like Nankin Road at Shanghai. But to their surprise, and often disappointment, they find sober shop-fronts, quite quasi-European in character; for the Pasar Baroe is less Chinese in outward appearance than the streets of any country town in Java.

The reason is that the ingenious Chinese, born shopkeepers as they are, recognized that if they were to hold the patronage of a large, well-to-do white population in an important city, they must cater for European tastes and needs exactly as they would be catered for by Western

shops, only better, if possible. They therefore European-
ized their stores both inside and out, and the result is a
curious blend of East and West, to say nothing of a
glorious victory for the Chinese shopkeeper.

There are many fine Dutch shops on the wide avenues
adjoining the canals, and they all have their clientèle, of
course. But competition on a large scale with the wily
Chinese shopkeeper is impossible. Whatever is wanted
for household and everyday use, mijnheer and mevrouw,
and all the Eurasian population (to say nothing of the
Chinese), go to look for it in the Pasar Baroe as a matter
of course, and almost as certainly they find what they are
seeking.

It is a long, straight, narrow street, with nothing more
individual in its appearance than there is in that of Bond
Street, and it is crowded at all hours of the day. It is the
only street in Weltevreden whose pavements are as full as
those of a Western town of white (or approximately
white) people, and those people are almost as entertaining as the shops themselves. You see few natives, and
suddenly find yourself surrounded with a race several
sizes larger, in every dimension, than the one to which
you have grown so well accustomed, and they are all in
European dress.

Buxom Dutch ladies with their robust offspring jostle
amiably against you on every side; chattering Eurasians
in over-bright colours and painfully high heels push past
in twos and threes; American and Australian tourists
stand all over the pavement in excited groups, holding
up the foot traffic; cars creep slowly down the centre of
the street, looking vainly for a space in which to park;
and when office hours are over, mijnheer too joins
the throng, making his purchases with the support of
mevrouw and all the children, before settling down until

dinner-time at the "Harmonie" Club, or at one of the fine open-air concerts which are such a pleasant feature of everyday life in this town of Well Content.

Motor congestion is so great in the Pasar Baroe that it is a "One Way" street from early morning till late afternoon, and an ingenious scheme to equalize business on both sides of the road ordains that cars must all park on the left during one week, and on the right the next.

The shops in this European-looking street are nearly all Chinese, but there are a few exceptions, notably the "Bombay shops" run by Indian merchants. These alone are truly Eastern in character, and by some mysterious arrangement between them and the Chinese drapers they have a monopoly of the retail silk business, while the Chinese have a corresponding monopoly in cotton goods. If, for instance, you should ask for a yard of silk in the establishment of Mr. Tjeng Guan, or for cotton "zephyr" in that of Mr. Wassimal Assomal, either will sorrowfully wave you away, and direct you to his rival, with as pitying an expression as the one you might expect to see on the face of a greengrocer whom you had asked for a tender mutton chop.

These Bombay shops monopolize the dressmaking business, as well they may, for the Indian "tailors" who make up the beautiful silks their masters sell are faultless at their work. Ordering a frock from one of them is the pleasantest and easiest of affairs. You choose your silk, and an emaciated, most unpromising individual with a tape measure round his neck is summoned from the back regions. He takes your measurements, produces a bundle of well-thumbed fashion books, and stands by while you choose (it may be) the skirt of one, the collar of a second, and the sleeve of a third, adding a few variations of your own. He does not even note them down, but when next day you go to try on the result, all your instructions will have been carried out, the dress will fit, and be beautifully "finished"; that, at least, has been my own experience in all the years I have known Indian tailors.

The charge for making an ordinary dress is from about ten shillings upwards, and another useful characteristic of these "tailors" is their ability to copy any model to the last stitch, or with any modifications the customer may desire.

The Chinese drapers' shops are hives of activity. Their astute proprietors were quick to adopt the modern method of display in open show-cases, and these stores are in other ways as up-to-date as a London "emporium." They carry a wonderfully chosen stock, for German, Dutch, English, and American "travellers" all visit Java, and the Chinese are skilled buyers. I have actually sought London in vain for various small items of everyday usefulness to be had in the Pasar Baroe—such, for instance, as the German "Farbe-Seide," with its hundreds of tiny spools of silk in finely graduated shades, displayed in a tall glass-fronted case—an adjunct which ought to be in every draper's shop in the world. By its aid silks are matched in a moment, and "thrown in" with any material purchased, or sold separately for a penny, at great saving of feminine time and temper. Whereas in a London shop all the trouble of a separate transaction in another "department" is involved.

There are shoe stores displaying a variety of styles undreamed of elsewhere, with a presiding genius always ready to invent or carry out a new one at a moment's notice. There are furniture shops where wardrobes or sideboards, like shoes, can be made to measure. There are opticians where immaculate Chinese in Western dress, wearing enormously powerful horn-rimmed glasses, are a walking advertisement to the wares they sell; and men's outfitters where displays of "Spring Suitings," scarves, and pullovers awaken thoughts of "leave" in Europe, and of the kit that will be needed once Port Said is passed.

There are shops filled ceiling-high with mattresses, and a snowy mountain of kapok beside them to remind you of the inviting material that fills them; there are "music" stores, advertising themselves with the loudest of loud speakers, whose raucous tones mingle with the pandemonium that pours out from within the shop, where a crowd of eager purchasers are trying over a dozen different dance-records on as many gramophones, amid a welter of glittering zither-banjos, guitars, mandolines, and divers jazz-band horrors.

There are shops gay as flower gardens with silk lampshades, piled up and hanging in dozens among the electric lights, in every conceivable shape and colour; there are stationers and bookshops, where you can buy books in half a dozen languages; chemists, selling patent potions for every ill, according to Dutch, German, English, American, or native prescriptions; cutlery shops, stocked with the fine tools and blades of Solingen, at half the price you would pay in England; china and glass shops, displaying the gaudy atrocities beloved of Eurasians; and perfumers, offering every possible aid to feminine beauty.

Then there is a Japanese photographer or two, whose windows are galleries of awkward bridal couples, and a few modest native "curio-shops," tucked shyly in among their foreign confrères.

The Pasar Baroe ends abruptly in the real native "pasar" (market) from which it takes its name; and at this point you will find that the crowd all about you has changed with equal abruptness from white to brown:

A VENDOR OF SMALL FLAT PINK OR YELLOW CAKES, MADE OF RICE OR CASSAVA FLOUR, MUCH IN FAVOUR WITH THE JAVANESE. THEY ARE DRIED IN THE SUN ON ROUND TRAYS, WHICH ARE THEN PILED IN THESE HUGE TINS AND CARRIED ROUND THE KAMPONGS FOR SALE.

BIG BAMBOO FROM THE MOUNTAIN JUNGLES AWAITING

without any warning you are out of the great Sino-European shopping street and are back in familiar Java again.

Just here, beside the market, under the spreading branches of some fine old trees, is the favourite rendezvous of the town's peddlers and hawkers; and all round about, apparently abandoned by their owners, are loads of fruit, perfumery, mats, cigarettes, chairs, stationery, or the marvellous miscellany from which visitors and residents are wont to replenish their store of "oddments." They are all dumped by the roadside under the trees, while an endless stream of natives threads its way among them. Nothing is ever touched. The Eastern native may be a thief. Every one says so. And yet I cannot imagine the London street hawkers trustfully depositing their goods, say, in St. Paul's Churchyard, while they go off to get a "snack," nor, if they did, that they would find them intact when they came back again.

There are very few French people in Java, but it is to a Frenchman that Weltevreden owes a flourishing native industry, and one that is not without its amusing side: the leather-work factory in the Nordwijk.

Every now and then, coming along one of the side streets leading to the river, you will meet a small native boy dragging some such object as a large dead lizard, by a string round its neck, its claws and tail coated with mud and blood, and head sagging forlornly on its broken neck; or perhaps you will see a couple of natives carrying a big snake between them. If you follow, you will see them stop at a neat little building, on the wall of which is painted, in Malay, in letters two feet high: "All kinds of animals' skins bought here." So here the natives bring their trophies, to be turned from the unsavoury-looking specimens, for which they are paid a few pence, into the beautiful leather goods for which the factory is famous, and which are sold at high prices.

But the biggest of the towns are only incidental to the real Java after all, and if you follow the road out of any of them you will find yourself at once among the rice fields. Most of Java's huge population is engaged in cultivating the soil, and once on the country roads there is evidence of it all about you.

Pony and bullock carts, laden with rice in golden bundles, pass every few minutes; farmers laden with all kinds of vegetables and farm produce, in big twin baskets slung from bamboo shoulder yokes called "pikoelan," pass in an endless procession that is a never-ceasing reminder of the island's extraordinary productiveness.

The markets to which all this produce goes are a mirror to modern native life. The Dutch have encouraged the Javanese in every possible way to cultivate crops for sale as well as for their own family consumption, for fruits and vegetables from almost every latitude can be grown in this fortunate island, owing to its variety of climates and the wealth of fertile land that it possesses at different altitudes. These foreign crops are now planted in many parts of the regions best suited to them, instead of rice (which was formerly the natives' only crop); and thus supply the constant demand for them for European consumption, both in Java and Malaya, greatly to the profit of the native farmers and to their country at large.

The native has taken enthusiastically to the innovation, for he finds it much pleasanter to have a little money to spend, and a more varied diet, than empty pockets and an eternally unchanging menu of rice. And as his purchasing powers are correspondingly increased, the shopkeepers too are benefited, and everybody is pleased.

There are villages or small towns at very frequent

intervals along the Java roads, and a market in every one of them. And daily towards them, in a tireless stream, flow the native farmers and their families afoot, each with the bamboo carrying-pole across the shoulders, bearing the fruits of their toil to be turned into guilders; even the toddler of five or six often carries a tiny "pikoelan," for every member of the family is laden according to his or her capacity.

The markets are a blaze of colour. There is the green and gold of firm, shapely carrots, tied together in bunches of exactly matched sizes; there are piles of scarlet or yellow tomatoes, and palest green lettuce; tiny pale pink onions; celery, beans, peas, spinach, nuts of all kinds, melons, pumpkins, pineapples, bananas, mangoes, and flaring red chillies mixed with others of the most vivid green. There are cabbages, cauliflower, beetroot, cucumber, yams, taro, lobak (a white root rather like a giant radish), grindjol (a huge green pod) and glowing purple tarong (the "aubergine" of France), mandarin oranges, bunches of red and white radishes, mangosteen (some of them split open to show the pure white heart lying in its crimson bed), and ramboetan in flamboyant bunches, looking rather like red, hairy horse-chestnuts, and a hundred and one other good things; even strawberries are not missing from the list.

The vendors, each in his best sarong, spotless white shirt, and jaunty Batik head-dress, sit cross-legged and smiling on the sloping benches in the midst of their wares, looking like benevolent little Buddhas.

In every market there are meat, fish, and dried fish sections—the latter never by any means difficult to locate; and also stalls for the sale of fish-fry (not fried fish, but baby fish, just hatched), for the benefit of fish-breeders. There are small stalls or shops innumerable which sell

Batik sarongs and selendangs and kain kepala, dress materials, shoes, shirts, sandals, belts, and everything else you can think of, from hairpins and braces and electric torches, to padlocks and pencils and Primus stoves, to say nothing of coffee electrically ground while you wait. Round every one of them there is a chattering, chaffering, little group, bargaining shrewdly so as to get the very best value for every hard-earned cent.

The buyers are as interesting as the sellers and their wares. In their brilliantly coloured garments, moving softly on their bare feet, and blessed as they are with low voices and a musical language, there is none of the clatter and hubbub of the West; nothing but a sort of murmuring chatter. The Javanese never shouts. And the colours seem to merge and weave and mingle themselves into ever-changing patterns as though they were part of the transformation scene at a pantomime.

CHAPTER

Kampong Dwellers & the Peddlers

JAVA is roughly the same size as England without Wales—about fifty thousand square miles—and has a rather larger population: some forty-one million as against England's thirty-six million.

It is hard, however, for the newcomer to Java to realize how densely it is populated. There are no huge overgrown cities, and only a few large towns, and those, despite the infinite variety of their traffic, are not crowded as we know crowds in the Western world. And the people are so well distributed that in no part of the island is one oppressed with a sense of overcrowding. On the contrary, Java is one of the most quiet and restful places left in a noisy, nerve-racking, modern world.

The secret of it all is that the Javanese are an agricultural people, and are scattered here, there, and everywhere throughout the length and breadth of the country, all around and among the fertile fields and hills and valleys in which they toil so unceasingly. Wherever you go, up and down the shady main roads or the narrow by-lanes, you will see their snug little brown houses, along the roadsides or tucked away among the trees, peeping out through the thick foliage from behind their neat split-bamboo gates and fences. Down every winding pathway, in every corner, wherever there is a space between the rice fields, the vegetable gardens, the tapioca or the flower fields, or wherever it may happen to be, there you will houses, in twos and threes and little groups; "kampongs," as they are called.

Every house has its own tiny garden, gay with scarlet hibiscus or golden alamanda, or some other brilliant flowering shrub, with an extra touch of colour added by the family sarongs hanging out to dry. The Javanese adore colour, and never seem able to get enough of it. They are as neat and clean as they are ornamental, too, and the dainty little women who live in those picturesque dolls' houses sweep every speck of dirt away from their trim gardens and backyards with home-made rice-straw brooms; and, what is more, they have the enviable gift of never looking slovenly while they are doing it.

The Javanese have a passion for washing, both themselves and their garments. They are for ever to be seen busily soaping sarongs and badjoes and fat brown babies in little bamboo-fenced washing places, ingeniously cut out and deepened in convenient angles beside the bed of a running stream; or taking a bath themselves (discreetly draped in a sarong), with much soft chatter and laughter in between. There is always one or more of these "bathrooms" near every group of native houses.

The houses are built of a material known as "bilik," which is nothing more solid than split bamboo interwoven into sheets and nailed on to a timber or bamboo framework, much as Europeans use fibro-cement and similar materials. These bilik sheets, which may measure anything up to about twelve or fifteen feet square, are damped to make them pliable, and doubled over in a wide curve on bamboo crosspieces, so that one man can quite easily carry the whole side of a house, if required, from place to place. And when a native builds a house he simply lays the sheet flat on the ground and cuts out the spaces for doors and window-frames with a sharp chopper.

38

Kampong Dwellers & the Peddlers

Bilik is an invaluable material. Light as it is, it is so tough that bridges floored with it will carry heavily laden pony or bullock carts, and wear for years. It is much used in European houses for ceilings and wall linings, for which purpose it is extremely decorative, for the native knows how to weave it into patterns almost as elaborate as those in a modern knitted jumper.

It is also used with concrete or brick foundations in the building of small European bungalows, garages, and sheds. When painted over it is absolutely waterproof.

Native houses, as well as almost all European homes in Java, are roofed with native-made red or brown tiles. For the outhouses they use "kajang," a thatch made of palm fronds. There is usually a pony stable with a corduroy bamboo floor, and a sheep-pen rather like a big bird-cage, raised three or four feet from the ground, where the inmates, though uncomfortably crowded, are safe from night prowlers.

It is obvious that the womenfolk of all these scattered kampongs could not possibly be always trotting off to town, or even to the nearest village, to do their household shopping. So the shops come to them, and the everyday needs of kampong life have brought into being one of the most familiar figures on the Java roads: the "peddler."

It should be said at once that the Javanese peddler or hawker has nothing whatever in common with the street hawker of England, the sort that we try (but generally fail) to discourage by putting up such notices as "No Hawkers," or "Beware of the Dog," on the gate. "Peddler," in fact, is scarcely a fair name for these indispensable, tireless folk, who trot endless miles day after day, up and down all the highways and byways of the country, with stout bamboo pikoelan across their shoulders, heavily laden with every imaginable article that may be needed by the humble kampong people. They supply a genuine need that could not possibly be met in any other way.

So there are walking ironmongers, drapers, haberdashers, confectioners, grocers, slipper- and sandal-vendors, and vendors of mattresses, chairs, woven mats, tables, and even iron bedsteads (these last carried by two men). I would be willing to wager a considerable sum that if you sat in your car by the roadside on any well-frequented country road, and waited for an hour or two, every possible article of everyday human or domestic necessity that you could name, from a safety-pin to a kitchen table or a garden rake, would pass you by in the course of the morning.

A faint clinking of metal announces the peripatetic hardware merchant, one of the most important of all. His twin baskets are piled high with kettles and cooking-pots, saucepans and frying-pans, and all sorts of queer-shaped kitchen gadgets dear to the native housewife.

Another will have enamel goods of all kinds; another, with big twin tin boxes painted bright blue, is a baker and confectioner, for the Javanese, though a rice-eater, likes bread occasionally when he can afford it, and is extremely fond of sweet cakes.

The haberdasher is always in great demand, for women are women all the world over, and those coils of dark hair at the nape of every little nyonya's (lady's) slender neck are the source of a roaring trade in hairpins. Native women, too, are great dressmakers, and needles and pins and all such trifles find a ready sale.

Of all the wares that you might least expect to see hawked for sale in remote corners of the country-side in a tropic island is surely fresh fish. Yet in Java you will meet peddlers whose big round baskets, lined with smooth green banana leaves, reveal great shining silvery fish as big as salmon, their freshness proven by an occasional spasmodic twitch.

The explanation is that freshwater fish-breeding is an important native industry, warmly encouraged by the Dutch, both because it ensures a supply of fresh fish for European tables, and because it supplies elements deficient in the natives' rice diet.

The fish are bred in artificial ponds surrounded with mud embankments, like the rice fields, and also very often in the rice fields themselves, between the crops. Many varieties are bred, but the two most popular are the Chinese "golden carp" (the goldfish that we know best in glass bowls) and "goerame," also one of the carp family. They grow to be as big as a fair-sized salmon, and bring good prices, for they are always in demand. The goerame is the kind most eaten by Europeans.

The "fry" are caught in fine nets (or even more often in that native all-purposes garment, the sarong) four days after spawning, through an outlet made in the mud embankment. They are then transported in flat baskets, waterproofed with tar and covered over, hung from the usual shoulder-pole, to larger ponds which have been prepared for them. A load (two baskets) of the fry costs from one to two guilders.

Before the fish are put in, the ponds are drained and under-water plants beloved of the fish are planted. In addition the fish farmer carefully feeds his "flock" daily with leaves, tapioca, and water-larvæ. So lucrative a business is fish-breeding that very high rents are paid for the ponds—from a hundred and fifty to four hundred guilders a year, in addition to land tax. The farmer is taxed also on the yield of his fish pond.

When the Javanese goes a-fishing there is no nonsense

about flies or casting, or sitting drowsily in a punt with rod and line. His procedure may not be so sporting, but it is far more practical.

First he calls together his family and a few friends to help him, scoops a hole in the "bund," or mud bank, and drains his pond, which is perhaps fifty or sixty yards square, until there are only a few inches of water in the bottom. Then he dams up the outflow, and digs a channel across the pond about eight inches deep, running in the direction of the outlet. Into this all the fish, which are floundering in the mud and water all over the pond, are pushed.

Then the rest of the water is drained off, the helpers standing by the outlet to see that no fish go with the water, and the great fish lie struggling helplessly, packed in the narrow channel like giant sardines in a tin. They are lifted out like babies, plumped into baskets, and hurried off to market, gleaming and golden as they turn and twitch in their last fight for life and breath.

The peddlers of Java, with one exception, are all natives. The Chinese have "cornered" the drapery and dress-materials trade, and they too perambulate the country-side and do a brisk business among the kampong ladies. It is quite a usual sight to see one of them with his pack open on the grass by the roadside, bargaining over a badjoe-length of scarlet or yellow muslin with a couple of village belles, who have laid down beside them whatever they happened to be carrying, whether it be a baby or a bunch of ripe golden rice.

The Chinese peddler, in his "flared" black or white jacket and floppy trousers, with an old straw "boater" on his head, and his pack tied up in a sheet of tarpaulin on his shoulder, is a curious contrast to all the others on the road.

The peddlers do much, too, to make the daily round of the Europeans in the Java towns an easy one. Everything in the way of haberdashery, perfumery, stationery, cigarettes, matches, and all such small articles of every-day use are brought to your door; and if the particular one that you desire is not in stock, the obliging vendor trustfully leaves his whole shop in your care and trots off to the town to fetch what you need, even if it is only two- or three-pennyworth.

The shoemaker calls daily, and will mend your shoes, squatting on the doorstep; and the watchmaker would do as much for your watch, if you cared to let him.

Fowls, ducks, and geese, in round shallow baskets with a hole in the top, rather like crab-pots, are brought round alive, and sold to the housewife "on the hoof," the sales-man pulling the poor creatures out by the wings and prodding them all over to prove their plumpness, and inviting you to do the same. And when he has sold you one he will tie its feet together and lay it carefully in the rain gutter to "keep it cool."

There is one relatively small group of peddlers who, although they are confined chiefly to one limited area, provide such royally brilliant splashes of colour when they appear on the scene (usually in the streets of Samarang) that they certainly cannot be omitted from the Java pageant.

They come floating towards you along the wide pavements, orange and crimson and rose-coloured against a dark background of evergreen trees, their light silken draperies lifting and rippling and wavering in the drifting zephyrs created by their own movements, and it is not until they stop beside you (with an eye to business, of course) that you see that what had appeared to you to be stray members of the Russian Ballet are, after all, only sellers of the silk lampshades which are made in great numbers hereabouts.

These shades contribute not a little to the charm of domestic interiors from one end of Java to the other; for there are few rooms in European or Chinese houses in which one of them does not shed a mellow gleam after dark. They are made in every conceivable shape and shade (some of them three feet across), and are sold for a few shillings, though there is not one of them that could not easily rival the costliest productions of London or Paris. And if you happen to catch sight of a group of these peddlers in the distance, standing gossiping on the emerald-green lawn of some garden, they look like nothing so much as a clump of impossibly gigantic poppies.

There are many other jog-trotting, heavily laden figures on the roads of Java who do not "peddle" the wares they carry. Among the most familiar of them are the grass-carriers. Ponies are many in Java and land is precious, and it cannot be spared for pasture as it is in England. Happily in that generous climate grass grows fast, and not a blade is lost. It is cut from every corner where it can find room to grow—along the roadsides, on the steep banks, and on the narrow mud "bunds" between the rice fields. It is then piled into two skeleton bamboo carriers, about five feet deep and two feet square at the top, tapering slightly towards the base, and carried in the invariable Javanese way, at each end of a bamboo across the shoulders.

Watercress, too, you will see being carried in the same way from the mountain-side beds, where it is grown on water terraces in the same way as the rice, and the weight of these big loads of tightly packed, thick, wet bunches, as can be imagined, is tremendous. Yet these sturdy, indefatigable people will trot with them half the night to get them to market in the morning.

But best of all the burdens that are carried on the country roads of Java are the flowers. The Dutch, as all the world knows, are the great horticulturists of Europe, and in Java they have a natural forcing-house ready to their hand, where every lovely bloom that we cultivate with such tenderness in colder climates has only to be planted and watered to grow as heartily as an English dandelion. So seeds of every kind were brought to the island, and on the high cool plateaux, where it is always summer (the kind of summer that in northern Europe we dream of, and never quite cease to hope for, but so very seldom see), they have encouraged the natives to grow flowers for market.

There are not mere gardens, but fields, of flowers, acres of deep crimson, rose pink, and creamy gerberas, tall and gallant and gay on their lusty stems, as they never grow elsewhere, magically changing from plump round buds into wide-open blooms almost while you look at them. Pink, blue, and mauve asters spread out in a wide square edged with green, shade themselves into a vague lovely pattern like a giant Persian carpet; and on wide terraces carnations of every hue, scarlet, yellow, pink, speckled crimson and white, peer out through the web of their spiky grey-green foliage.

There are masses of chrysanthemums in russet and gold; dahlias of every shade and variety; roses, tiger lilies, agapanthus, azaleas, gladioli, arums, verbenas, stocks, cannas, marigolds, sunflowers, irises, and a hundred others all growing in a virile luxuriance it is hard to imagine and impossible to describe, as though they were actually bursting with the wealth of life infused into them by the sunshine and the moisture and the rich volcanic soil.

Always their setting is the same: the steep, terraced hill-side and lush green foliage, with the crystal-clear stream that has watered them singing its murmuring song as it hurries away to bring the same gift to the rice fields below; and beyond, secret and mysterious in the distance, the swelling curves of the jungle-clad mountains.

To the Javanese, as to the Provençal peasant, flowers are a commercial undertaking, and he is no more senti-mental about them than he is about rice or onions. And just as the Provençal prosaically piles his glorious golden jonquils in a flaming mass on his wheelbarrow, so the Javanese fills up his bamboo carriers with as many flowers as he can possibly cram into them, and jogs off down the hill to market. It is then that you will meet him, trotting along, humming softly to himself, between two man-high masses of living colour, looking truly, if ever a man did, a thorn between two roses.

If you stop him he will always sell you an armful for a few pence, or you can go into a field and pick as many as you can carry, and the farmer will be all smiles if you offer him the same modest sum. Flowers, happily, are not an extravagance if you are fortunate enough to live among the hills of Java.

The Dutch love to "say it with flowers," and accord-ingly the florists in Java do a lively business. Never a birthday or wedding anniversary, nor an "occasion" of any kind, goes by ungreeted by flowers, and the mes-sengers, mounted on bicycles, carrying big bouquets or baskets, add one more touch of colour to the streets of the towns. Flowers are always sent, too, on the arrival home or departure of friends, and the after-hatch of the weekly mail-steamer for Europe, piled high and com-pletely covered with tributes for the passengers, is as well worth going to see as any flower show. Great baskets of every kind of bloom, delightfully arranged, are massed together in one glorious medley of scent and colour, doomed, alas, to die far too soon from the buffets of the strong sea breezes, so different from those of their native hills.

The pity is that all this flower-giving is a rather empty custom. The number of bouquets is a measure of popularity, but the flowers themselves are left to die, unwatered and uncared for, and very soon pitched overboard.

The florists' trade is active, too, in Singapore, and every flower in their shops comes from Java. Twice a week the "ferry" from Batavia lands its fragrant cargo, and a stream of coolies flows endlessly down the gangways, laden with long flat baskets full of the flowers that shame the uncultivated mountain-sides of British Malaya.

A minor village industry which the traveller in Java cannot fail to notice sooner or later is the manufacture of "koeweh"—a word meaning any kind of sweet, but specially applied here to a thin, pancake-like biscuit made of rice or cassava flour, sweetened, and either coloured bright pink or yellow, or left snow-white. These (and also a rather similar-looking biscuit, flavoured with pounded prawns instead of sugar) you will often see drying in the sun on big round trays by the roadside, in front of native houses, or else on bamboo stands in an open space, where the home of the maker of these delights has attained the status of a miniature "factory."

Javanese Mythology & the Wayang

JAVA possesses a mythology of its own, a mythology
as characteristic and almost as elaborate as that of the
Greeks and Romans. It is less concerned, however,
with gods and heroes, than with the adventures and
domestic affairs—some of them extremely indiscreet—of
princes and common folk with their relations, and
particularly with their relations-in-law.

The true source of the myths is obscure. That they owe
something to Hindu influence is certain, for some of the
best known stories are taken from writings of the Hindu
period in Java. But the figures of the various characters
in the stories, grotesque and even hideous though some
of them are, have a mild, benevolent, Punch-and-Judyish
sort of ugliness, very far removed from the horrible and
often obscene hideousness of so many Hindu idols and
images in India.

The stories as they are now told, whatever they
may have been originally, are unmistakably Javanese in
character. They are childishly ingenuous, full of an airy,
inconsequent magic, like that of Grimm or Hans Ander-
sen, in which human beings are transformed in the
twinkling of an eye into beasts or mountains, or brought
back to life after the most mortal of death-thrusts.

The powers of Nature—storm and flood and earth-
quake—which are ever present in the minds of people
who have always lived under the shadow of potentially

SOME *WAYANG* STARS AT PLAY

THEY ARE ALL CHARACTERS WELL KNOWN TO THE JAVANESE PLAYGOER; BALADEWA, ARDJOENA,
LASMANA, SOEBADRA, GATOK GADJA AND BIMANJOE.

A SHEET OF BILIK

IT IS BEING CARRIED BY A NATIVE TO THE SITE OF HIS NEW RESIDENCE, WHERE IT WILL BE LAID
ON THE GROUND AND THE WINDOW AND DOOR SPACES CHOPPED OUT WITH A KNIFE.

active volcanoes, are, as might be expected, much in evidence.

Some of the stories have been immortalized, as no written record could have preserved them, by the "Wayang," or native theatre, which for countless generations has been so much a part of Javanese life that the fifty or sixty chief characters which adorn the tales are as familiar to every native as Jack and Jill and Mother Hubbard, and the rest of our nursery rhyme characters, are to us, probably far more so.

These queer figures, awkward and angular, with noses like the beaks of birds, and arms longer than their bodies, are more or less familiar to every visitor to the East Indies. They appear in every native design: in Batik, in wall-paintings, in buffalo-horn ornaments and utensils, and on silver spoons, but their place *par excellence* is in the Wayang.

Of this Wayang there are several kinds. The oldest, the true theatre, or "Wayang Wong," in which the parts are played by human actors, now survives only in a comparatively few companies of strolling players, and at the Courts of the two remaining reigning Sultans, Soerakarta and Djokjakarta.

At these Courts a performance is given from time to time on State occasions, and is a most elaborate affair, lasting for several days. It starts early in the morning, and goes on till late at night. There are no intervals for meals; refreshments are served all day long, and when either of the Sultans entertains a party of European guests, these are regaled at a luncheon which lasts for many hours. The royal host and his friends sit in a great reception room open to the air, and the Wayang takes place in a covered temporary extension, built out in the grounds, in front of it. The plays are presented with almost unimaginable

Javanese Mythology & the Wayang

splendour. All the performers are members of the Court, and the gorgeous silks of their robes and sarongs are stiff with jewels; and the kris with which each stiff, jerky mock death-blow is struck is probably almost priceless.

The Wayang of which most seems to be heard outside Java is the "Wayang Koelit," a shadow-show in which the figures are cut out in stiff buffalo hide, and the play performed in silhouette thrown on a screen by a light from behind. This form of Wayang is much performed for the benefit of tourists to Djokjakarta, which doubtless accounts for its being the best known.

But the true Wayang of the people, the one without which it is impossible to imagine Javanese native life, is the "Wayang Kayoe." In it the actors are wooden puppets about eighteen inches high, really beautifully carved and elaborately painted in many colours by village craftsmen. No village of any size in Java does not possess one of these and, accompanied by the "gamelan," a primitive sort of orchestra which supplies the musical accompaniment, it is an essential to village life, and in demand at all native weddings, anniversaries, and celebrations of every kind.

When an occasion of this sort arises, say a wedding, it is the bride's father, as with us, who has to provide the entertainment. And it goes without saying that that entertainment must be the Wayang which, with the gamelan, will cost him at least twenty-five guilders (over £2 at par), and probably more.

The proprietor and operator of the Wayang is the "Dalang." He is a most important person, for he is, in fact, the unwritten book in which the "tjerita-an," or stories, are bound up. He is often the descendant of a long line of Dalangs, through which the tales have been handed down, word for word, from father to son; or else

he may have been in his youth one of the little boys who
act as attendant sprites at the show, and hand the Dalang
each new character as it is wanted.

The "stage" on which the Wayang Kayoe is performed
is a very simple one. It consists of the stem of a banana
tree, resting on two bamboo trestles. The little sarongs of
the puppets conceal a long, sharp, wooden spike, which
serves them instead of legs, and this is plunged into the
soft banana stem, enabling them to "stand" quite firmly
on the stage, and to be moved and replaced easily at will.

When the performance is about to begin, the figures in
their gay Batik garments—the female characters wearing
scarves, and the male ones armed with tiny wooden krises
—stand in two crowded groups, one at each end of the
stage, with a space in between, in front of which the
action of the play takes place. The Dalang is squatted at
one end, and a small boy helper, alert and bright-eyed
(for woe betide him if he makes a mistake!), at the other.

The Dalang starts in dramatic fashion. Seizing a
figure (with one hand concealed under its sarong con-
trolling the head and body, and the other manipulating
with amazing dexterity the slender sticks attached to the
jointed arms), he declaims its part, picking up each
character in turn and plunging its hither end back into
the banana stem when its turn is over, changing his voice
for each, and working himself up into a state of great
excitement. His assistant manipulates the characters
playing opposite, but the Dalang speaks for both, for
this is an honour not to be left to lesser men.

Meanwhile the gamelan plays unceasingly its queer,
tuneless, rhythmical accompaniment, a sound almost as
familiar to country-dwellers in Java as that of running
water. For the gamelan is less costly than the Wayang, and
even the humblest kampong usually possesses one. So

that at dusk, and all through the long warm evenings, it is rarely that you will not hear its vague, oddly restful, mellow music. There is no tune, only an indeterminate sort of rhythm which yet has no definite beat. It has no beginning and no end, and when it has ceased it is usually some time before you realize that it has faded away into silence, so naturally does it harmonize with all the soft little noises of sleepy birds and insects, and the drowsy puffs of scented breeze that play through the darkness.

The chief instrument of the gamelan is six or eight feet long, and built somewhat on the principle of our xylophone. Small pieces of split bamboo or of metal, each one a little shorter than the last, are fixed across two slightly converging bamboos, and tuned to something roughly approaching a scale. They are gently struck with a small wooden mallet. This instrument is usually accompanied by one or two small buffalo hide drums, which are very softly strummed rather than struck with the fingers.

It is doubtful whether any European is very likely to become an ardent Wayang fan. But if you have never seen one, and a native friend honours you with an invitation (for there is no other way of seeing the true kampong Wayang), I would strongly advise you not to refuse. Even though you may feel that a kind of *noblesse oblige* demands that you see it through to the end, in order not to hurt the feelings of these humble people—and that end will probably be at about five o'clock in the morning!

Being bidden by a good friend of mine, one Si Irpan, to his daughter's wedding party, I arrived to find the little kampong totally transformed. The whole of the open space in front of the group of houses had been roofed over with kajang on bamboo supports, trellised round with split bamboo, and decorated with palm fronds, paper streamers, and spangles, all of it having appeared as though by magic since the morning.

There were rows of long trestle tables and chairs set round an open space for the Wayang. On a low platform, seated at a small table, sat our host, in stiff new brown and yellow sarong, spotless white shirt, and smart new head-dress; on the table beside him was a big cardboard chocolate box, covered with an elaborate lace doily, and as each guest arrived (or, more rarely, this ceremony was deferred until departure) he or she walked up to the platform and shook the host's hand. But this was no mere ceremonial handshake—far from it! At a Javanese wedding you must "leave a kiss within the cup"; in other words, you must "palm" a coin and pass it dexterously into the palm of your host while you greet him and murmur your good wishes for the young couple's happi-ness. And equally neatly, before greeting the next guest, the host slips each offering (after a shrewd, appraising glance) into the box.

He sits at his post all the evening; that is, from about seven in the evening until five o'clock next morning. But he doubtless feels it is worth it. In the first place the Javanese are the most polite of people, and it would be discourteous to miss either welcoming the coming, or speeding the parting, guest. In the second place it would be most unwise, for one never knows! They keep drifting in and out all night. And every now and then, when the Wayang is in full swing, and he thinks no one is looking in his direction, if you steal a quick look at your host you may catch him furtively lifting a corner of the lace covering the chocolate box, to see how the contributions are mounting up.

After all, how little difference there is in human customs.

Who would dare to go to a wedding in England without having sent a wedding present? In Australia there is that most practical institution, the "Wedding Tea," to which all the bride's friends bring the utensils that will be needed in the culinary department of the new *ménage*. And in Java the contributions of the guests go to help to pay for the hire of the Wayang, the refreshments, and the bride's and her parents' new finery.

The bride does not appear. She sits on the floor in the bridal chamber, just inside the door of her house, dressed in a new sarong and silk coat, her head bowed under the weight of a bridal wreath made of beads and artificial flowers which must weigh several pounds. Behind her on the ground is a fine new kapok mattress, with snow-white sheet and frilled pillows, and mosquito-net garlanded with flowers and spangles. She extends a limp, slender hand to the women guests, who are led in one by one by her mother to gaze at her finery and wish her "salamat" (good luck). She looks utterly bored by the whole proceeding, as no doubt she is. For the bridegroom is making merry with his friends outside, and she may not so much as see the Wayang.

The Wayang had started with the arrival of the first guest, and went on tirelessly hour after hour, with every now and then a brief pause, during which the Dalang fortified himself with a little refreshment. The tables were loaded with dishes of highly coloured and very sticky cakes and sweetmeats, and with bottles of fizzy pink, yellow, and green drinks. These delights were constantly being urged upon us by our too hospitable hosts, greatly to my embarrassment. For they would take no refusal, and I am afraid that a whole collection of those terrifying eatables found their way under the table. I have always hoped that my place was not located by them next morning, or that the kampong dogs found them before anyone else did.

No one seemed to take much notice of the Wayang performance. Baladewa, Ardjoena, Soebadra, Gatok Gadja, Bimanjoe, and the rest came on and played their familiar parts. Every now and then a favourite passage seemed to please the audience, but for the most part the guests went on eating and drinking and gossiping in low voices, moving about and greeting each other, depositing their coins with the bride's father, or paying formal visits of inspection to the bride.

But this apparent indifference in no way damped the Dalang's ardour. Like all true artists, he was carried away by his art and independent of his audience, and his dramatic fervour was as great after seven or eight hours of talking as it was at the beginning, even though his voice was a trifle hoarse. He seemed to be in a sort of dream, and for him the little figures that he handled so dexterously, making them mince or strut across the stage, expressing unmistakable defiance or arrogance or supplication, or any other mood the play demanded, were alive and breathing, and the old stories actual happenings.

The making of the puppets is as great an art in its way as that of the Dalang. The differences in their elaborate head-dresses and other details must be absolutely exact, for they must be recognizable to the smallest native child in the audience. They are carved out of a very soft wood called "kayoe lameh," and the men who make them are regarded, like the Dalangs, with great respect.

They use the simplest of tools; equipped with nothing but a couple of slightly curved, short-bladed knives they will produce an immortal character from a shapeless block of wood with a speed and ease that many a Western sculptor might envy. The dolls are enamelled in gold and many colours, and dressed by the kampong ladies in scraps of discarded Batik, or by cutting up the tiny sarongs sold for children in any native market for fifty cents (tenpence). One of these is enough to provide sarongs for quite a number of the "caste."

All the different figures, to European eyes so very much alike, are known to the simplest Javanese. If you have wall-hangings on which the characters are woven or painted, or Wayang puppets hanging up in your "voor-galerij," they are sure to catch the eye of any native who comes to your door. He is certain to comment on them, and, given the slightest encouragement, will name every one, explain their very unconventional domestic relationships, and tell you some long rambling tale about them that you have never heard before.

Sometimes, as you travel the country roads, you will meet a small party of natives, one walking alone and empty-handed, two carrying a big coffin-like box slung between them from a bamboo resting on a shoulder of each, and others laden with the various instruments of the orchestra. It is the Dalang who walks alone, rehearsing, no doubt, the stories that he is presently to tell again for the hundredth time. The box contains all the classic characters of Javanese mythology. And they are all on their way to celebrate the founding of yet another busy and contented little branch of Java's ever-growing, enormous family.

A Motorist's Paradise

JAVA is certainly a motorist's paradise. But there are angels at its well-barred gate, and each of them is thrice armed with a flaming sword.

The first is the Customs Officer, and his sword is a very flaming one indeed. The first time I took a car into Java, it was nearly seven hours, spent on the wharf in the Equatorial sunshine, before he lowered his weapon and let me pass, and even then I was scarcely over the threshold when even stronger forces were arrayed against me.

I arrived one exquisite morning by one of the "K.P.M.'s" admirable steamers, complete with car, and with a hundred dollars in Straits currency to cover the twelve per cent. *ad valorem* duty required by the Customs, —a sum, by the way, which was a handsome compliment to my shabby, faithful old "Chev," whose market value, I well knew, was far from being in proportion to my affection for it.

The ship tied up, the car was slung ashore with admirable ease and efficiency, my luggage was put in it, and off I drove down the long line of busy wharves to the barrier, where I left the car, and went into the office to pay the duty and be "cleared."

I spoke no Dutch in those days, and having been warned that it is extremely tactless to address a Dutchman in Java in Malay (which he is apt to take as a suggestion that you suspect him of Eurasian antecedents), I started by asking the officer in charge if he spoke English. He assured me, not without a touch of asperity (for the Dutch are good linguists and proud of it), that he did. I thereupon explained my car was outside; would he be so kind as to assess it for duty?

He merely chalked my baggage without opening it. and then, after a pause, asked very courteously if there was anything further he could do. "What . . . Oh! . . . I see . . . a car . . ." he said. "You will find plenty outside"; and added, waving away the bundle of dollars I had proffered in token of my willingness to pay the duty, "No . . . no . . . the fare is only four guilders." Then, raising his voice, he called to the group of native taxi-drivers awaiting fares at the entrance, "Heh . . . the nyonya wants a car!"

But the nyonya didn't. This time I sat down firmly on the counter and, regardless of his feelings, explained in my very best Malay. Light dawned at last in the official eye. "Ah . . . Quite. . . ." he said airily. "Your own car. Why didn't you say so? Please give me the Import Pass."

"Import Pass"? What on earth was that? I had never heard of it. But it seemed I ought to have got one from the Dutch Consul before sailing.

"No car can enter Java without an Import Pass," said the official severely. "You must hire a car, and leave yours here till I get the papers from Singapore."

Now I had no mind whatever to depart in a hired car, leaving my own standing on the wharf for a week. It occurred to me that the right people to extricate me from the tangle were the firm who had shipped the "Chev." I learned that they had an office at the port, and set off (on foot in the blazing heat, for I was not allowed to take the car through the gate) to see them.

A Motorist's Paradise

I found the office, and after long explanation the affair was duly located. Innumerable papers were filled in; every one was most kind, if a trifle slow. At last I was given an imposing document, all in Dutch, with which I walked gaily back to the Customs, confident that now I should soon be flying along the smooth wide road to Weltevreden, bound for a bath, lunch, and all the comforts of civilization.

I greeted mijnheer of the Customs like a brother, so pleased was I to think that soon I should have seen the last of him. But, to my horror, he only glowered at the paper I handed him. "This is nothing," he said coldly. "I want the *Import Pass*. Go back and tell them."

I was half-way down the steps before he finished, and I "went back and told them" so eloquently that a smart young man was sent back to the Customs with me to fix the matter up. It would take only five minutes, they said.

What a flow of gutturals followed! What a turning over of folios and regulations! And then the Smart Young Man turned to me with the air of one in whom a brilliant and entirely novel idea has just been born. "We have found it!" he announced triumphantly. "You must pay twelve per cent. of the car's value!"

What was the good of saying that I had tried to do that an hour or more ago? So I handed over my bundle of dollars in silence.

But it wasn't so simple as all that. Again they were waved away. "The necessary papers must now be made out. It is a long affair. It may take all day. . . . You had better hire a car. . . ."

I glared. Nothing would induce me to hire a car. I had one. My luggage was in it, and I intended to drive ashore in my car and no other. . . . They gave in, and the papers were promised in an hour.

I decided to go back to the ship, which promised more comfort than the car or the Customs shed at midday in these latitudes. So back I went, walking dispiritedly down the long, busy, scorching wharf, up which I had driven so gaily a couple of hours earlier. Back to the empty ship, where the Chinese "boys," not unnaturally, regarded me with considerable suspicion. But the time passed and, punctual to the minute, came the Smart Young Man, waving three sheets of foolscap, covered with the finest script, which I signed where I was told, in blind, beautiful faith that all would now be well.

Back to the Customs we trudged, along those endless wharves, and once again I tendered my bundle of notes, looking now rather the worse for wear. "Dollars? What was the good of dollars? You use guilders in Java. You must change them. Where? Why, at the Post Office, about half-way down the wharf!"

So to the Post Office I obediently repaired. But apparently that institution had never seen a dollar before. They looked at them with the utmost dislike. "Possibly you could change them at Weltevreden. . . . You had better take a car. . . ."

I fled. And then the Smart Young Man came to the rescue once more. He would change them in five minutes. "Splendid!" I said. "I'll sit in the car and wait for you, and then I shall get to town in time for lunch after all." "B-b-but," he stammered, "I have still to get the signature of the Head Controller. It is very far away. It may be many hours. . . . You had better take . . ."

It was the last straw. But nothing could move me now. "If it takes many hours—or a week—or a month," I said bitterly, "I shall still be here when you come back." I bought some bananas at a native stall, and climbed into the old "Chev." There was to be no bath, and no lunch;

but this one refuge I could claim in an inhospitable country. I would stay in it till I died.

An hour passed Two hours. I ate my bananas and longed for a drink. The sun blazed mercilessly down. I grew drowsily interested in the doings of the gatekeepers, in the jokes they cracked, the cigarettes they smoked, and the amazing expertness of their expectoration. I began to feel as though I had known them for years. I noted the instinctive politeness of the ever-passing natives, bound upon this, that, or the other of their lawful occasions, and rejoiced that I was not in the same predicament at Liverpool or Sydney. I was almost enjoying myself; at all events the thing had become a habit. I rather think I must have dozed . . . for suddenly . . . there was the Smart Young Man at my elbow.

"I tell you it's no good," I said sleepily. "I will *not* take a car. . . ." He looked hurt, and handed me a slip of paper and the change—for all the world as though it had been only five minutes instead of half a day since the affair started.

I could scarcely believe it, but that really was the end— of that chapter. One more short interview with the Customs man (whom we found fast asleep) and at last I drove through the gate of paradise, thinking that all my troubles were over. But there was worse to come.

I had been warned that the hand of the Law was apt to be heavy upon the motorist caught driving without a "rijbewijs" (driving licence). This would, however, be merely a formal matter in my case, I felt sure, for I had been driving cars for more years than I cared to remember, and had a whole assortment of licences of various countries to show to whom it might concern. So with a light heart I presented myself at the appointed place: the Parapatten Politie Kantoor.

The first snag was the discovery that Thursday (on which I happened to arrive) was an "off" day; I must wait until the next morning. However, that was nothing. At the appointed time duly I returned, and it was not long before I realized that getting a driving licence in Java was no mere straightforward matter of demonstrating that you can drive a motor-car.

First, so the Dutch officer told me, I must go to the Post Office and get a form with a one-and-a-half guilder stamp, bring it back, and he would fill it in for me; then I must go and have two photographs taken and bring them back to him; then I must be "examinated" (he spoke perfect English), and if I passed the test I must come back and apply for the rijbewijs in duplicate, and with that he went back to his desk.

Well, there it was. It sounded as though it would take a week, and I wanted to start up country the next day. But suddenly I had an inspiration: a dozen or more "mata-mata" (native policemen) were sitting outside, apparently awaiting orders. There was no fear of offending them by speaking Malay, so, addressing one at random, I asked if he would come with me and show me where to get a photograph taken. He jumped into the car, obviously delighted, and off we set.

The Post Office was easy: the little mata-mata got the form in a mere twenty minutes or so. He knew a good place to get a "portret," and directed me to a queer, low-browed little shop in a side-street, where I "sat" to a small, kimonoed Japanese, while her two tiny, yellow scraps of children fixed me with an unblinking stare almost worse than that of the camera. That little lady could have given points to many London photographers. There was no fuss and no posing. She sat me down, smiled engagingly, focussed, trotted across and laid one soft little finger on my chin to press it gently aside, and trotted back to her camera. There followed the muffled click of the shutter, and she vanished into the dark room, whence she returned in due course with the negative in the hypo. dish for inspection.

It appeared excellent—distinctly flattering, I thought—and when it had been "passed" by my friend of the police, who took entire charge of the affair, and impressed on her the urgent need for haste, she promised gravely that two prints should be ready in an hour: the price was three guilders.

At this the police escort broke in with indignation. "Much too dear," he told her. "The nyonya could have a dozen copies for that! . . ." But she only looked at him very gravely, and said softly but firmly in her pretty Malay, "You wish for them in one hour, yes? I will give them to you. The price is three guilders." It looked as though an argument over a guilder might hold me up over the week-end, so I hastily laid down three shining coins, took the Law by the arm, and drove back to the Police Station.

Here there was a new development. The friendly Dutchman had vanished from his desk, and in his stead sat a tall, coal-black gentleman from the West Indies, in magnificent uniform and shining top boots, who told me, "The other toean has taken your papers. He may not be back to-day." It looked like a deadlock. But my little escort was determined to see me through, and poured out such a stream of eloquence concerning my many virtues and the extreme urgency of my affairs, that at last the dark gentleman, with a shrug, jerked his head in my direction, with, "Get your car. I will come."

I got it, and sat there, waiting. Presently out came His Dark Magnificence, chatting with a Dutch policeman and roaring with laughter over some joke which (perhaps happily) was lost on me. They entered the car, slammed the door, and continued their conversation without a word to me. "Which way?" I asked; and thereafter, at every turn or crossing, I would inquire over my shoulder for directions, which they gave a trifle impatiently, as though it were rather rude of me to interrupt. We went round and round, through labyrinths of suburbs, through streets wide and narrow; it seemed as though we were going on all day, when suddenly there came a new order: "*Stop!*" We were in the very middle of a crowded street, so I disobeyed to the extent of manœuvring to the side, stopped, and waited.

Nothing happened. The conversation behind me flowed on. With deplorable rudeness I interrupted. "What now?" I asked. A gust of laughter greeted me, followed by a long pause. Then: "You drive much too fast!"

Now, in comparison with Batavia's "flying taxis" (which fully justify their name), I had been crawling. But my heart sank like a lump of lead. Was I to be refused a licence after joy-riding these two loquacious policemen round the town for the best part of an hour? Obviously the soft answer was my only hope. I apologized abjectly. There was more laughter and then silence. "Well?" I said nervously. "Turn the car round," came the order. I turned, and drove on—very slowly this time. "*Stop!*" I stopped. "We will get out here." "And the licence?" I said, rather faintly. "Oh yes . . . of course, the licence. Take this" (scribbling on and tearing out a leaf from his notebook) "to the Kantoor. They will see to it." And out they both got and disappeared through a gateway, without another word.

I was completely lost, but I found my way back at last

A NATIVE CHAIR VENDOR

THE CHAIRS ARE OF SOLID TEAK AND SO HEAVY THAT ONE ALONE IS HARD TO LIFT. YET THESE
MEN TROT FOR MILES CARRYING A PAIR. THIS MAN ADDED A WEIGHTY METAL GONG.

ONE OF THE ROADSIDE WARNINGS OF THE JAVA MOTOR
CLUB WHICH GREET MOTORISTS AT EVERY CORNER

SOMETIMES, AS IN THIS CASE, ON A PARTICULARLY EXCITING STRETCH OF ROAD, THEY WAX
ALMOST INCOHERENT IN THEIR KINDLY ANXIETY.

to the Parapattan, and presented my talisman. Alas, no one was in the least interested. There was only one hope: it seemed the time had come for action. I abandoned all deference, and, raising my voice, spoke with chilly hauteur. "Mijnheer —— gave me this" (reading out the name on my scrap of paper) "and said my licence was to be made out at once. Be so good as to see to it. I am in a hurry."

It worked. Someone took the paper and the photographs (which I had called for on the way) into an inner office, whence there issued forthwith the quick rattle of a typewriter. Then I was led (again under police escort) to yet another room, where I was invited to press my thumb first on to an inky pad and then on to the space reserved for it on the licence (turning it from side to side so that none of my criminal tendencies should go unrecorded); then I was waved to a small tin wash-bowl hanging on the wall, where with a grimy bit of soap and still grimier towel I tried to remove all traces of the crime. Then came the final gesture: "One guilder fifty, please"—and most thankfully I handed it over. Where else in all the world could you get so long and varied an entertainment for so low a price?

And so at last I had a rijbewijs, a green card stating that Mevrouw ——, aged—but no, I shall not disclose that, and neither does the licence, for that matter!— was permitted to drive a motor-car in the Dutch East Indies from this time forward for the term of her natural life. Below was a portrait of feminine beauty whose anguished expression and staring eyes could scarcely fail to move the stoniest policeman's heart to compassion, however heinous a breach of the traffic regulations the original might have committed. And the final garniture was a blurred black smear, purporting to be the imprint of what I had hitherto always believed to be a rather shapely thumb.

However, it was just as well I had it. I had barely passed the outskirts of Batavia when a determined-looking Dutchman barred my passage. "Your rijbewijs," he said. I handed it over. He took it, looked first at the portrait and then at me, smiled (sadly, I thought), handed it back, and waved me on my way.

Ruritanian Royalty—Pawnshops—& Prisons

TO arrive at Soerakarta (or Solo, as it is often called) by chance, as I once did, when a big native fair was in progress and the whole place *en fête*, was rather like straying inadvertently on to the stage at Drury Lane during the Christmas pantomime.

Javanese dress is picturesque enough at all times, but as I turned the car into the wide main street of Solo I found myself hemmed in on every side by the most fantastic, richly dressed crowds I had ever dreamed of. Some, evidently the *élite*, were in silken sarongs of deep claret or purple; others, belonging to the Court, in stiff sugar-loaf head-dresses and black coats; and all around, as far as I could see, were hundreds, if not thousands, of humbler folk all dressed in their best, all the more effective in that their sarongs were almost uniformly mixtures of rich blue and two shades of warm brown— the favourite colours of the Soerakarta Batik makers.

Most striking of all was the fact that there seemed to be scarcely a man of them but wore a kris tucked into his belt at the back, which is a sight not often to be seen except in the Wayang. Every hilt was a work of art. Some, worn by the nobles, glittered with gold and gems, and many scabbards were of silver, elaborately embossed or chased. Every now and then a "personage" would appear, with an umbrella of red, green, or some other colour held over his head by an attendant, according to his rank, the crowds making way with exaggerated respect. And then, when an imposing motor, wearing a small golden umbrella on the radiator, swept down the street with a magnificently uniformed flunkey haughtily waving the common herd aside, the car and I, in common with the rest of the crowd, lost no time in squeezing ourselves into the smallest compass possible, so over-powered were we with the splendid vision of royalty in all its glory of robes and jewels that flashed upon us as the car rushed past in a cloud of dust.

Javanese royalty—what is left of it—is nothing if not up to date. It would be unthinkable to sally forth without the Royal Golden Umbrella, and equally unthinkable to take the air in anything but a motor-car. So East and West combine for once; royalty travels in the car, and the royal umbrella (in miniature) on the radiator-cap.

Soerakarta is the capital of one of the only two remaining Sultanates in Java. The Sultan, or "Susuhunan," as he is generally called, retains his title and his Court by virtue of a treaty made with the Dutch East India Company in 1750. The other reigning prince is the Sultan of Djokjakarta, whose territory was formerly part of the kingdom of Soerakarta. He, too, holds his throne by an ancient agreement. Each of these two toy kings reigns in magnificently staged splendour over a kingdom just about as real as Ruritania. Each of them has, literally, thousands of courtiers and dancing-girls and officials and satellites; a fine palace, horses, carriages, motor-cars, silks and jewels and swords galore—all the "properties," in fact, of the stage potentate that he is.

All these things may be his, because under the treaty he receives a handsome proportion of his own revenues. But power he has none. Life has lost its old-time savour. Not one dancing-girl may he throw to the tigers or the crocodiles; not a single courtier can he have strangled, or hung head downward in the well. His hands are tied, and in all things he must refer to his Dutch "Elder Brother," the Resident, who advises him upon these and all other matters of State.

But for all that, the stage crowd play up to him well. As in the palmiest days of the Sultans, not a soul dare stand upright in the royal presence. No head may be raised as high as his. And he has the satisfaction, as his forefathers had, of seeing his whole Court crouching before him, and the servants that serve him with food serve his pride as well, by crawling in like ungainly monkeys, bearing his priceless gold and silver dishes as best they can.

Not even the Queen of Holland herself has a better State coach than the Sultan of Djokjakarta. About twenty-five years ago, when a new one was built for her, the Sultan saw photographs of it in the papers, and promptly ordered a replica for himself. It is an exact copy, except where it has been improved upon with Javanese ornaments and carvings, and the native driver and postilions are disguised in cocked hats and European uniforms.

Another royal prerogative dating from very ancient times, of which Dutch rule has not deprived either of these monarchs, is the Bodyguard of Women, though whether the princes are grateful for the concession there is no satisfactory means of ascertaining. The bodyguard itself stands in the way, and it consists of fifty ladies, specially selected for their age, hideousness, and general decrepitude, who are designed to protect the royal person from the dangers of Court intrigue.

The difficulties connected with precedence, which are not altogether unknown even in Western society, are apt to be aggravated at a Court wherein there is a multiplicity of royal wives. So on State occasions, when the Sultan has found it expedient for one reason or another to refrain from raising any of these ladies to be Wife in Chief, the difficulty is tactfully surmounted by handing over the duties of hostess to the Sultan's sister, or some other female relation.

No king, not even a stage one, would be complete without an army, and this, too, the Dutch have not forbidden. So each of the Javanese Sultans has a perfectly good standing army of his own, not noticeably (at all events in appearance) so very much more comical than the official Dutch Colonial one. So what, after all, could a monarch in a Land of Wayang want more?

The crouching position assumed by the Javanese as a mark of respect at the Sultan's Court is the remnant of a very ancient custom, and no doubt dates back to the times when those in power trod literally on the necks of their unfortunate dependents.

Not only was it demanded by royalties and chiefs from their subjects, but was for centuries the conventional gesture from an inferior to a superior, through all ranks of society, from the humblest coolie upwards. It was taken over, with the other native rights, by the old Dutch conquerors, who crushed the wretched natives into at least as crawling a servility as had their own former rulers.

The custom was general up to the time of Raffles, who in his five years of whirlwind reform, tried to sweep it away with a thousand other repressions. And the Dutch rulers who came after him, more enlightened than their predecessors, also came more and more as time went on to discourage the custom, until now it has practically disappeared except at the Sultans' Courts.

It has certainly died out as regards the native attitude

to Europeans, but the Javanese still instinctively reveres his own native aristocracy, and in this connection I recently saw an interesting survival of the old custom.

I made the acquaintance of a Dutchman in the Government service and his dainty little wife, who is a member of an old Javanese family of very high rank. Their house is a European bungalow, luxuriously appointed in European style, for Mevrouw X. is completely Westernized and speaks perfect Dutch, and the servants are the usual native "boys." To my surprise, on being entertained there one evening, the boy who handed round the drinks suddenly crouched down on approaching his mistress, and offered her the tray, precariously balanced in one hand, while he steadied himself on the floor with the other. The little lady accepted it as a matter of course, and told me afterwards that she would not dream of allowing her servants to approach her otherwise.

The kris, the favourite and traditional weapon of the Javanese, was formerly worn universally throughout the island, but it has now long been prohibited except at the Sultans' Courts, whose members, down to the lowest servants, are permitted to wear it.

But although it is no longer universally worn, it is still an object of special veneration, and there are few native households that do not possess at least one, which is treasured as an heirloom, and passed down from father to son, together with the tales of great deeds it has accomplished in the hands of their ancestors. With those stories, as often as not, there will be whispered others of the magic powers the weapon is believed to possess. For to the Javanese the qualities of a kris are not by any means only the tangible ones of a trusty blade in an ornamented scabbard.

He can also tell you, if he will (but fear of its magic

71

sometimes seals his lips), whether its spirit be a good one or a bad. If it be bad, then, however delicately wavy the blade, and however beautiful the hilt and scabbard, it would be mere foolishness to let it come into your house, for it would certainly bring evil upon it.

"Krises" of sorts, machine-made for the passing tourist, may be bought in the streets of any port in Java. But the true kris, native-made, by the time-honoured hand processes known to no one but themselves, are not so easy to come by, especially old ones that have been worn and used.

The native who possesses one hates to part with it. But it does happen sometimes that a daughter's wedding, the loss of a water buffalo, or some other financial crisis may force him to stifle sentiment and take his treasure to the local "pandhuis," or "roemah gadean" (pawnshop). Knowing this, I seldom pass through a country town without pulling up at the pandhuis to ask the "mandoer" (head man) in charge whether by chance there is a kris among his heterogeneous collection. For years I never saw one, and then one day at a small village in the hills at last I came across a treasure.

It was evidently very old, and the heavily chased silver-covered scabbard was rubbed right through the middle, whether with wear or polishing, who shall say? Anyway, I bought it for the sum of one guilder, and had no sooner brought it home than it vanished, and I thought it was lost to me for good. But my "boy" had only taken it home to his kampong, and brought it back later, gravely assuring me that the "doekoen" (witch-doctor) had told him it was a very good kris indeed! That doekoen was a palpable invention to cloak the "boy's" desire to show off the treasure, but the kris had at least the virtue of coming back to its lawful owner.

The roemah gadean is an indispensable feature of Javanese life. The native is always in financial difficulties of some sort: every cent he earns is heavily mortgaged beforehand; he is an inveterate gambler; and to deny himself anything that he wants, unless it is manifestly unobtainable, is entirely foreign to his nature. So, with this shrewd knowledge in their possession, the Dutch wisely made the pawnshops a government monopoly, and a very valuable one they are.

The familiar sign "PANDHUIS—ROEMAH GADEAN" greets you in a conspicuous place at the entrance of every village, and there are at least two in every larger town, and a constant stream of natives, putting their possessions "up the spout," to get a few cents towards their immediate necessities, flows almost unceasingly in through the entrance.

The numbers that go back to redeem their treasures can hardly be described as a stream. There are not even enough of them to trickle. A few now and then may ask for their Lares and Penates back again, but for the most part they go to swell the huge collection of "unredeemed pledges" with which the shelves and cupboards are crammed.

Batik is the mainstay of the pandhuis. The native usually has a spare sarong or so, and to pawn a garment that he is not actually wearing, if he is in need of a little ready money, is the first thing that occurs to him. So on every side piles upon piles of sarongs are stacked up, most of them to be sold eventually for a ridiculously low price, then to be worn for a time, then pawned and sold again, and so *ad infinitum*.

Nearly always there is a rackful of bicycles, but these are an exception to the general rule, in that they really do represent "temporary accommodation," and are almost invariably redeemed. The native method of buying a bicycle is peculiar. He does it on the hire-purchase system: pays a deposit and perhaps the first monthly instalment, and after that, whenever he has no money to pay the instalment (or possibly the licence), he puts the bicycle in pawn. But somehow or other it seems to work out all right, and though the bike will certainly have seen its best days before it is paid for (if it ever is) it troubles him not at all. He will always manage to raise the money to redeem it by hook or by crook, probably by pawning something else, when he wants it to ride on some special occasion.

A good deal of queer old brass finds its way to the government pawnshops; you will sometimes see clumsy "chewing sets," with compartments for betel-nut, leaf, and lime, snuff and tobacco boxes, odd-shaped ladles, and other utensils. More rarely a bowl or plate in thin, roughly beaten, native silver is to be found among the medley of rubbish, and when it is, it is usually well worth buying, for there is no attempt at exploitation in the fixed pandhuis prices.

The partly Westernized youths in the towns are fond of buying European musical instruments, only to discover that a lifelong acquaintance with the gamelan does not help the unskilled player to wring music from them. So these, too, find their way to the pawnshops, and a selection of nearly new violins, zither-banjos, accordions, and an occasional stray from some jazz band are quite often among the bargains, as are also a fine variety of European pattern shoes and native sandals.

It is to the pawnshops you must go in the forlorn hope of tracing stolen property; and like most things in the East it is a business requiring infinite patience. Descriptions of stolen articles are sent by the police to all the hundreds of pawnshops in Java, and it is sometimes a year before a thief, thinking that by then everybody concerned must surely have forgotten all about it, goes to "pop" his booty. Then (if the system works, as I have been told it has been known to do) he is caught, and the victim of the robbery recovers his property. I must confess, however, that I have yet to meet one of these fortunate persons.

Though thieves are seldom caught, other malefactors are swept in from time to time, in Java as elsewhere. I once paid a visit to one of the prisons, and found there so apparently contented a community that I was reminded of the old jail at Suva, Fiji, from which, though it possessed only a front and two side walls, and no back, not a single prisoner had ever been known to escape. The moral effect of the imposing entrance through which they were marched and the pleasant life they led within its three high walls were sufficient combination to keep them there!

The jail I visited in Java had its proper complement of walls, but I doubt if it would have mattered much if it had not. No one inside seemed in the least discontented, or displayed the slightest desire to escape. A kindly Dutch-woman was in charge of the women's side, and the groups of native women over whom she held sway might to all outward appearance have been the employees in the various departments of some factory or institution.

A whole roomful, squatted on the floor in front of their hand sewing-machines, were busily stitching shirts, and a low hum of voices mingled with the hum of the machines. Some were working in the well-kept garden, others doing laundry-work at big concrete tubs, and some weaving, but most were in the big Batik factory, turning out sarongs and selendangs and kain kepalas in delightful colours and designs, and one of the women occupied in each process demonstrated it for the visitors under the

75

direction of the matron. Such a pleasant, quiet, gentle set of women were they, that it came as something of a shock to learn that the "little slip" which had brought many of them to prison was one that we by no means associate with those amiable qualities, and that was— murder!

A diminutive creature, who looked up at us with a smile from the blue cotton garment she was stitching, had, so the matron told me, divested herself of her husband by putting powdered glass in his rice, and everything pointed to her having made several earlier attempts on the unlucky man before she finally pulled it off.

One would have thought it was scarcely worth while to go to all the trouble of murdering a husband, however tiresome, in a country where divorce is so simple a matter as it is in Java. Yet quite a number of them had done it by one means or another, mostly with poisons of various kinds, in which the Javanese, being skilled herbalists, are adept.

The reason undoubtedly is that life is far less sacred to Eastern than to Western minds. Under the old native law a murderer got off lightly, but the most barbarous and horrible punishments, such as imprisonment for life in narrow cages, were inflicted on defaulters in debt. The Javanese are civilized nowadays, but it does not rid them of their extraordinary sensitiveness to insult or injury, and its concomitant instinct for revenge, or the determination to be rid of an undesirable human associate.

This same quality of supersensitiveness makes them very prone to suicide. They can no more face unhappiness than they can physical illness; homesickness, for instance, is a quite sufficient cause. Coolies, women especially, who have emigrated to Sumatra or the other islands to work in the plantations, not infrequently put an end to themselves; and sometimes an assistant on his morning rounds will come upon a pathetic little object in a draggled sarong hanging limply by a rag of twisted Batik to the gaunt branch of a felled jungle giant.

Even among the native children suicide is quite common as the result of nothing more than a few harsh words. So perhaps it is not surprising if, among people of such a temperament, a quarrel ends now and then with a dose of crushed glass or bamboo scrapings, or an insult is wiped out with a slash of the parang.

CHAPTER SEVEN

A Few Native Foibles

IT is an accepted tradition among Europeans in the East that the native is incorrigibly lazy. Of course he is. Any novel about that part of the world will tell you so, and so will Mr. Jones, of Tooting, as he lies at his ease in a lounge chair, with his feet on another, after the toil of the long weary day, while Mrs. Jones interjects faintly now and then that these native servants are "really quite impossible."

After all, who should know better than Mr. Jones? He has been in contact with the idle wretches since soon after sunrise, when Ah Wan brought the early morning tea, and, a little later, his shaving water. Then, having bathed and donned the clean linen and immaculately starched white suit laundered by the native "penato" (washerman), breakfasted on fare prepared by a native cook, he was driven to the office by a native chauffeur, and sat at his desk all the morning and afternoon giving orders to natives and Chinese. And now, here he is, in another clean white suit, shouting to the "boy" for a cool drink. Lazy devils, these natives . . . and yet . . . how strange it is . . . our houses are swept and garnished, brass polished, linen spotless, the lawns shaven, and every garden a delight to the eye, though we do none of these things for ourselves in Java.

The simple fact of the matter is that the speed craze that has fallen like a blight over the Western world, and driven out leisure and repose, has not yet infected the Javanese (except when he is driving a car!). He comes of a people who for centuries have toiled from dawn to sunset, taking their own time, and yet covering an astonishing amount of ground in a day. It has never occurred to him to hurry. The rice field had to be ploughed or reaped, but not another bunch of grain would it yield for being finished a few hours earlier. So, instinctively, he applies the same principle to all these strange new occupations into which we Europeans have forced him and, all things considered, he makes a very creditable job of it.

There is an old tag, moreover, that applies very aptly to life in the East: "Like Master" (or perhaps it would be more appropriate in this case to say "like Mistress") "like Man." For, given proper training and supervision, the Javanese servant is a pearl of great price. But under a nyonya who is too lazy either to learn his language or try to understand his ways he is hopeless. And, once back in England, a very brief experience of the services of a pert, high-heeled "Gladys" makes even the worst of your Javanese "boys" seem desirable.

I have often wondered how we Europeans in the tropics manage to convince ourselves of our superior energy. Even in our most strenuous game, tennis, we cannot even pick up our own balls. They are handed to us by two nimble natives, who run hither and thither unceasingly throughout the game; and woe betide them if two balls are not held out ready to the player's hand for every service!

It is all rather absurd. Javanese industry needs no other monument than Sir Christopher Wren's "Look around you!" Every foot of the countless miles of intricately irrigated and cultivated land that you see on every side as you drive about Java is a testimony to the skilled work of human hands—the hands of the "lazy native."

Generalizations are foolish, and often dangerous, but it is safe to say that the Javanese is a curiously childlike person, up to a point. He has a child's intense sensitiveness; he is deeply affronted by ridicule, and very apt to cherish a grievance. But his allegiance and affection are not hard to win and, once won, he is capable of great devotion, and can be the most thoughtful and kindly of nurses in time of illness. He is full of curiosity about anything and everything, especially about anything that concerns money. He never fails to inquire, when anything new is bought: "How much did the toean pay for it?" and his bargaining capacity is boundless. Money is his ruling passion, as it is that of the French peasant; and as you pass natives chatting in the streets or market, nine times out of ten you will catch such scraps as: "Dia mints satoe roepea" (He wanted a guilder), or: "Sahaya kasi tigapoeloe sen" (I gave thirty cents). And doubtless it is to this avarice of his that the Javanese owes his worst fault: a tendency to thieving. And yet, after all, thefts have been known to occur in other places! And I think that on the whole your small change is as safe in Java as it is, say, in London.

Childlike though he is, the Javanese native will often surprise you with his intelligence. An old "boy" I once had, when asked the Javanese word for any object, would always reply by reeling off the Malay, Javanese, Soendanese, and Madoerese names, occasionally adding, with a little shy chuckle, the Dutch one, all in a faintly deprecating tone, and twiddling his bare toes in a comical way he had when embarrassed, as though apologizing to the nyonya for venturing to know something that she did not. I have often tried to imagine an English servant

AN OLD *DALANG* (WAYANG SHOWMAN) WITH *BALADEWA*
HE IS ONE OF THE MOST POPULAR CHARACTERS IN THE JAVANESE PLAYS.

instructing a foreign visitor in the name of any desired object in a selection of three or four languages as well as his own. But imagination breaks down at the attempt.

Every now and then you will come across a native who is exceptionally clever with his hands; a descendant, perhaps, of the almost vanished craftsmen who flourished in the spacious days of the old Sultans. A Dutchman of my acquaintance has a chauffeur who is not only a first-rate mechanic and electrician, but repairs his master's shirts on his sewing-machine, and makes his own very smart khaki drill uniform suits. He sits on the ground, working the machine by hand, and pulling the material into place with his toes. I have known him finish a suit in half a day, buttonholes and all; and, a few days later, he would be putting the finishing touches to a bilik stable, with concrete floor and drains complete.

Another childlike trait is the native's disconcerting trick of observation. An old mandoer (head boy) in a Batavia hotel told me one day that he could tell Dutch, English, or American people apart at once, from the way they used their knives and forks. He then proceeded to give a graphic demonstration: "When the Dutchman has finished eating he does like this": (laying the knife and fork with their "business ends" facing each other, at opposite sides of the plate, and the handles resting on the table); "the English toean puts them like this" (laying them side by side on the plate in the conventional English way). "What does the American do?" I asked. This was much more dramatic. The old man gave an excellent imitation of Uncle Sam cutting up his food with his knife and fork, then laying the knife aside, blade on the plate and handle on the cloth, and eating with his fork. It is almost superfluous to add that the old scoundrel was

F

diplomat enough to express warm admiration for the English method!

The Javanese is a great talker. He loves an audience, and sometimes he is quite worth listening to. Out on photography bent one day, I came upon an elderly philosopher whose observations on men and things, and perhaps even more so on women, were as picturesque as he was himself, as he sat on a rock in the shade, in his faded badjoe and sarong, smoking innumerable cigarettes. (Mine, of course!)

We had been chatting for some little time when, by way of a new conversational opening, I asked after his family. Had he a wife? . . . No. He had not. But (and here he smiled a queer little reminiscent smile) he had had several, five of them, in fact, in his time. I tried to clothe my features in a suitably non-committal expression, and inquired politely how this had come about. Had they all died? He smiled again, and waved a hand airily: "Oh dear, no. He had only 'thrown them away.'" He used the phrase "soedah boeang," meaning literally "thrown away," a commonly used colloquial term for divorce; and as divorce in Java is a simple matter, costing but the modest sum of two guilders, the native attitude to it is quite well expressed to it by the phrase.

I felt I might be treading on delicate ground, but I ventured presently to seek information as to what might have led to the discarding of such a long succession of ladies. Once more he smiled, and spat meditatively, his gaze fixed on the tops of the lofty trees in the valley below. And, as is the custom of the East, his reply was indirect.

"It seems to me, toean," he said, "that the marriage customs of the Java people are better than those of the white folk. For, when a white man takes a wife, whether she be good or bad, whether his heart be light or heavy because of her, he cannot by any means be rid of her. He must keep her always, and therefrom there ensues many times much trouble. I am an old man, toean, and often have I seen this thing when I was servant to Toean Be-rown (who was as a father to me, and whom I followed from place to place for many years, till he went to his own country, when I returned to my village). There be very many women in the world, toean; and since a man must have peace and contentment in his own house—or why indeed should he live?—then if the woman he has does not bring him that happiness, he must try and try again, until, by good fortune, he finds one who suits him. Thus it was with me, toean. But, wah! . . . I had no luck. I found no happiness with any of them, and not one of them bore me children. And so at last, seeing that I grew old, I put the last one from me, and tried no more. And now my house is a place of great peace, where I can sit and smoke and eat my rice in comfort."

At this point there appeared from the direction of the village two stalwart young natives, carrying various small packages, each dangling from the string of tough grass with which it was tied. The old man waved a hand towards them, and went on: "These be young men, toean, and my limbs grow old, and they go to the village to buy such things as I require. For I have no son, as I have said. But these are the sons of two of the women who were formerly my wives: fine young men, toean, and very strong." And he looked at them with an appraising, quasi-paternal eye.

Here was a pretty little sermon for a drowsy afternoon, and a reminder that there may be other solutions than any that Western law has devised for matrimonial problems. Native divorce is so simple and straightforward a matter in Java, that it involves no sort of slur or "unpleasantness"; a lady who has been "boeang" is just as sure to marry again as the man. And if she can live amicably cheek by jowl in a small village which also contains her ex-husband, good-naturedly lending him her sons by a subsequent spouse to run his messages and look after him in his old age, it seems as though there must be a good deal to be said for the system. Not even in emancipated America do we hear of anything quite so "matey."

The average Javanese peasant is an expert naturalist. Ask him any question about the ways of birds, beasts, or plants, and he invariably proves a mine of information, which is all the more striking to one who went first to Java, as I did, from Australia. For there, to the average countryman, eight out of ten birds are "bush sparrows"; and any plant that is not immediately recognizable as wheat, oats, or maize, nor officially classed as a "noxious weed," is as nameless as any foundling child. The Javanese, on the other hand, not only knows the name of every habitant of the jungle, but will regale you, if you care to listen, with all sorts of wondrous fairy stories about them; from which he will switch off at a moment's notice to tell you how to treat a nut, just fallen within his reach from the tree above him, in order to extract its dye. And if he tells you to look out for bats, birds, or beetles at any particular time or place, you may be quite certain that there they will be almost to the minute, as though they were running to a time table that he had drawn up for them.

One of the most amusing characteristics of the Javanese is his innocent vanity. He loves above all things to be photographed, and the camera finds a very short road into his good graces. "Bikin portret" (make a portrait), as he calls it, of a native (and of his wife and family, whom he is sure to introduce for the purpose at the first opportunity), and there is nothing in his power he will not do for you, though he is as critical as a society beauty of the result; and if there is a shadow on his face, or a high-light on his nose, that he finds unbecoming, he will not rest until he has persuaded you to give him another "sitting." But I have found that money spent on this kind of photography (looked at quite frankly as an investment) brings an excellent return in native goodwill.

I remember meeting with only one exception, and that was on a tea-estate in Mid Java. A withered old native woman, laden with a huge bundle of prunings, was coming down the path, and I asked her, after exchanging greetings, if I should photograph her, expecting the usual eager response. I got it, but with a difference. "Of course the nyonya could bikin portret, provided the nyonya would give her fifty cents!" But I was buying no photographic rights that day, and the old lady went off muttering angrily to herself, quite unaware that I got an excellent snapshot of her retreating figure. And as her back view was much the most attractive part of her (she was certainly no beauty), I didn't score so badly after all.

The native is an ardent cinema "fan," educated to be so, no doubt, by the posters which appear even in remote villages, and by the leaflets describing the amorous screen exploits of popular stars, in highly picturesque Malay, which are distributed in the streets in thousands. These are scarcely calculated to enhance the native's regard for the "orang poeteh" (white man), and it seems to me very much to his credit that in spite of them he still treats the European with such consistent courtesy.

Javanese Seamen & Sportsmen

IT is so natural to think of the Javanese in connection with his rice-lands that the claims to notice of those of his race who live along the coast are rather apt to be overlooked. They have strong claims, nevertheless, for, like their cousins, the Malays, the coastal Javanese natives are accomplished "orang laoet"—men of the sea —whose art was doubtless handed down to them, as was that of the Malays, by ancestors who acquired it in the course of their piratical exploits among the early sea-farers. And their skill has been kept alive ever since by the difficulties and dangers of fishing in the stormy seas that beat on the shores of Java.

To realize what some of those difficulties are, you should travel some late afternoon, when the east monsoon is blowing hard, along the road that skirts the north-east coast, and see a fishing fleet coming home from the Java Sea. It is a very different sight from that of the North Sea trawlers hurrying home to Grimsby, or even from those almost forgotten days when the old brown-sailed fishing smacks slipped silently one by one into harbour at Lowestoft.

Near Kragan, on the Java coast, there is a miniature Lowestoft, with a "bandeng" (herring) fleet of big, heavy, wooden "prahoes"; but the shelter of its small harbour can only be gained at high water by a narrow channel, and the whole fleet is beached on the open sands that here for

many miles stretch unprotected, open to the full force of
the sea.

The homing fleet sails into the picture from the
distance, running fast before the wind, until it is within
a few hundred yards of the shore. There, one by one, the
prahoes heave to, and lie rolling awkwardly, awaiting
their turn; for each one has to be beached separately, with
the assistance of the whole village community.

On comes the first one towards you, running for the
shore at the speed of an express train, apparently heading
for certain destruction. Then suddenly, before you can
realize what has happened, with a smartness worthy of a
racing yachtsman, the big mat sails are down and stowed,
and the masts bare; the prahoe has turned broadside on to
the rollers, and then surges shoreward, pounding heavily
on the sand, as each crisply curling white-maned wave of
transparent pale-green water breaks against her side in a
shower of spray.

To the watcher it looks like a wreck, for half the crew
jump overboard, to be met by the men of the village, who
swarm round the helpless ship; and between them,
swimming and wading alongside, they push and pull her
round until they have manœuvred her stern-on to the
shore, where, lifted a little farther by each great roller as
it races in, she is safely beached at last.

There the men leave her to the women, who, meanwhile, have been hurrying along the sands in crowds,
carrying baskets for the fish. They climb aboard with the
agility of cats, fill their home-made baskets, and presently
depart again, heavily laden, for the town.

One by one the big prahoes are brought in by the same
perilous means, each of them crashing on the sands, as it
lies broadside, with a force that one would have thought
no boat ever built could survive.

But Java teak is staunch; there is never a hitch. All is done with almost mechanical precision, and at last the whole fleet lies side by side, as orderly and exact as a row of cars on a parking station; but how infinitely more pleasing to the eye! And the men who have accomplished it all nonchalantly wring out their soaking sarongs, light up their tiny native cigarettes (brought down for them by the women) with the flint and steel that every Javanese carries, and drift off quietly down the sands towards the village, to eat their evening rice, and sleep awhile before the rising tide calls them back into action again.

I wonder sometimes how some of us of the Superior Race, who talk so glibly of the "lazy native," would care to undertake this kind of work?

Fishing of this sort goes on all along the coasts of Java. The fish caught is mostly the bandeng, a very small member of the herring family. There is also a great deal of shrimp-fishing, which is carried on with curious round nets, like enormous inverted umbrellas, mounted on slender curving bamboos.

There is, too, an important seawater fish-breeding industry, but this is mostly in the hands of the Chinese, who raise the bandeng in big salt-water ponds along the coast. Most of this fish is dried, and there is an enormous demand for it; thousands upon thousands of tons are consumed by both natives and Chinese. You can go into storehouses stacked high with the unsavoury stuff, and the spacious sections necessarily given over to it in every native "pasar" are places to be hurried past with breath well held, for they advertise their wares in unmistakable terms to the shrinking nostrils of the European passer-by. But, needless to say, they are always well filled with a chaffering crowd of native and Chinese housewives.

A curious custom, undoubtedly a very ancient one, still persists among the people of the coastal villages: that of launching a "prahoe hantoe," or devil-boat. An old native fisherman explained it to me thus: "If evil comes to the village, nyonya; if our nets are empty; if our wives bear us no children; or if sickness comes upon us, then it is certain that a 'hantoe' must have come from the sea to dwell among us; and he will certainly stay till we build him a ship so that he can sail away. So we consult the doekoen (paying him money), and make a small ship as he directs, and place an image of the hantoe at the stern so that he can steer it. We launch it at night on the falling tide, with soft words, telling him that it is a fine ship, and will carry him safely to a richer village than ours. And if in the morning the ship is gone, all is well, and the evil will depart from us; but if the tide should bring him back, then are we very sad at heart, for we know that yet more evil will come upon us."

Once, on a lonely patch of sandy coast, I found one of these queer ghost-boats firmly aground. It was about three feet long, strong and seaworthy, and fit to bear the grotesque little figure that stood firmly fixed in it safely across any ocean. Whether it had been hopefully launched from the nearest village, and had drifted back unseen in the darkness, or whether some distant community had foisted its ill luck upon them, I never knew.

But happily the tide was ebbing. No one was in sight. So I waded out and set the little ship (with soft words to the hantoe, as directed) upon its way. I watched till it drifted out of sight, carrying its freight of bad luck, and prayed to the island gods that its course might be set for some distant land inhabited only by crocodiles.

No one has ever been able to explain why it is that the blow-pipe, or "soempitan," that mysterious weapon with which some of the aboriginal tribes of South America do their fighting, should be known only to them, and to people as far remote from them as those of Malaya. It is still used by the Sakais in the jungles of Malaya to kill game, and was well known to the Javanese in the Middle Ages, but it is generally supposed to have disappeared completely in modern times. It was all the more interesting, therefore, to come across a survival of this primitive weapon, not, as you might suppose, in some remote corner of Bantam, but within a very few miles of Bandoeng, one of the biggest centres of European civilization.

I was taking a short cut through a coconut plantation to a path leading through a native kampong when I came upon an elderly native shooting idly at a mark in the middle of a vegetable plot from which the crop had been cut. His weapon was a blow-pipe about eight feet long, an unwieldy-looking contraption with which accurate aim would appear to be an utter impossibility; and when the old man told me he was getting it ready to shoot the birds which were destroying the crop on his other field, I smiled to myself a pitying little smile at the poor, guile-less old fellow, thinking that for all the execution he was likely to do among them, those marauding birds were fairly safe.

Rather unkindly, out of sheer curiosity, I found a scrap of paper, fixed up a small white target half-way across the plot, and invited him to aim at it. He fitted a ridiculous dart, or arrow, made of a bamboo splinter about two inches long, bound with a wisp of kapok, put the pipe casually to his lips, and, with scarcely a glance at the mark, gave a little puff. He seemed to have aimed high in the air, but when I looked at my scrap of paper it was well and truly transfixed through the middle with that wicked little needle-pointed bamboo splinter.

The old man did it for me again several times in the same casual way, till the target was more holes than paper, and I wasted no more pity on the poor, simple native with his absurd childish toy. He told me that it was a favourite method of killing birds in the country round about; it was "so easy," he said.

But it occurred to me that even quite a small party of natives equipped with this unpleasant weapon and plenty of poisoned darts, sniping from cover, might be anything but an "easy" enemy to reckon with.

The Javanese has quite different notions of sport from ours. But he has taken very kindly to one European game, and that is association football. Every town has its team, and they visit each other, usually on Sundays, by motor bus, and play off a long programme of fixtures that lasts all the year round. They play a hard game, very entertaining to watch, especially when they play barefoot, and no European ever fails to marvel at the terrific force of the kicks of which those strong bare feet are capable.

A native football crowd is noticeably self-contained, compared with one composed of English or Australians. They applaud a goal lustily, but otherwise they seem to find the game a trifle dull, which after all is natural in a people whose forefathers had such full-blooded sports as tiger-spearing and buffalo-versus-tiger fights for their half-holiday diversions.

The same applies to horse-racing, of which there is plenty in Java, for there is a Turf Club in every large town. The native goes to the races in crowds, as he does to any other "show" that comes his way. It is a holiday, an occasion for dressing up and wearing his smartest sarong, but if he feels any particular enthusiasm for the racing, he certainly does not show it.

The races themselves, run by Australian horses, ridden

by Australian jockeys, are so entirely European that if you looked only at the track you might just as well be at Epsom or Randwick. Perhaps it is just that vivid contrast between East and West that makes the motley crowd all the more amusing, especially if, eschewing the more conventional delights of the Turf Club lawn, you drive to a road skirting the course, near one of the starting posts, and sitting at your ease in a small grandstand of your own, have not only a perfect view of the racing, but the added entertainment of watching a diversity of Eastern nationalities at play.

The Javanese, of course, predominates, but there are plenty of others to be seen. A smart young Chinese mother, her great "bun" of black hair impaled with long gold pins, stands close by, wearing a spotless starched white coat and full black trousers. In her arms is a plump, delightful baby, as clean and starched as his mother, his hair close shaven from the neck half-way up the back of his head, making the top look like a small black cap. An older boy, clad only in a pair of white shorts, executes catherine wheels and other mild gymnastic turns, to amuse his baby brother, watching us all the time out of the corner of his eye. They all decide after a while that we are harmless, and come to sit on the running-board of the car, where the baby presently draws our attention very gravely to the tiny gold ring and ear-rings he is wearing.

A party of Japanese, very smart and dapper in European suits, with bright brown shoes and silk socks, stroll by; then a sleek, slim Indian, also as European as a Chinese tailor can make him, speaking to no one, looking shifty and morose. A group of young Chinese, wearing spectacles so strong that they distort their eyes, lean on the rail deep in earnest discussion, probably of their country's politics; and when every now and then the conversation

takes a lighter turn, there is a flash of gold-filled teeth—
for the Chinese is almost as fond of a "golden smile" as
the American.

Everywhere, threading their way among the people,
are the peddlers. Some are selling bunches of red, hairy
ramboetan; others, air balloons, which float over the
heads of the crowd like big, multi-coloured bubbles.
Some sell sweetmeats; there is no limit to the varieties
you could buy if you were brave enough to try them.
There are sticky balls impaled on the ends of slender
bamboos; freshly fried cakes still sizzling from the pan
(which, with the fire that cooked them, hangs in the
portable kitchen at one end of the carrying pole). There
are "lucky dips," tiny parcels done up in scraps of newspaper, which all seem to reveal the same revolting caramel-
like mess when unwrapped, but which find a ready sale;
and sprays of paper flowers, with brightly coloured eggs
nestling among them by way of fruit.

One old Javanese offers Wayang puppets for sale,
giving so expert an exhibition with one or other of them
every now and then that it is pretty evident he must have
been a Dalang (showman) in his time. Another announces
himself as the "bird man," and sells birds made of
buffalo horns, the tip forming the beak, and the legs and
wings cleverly cut out in horn and added. Another offers
rough but attractive local pottery; another, Batik; many
sell cigarettes, and their cry of "Roko, roko," is everywhere, and one insists on opening a box and unwrapping
mysterious tiny parcels done up in pink tissue paper
containing native "silver" spoons shaped like Wayang
figures, which he lays out seductively along the running-
board.

All this and more, with brief flashes of racing, the start
of which we see, but never the finish, which after all is as

it should be, for if you never know which horse wins, you need never lose your illusions about the one you "fancied."

The Java natives' own sports are mild. They have not taken to cock-fighting like the Filipinos, but fights of a sort they have. They will spend hours grubbing in the ground for a certain pugnacious species of cricket, which they keep in tiny cages made of the inevitable bamboo, finely split, and feed with flies (for this is a carnivorous variety) to make it fierce, until it is ready to challenge an equally well-prepared antagonist.

These devastating combats are staged in the kampongs at all times and seasons, surrounded with deeply interested little groups of backers, whose exclamations of "Wah! Koerang berani, dia!" (He's a coward!) or a groan of "Kasian-lah!" when the favourite is finally dispatched, are about as near as the Javanese ever gets to "barracking."

Madoera, which is separated from Java proper by a narrow strait, but is really almost a continuation of East Java, is the one fortunate locality where two really exciting sports still survive.

One of these is goat-fighting, which is full of thrills (for the goat), but ends in anti-climax. The antagonists, big "he-goats," selected for their weight and strength, are held at each side of the arena in full view of one another. A signal is given, they are released, and charge, straight as arrows, head-on, coming together with a crash like a motor collision. The impact might be expected to have some effect, but nothing happens.

The goats continue to butt each other clumsily until they are seized and dragged back to their original places, to charge and charge again, ever less and less fiercely, until at last there comes a crash which finally dissipates the warlike ardour of one of the two. He simply shakes

94

his head to signify that he has done with the affair, walks away, bleating to himself, and begins to crop grass with his back to his opponent.

The victor of this bloodless contest is acclaimed, stakes are collected, and the show is over.

The other Madoera sport is bullock-racing, which also ends in something of an anti-climax, for nobody ever actually wins, but which always adds a few casualties to the fun. The handsome, creamy draught bullocks, gaily decorated, are yoked in pairs, with a kind of sledge lashed between them, one end resting on the yoke and the other dragging on the ground. On this stands the "jockey," gripping an upright pole with his knees, leaving his hands free for the rope reins which are passed through the bullocks' noses.

The clumsy beasts gallop at astonishing speed, and it is nothing unusual for a jockey to be hurled from his precarious perch and horribly trampled, or possibly killed.

Sometimes, when the harness breaks, or the jockey loses his balance, the teams run amok among the onlookers, breaking arms and legs, and even killing any spectators who are too slow to get out of their way; and as a pair of heavy bullocks in full flight is an awkward thing to dodge in a narrow space, casualties are common. But they damp nobody's enthusiasm except that of those immediately concerned. In fact, they are part of the entertainment. "The show's the thing" at the bullock races, just as it was at the tiger fights long ago.

Among native amusements, though it scarcely comes under the head of "sport," kite-flying is immensely popular. You can scarcely pass a kampong in the country without seeing half a dozen or so big paper kites fluttering in the sky. They are made in the villages, in every imaginable shape and pattern, and extremely decorative some of them are.

The best I have ever come across were at Pendjaloe, beside the lovely lake that has formed in the crater of an extinct volcano. A whole flight of them was rising one after the other, shining and glimmering in all sorts of colours, with long, fishlike tails undulating in the breeze, and the air was full of a murmurous humming sound, for which I was completely at a loss to account, for birds or bees there were none that I could see.

I asked a passing native if it was magic that made the music in the air, and he told me that it came from the "layangan menyanyi" (singing kites), which were the special pride of the near-by village where they were made. He explained that a section of small bamboo with a "reed" (evidently on the principle of our clarinet) was fixed at the base of the kite, so that "the wind sang through it as it flew"—rather a poetic idea to proceed from a simple old peasant! I wish I could say that the "singing kite" is universal throughout Java, but, sad to relate, I have never come across it again.

THE BUDDHIST TEMPLE OF BOROBOEDOER, SAID TO BE THE FINEST TEMPLE OF BUDDHA IN THE WORLD

EACH OF THE FOUR HUNDRED NICHES ROUND ITS WALLS CONTAINS A SEATED STATUE OF THE GOD. IT WAS COVERED WITH JUNGLE GROWTH FOR CENTURIES, BUT WAS EXCAVATED ABOUT A HUNDRED YEARS AGO.

A Chapter of Javanese History

JAVA did not make her first appearance in European history until the end of the sixteenth century. At that time it was not by any means Britannia that ruled the waves, but Spain and Portugal—so much so that the ship of any other nation that dared to show its hull above what they chose to regard as their private horizon was regarded as a pirate and, if possible, summarily treated as such.

Hence it was that Drake's voyage to the East, in 1577, was regarded by the two nations who had the Pope's sanction for dividing between them "all such lands as have not been heretofore possessed by any other Christian King or Prince" as a most outrageous trespass upon their lawful preserves.

The British then earned the right to sail the seas by defeating the Spanish Armada. After that the spice trade, formerly the monopoly of the Arabs, Spanish, and Portuguese, became the bone of contention for which the British and Dutch were to fight for the next two hundred years.

The history of Java from this time onward is bound up with that of the British and Dutch East India Companies, and that history is full of incident.

After the defeat of the Armada, in 1588, the merchants of London decided to fit out an expedition to investigate the prospects of trade with the East. Four ships set sail in 1591 under the leadership of a Captain Lancaster, and arrived off Penang, in the Malay Peninsula, in June of the following year.

I am afraid it must be confessed that the gallant captain was a pirate at heart, for he interpreted his orders to "investigate" by attacking any Portuguese ships he came across, stealing their cargoes of pepper, and then sending ships and sailors to the bottom of the sea.

Having in this way reaped a rich harvest of "trade," he sailed for home, but did not arrive altogether without incident, for two of his own ships were in their turn sunk on the way. However, he reached the Port of London eventually with enough pepper in the holds of his two remaining ships to convince the good City merchants that there was plenty of valuable trade to be had in the East Indies.

The famous company was thereupon formed, and Captain Lancaster was appointed its first Governor. He sailed in command of the first official fleet of four ships in 1601. They anchored off Acheen, in North Sumatra, in the following year, and were received with great friendliness by the natives, with whom they did a brisk trade in pepper, sending home many rich cargoes.

Meanwhile the Dutch also had sent out an expedition, under one Houtman, and formed their company in 1602. The British established a trading station and settlement at Bantam, in the west of Java, and the Dutch promptly settled close beside them, doubtless for the purpose of keeping an eye on their rivals. About the year 1611 both companies moved their stations to Jacatra, on the site of which Batavia now stands, and there the rival merchants traded side by side in anything but amity for many years.

A Chapter of Javanese History

But it soon became evident that the Dutch "carried too many guns" for the British. They had all the weight of the Netherlands government behind them, whereas the English company was an entirely private enterprise, a group of independent merchants; though it has to be admitted that the greed of those merchants must have had much to do with the failure of their representatives in the East against the Dutch at this time. In spite of their inferior resources, the Londoners could have resisted the Dutch far more effectively if the company had been willing to cut down its dividends and spend more on ships and forts. This they refused to do, despite the constant prayers of the luckless adventurers who were earning those rich dividends for them; and for a very long period they were only sending out scattered ships at long intervals, while the Dutch dispatched a constant succession of well-equipped fleets, which established them so firmly that the English were forced to give way.

As an example of the tremendous contrast between the companies' respective Eastern equipment at this time, their records show that in 1622 the Dutch had eighty-three ships in the trade and the English only twenty-eight. In Wilkinson's history of the period the London merchants are described as: "A sanctimonious company that supplied its employees with devotional literature, underpaid them, and sacrificed their lives rather than reduce its dividends."

In 1615 the Dutch had proposed that the rival companies should amalgamate, their shrewd reason being that they found the cost of maintaining a large fleet and army to hold their own against the Portuguese was seriously reducing their profits; they therefore suggested that England should carry part of the burden of fighting their mutual enemy, and that, when that enemy had been finally disposed of, the victorious allies should share the Eastern trade. The English directors in London, however, having profited hitherto by the Dutch army and navy without contributing a penny to their upkeep, saw no reason to alter so eminently satisfactory a state of things.

Unwillingness to sacrifice profits to their servants' security seems always to have been a characteristic of the English company's policy. They much preferred to let their unlucky representatives be insulted, imprisoned, or even murdered by native rulers or by the Dutch, than waste good money on protecting them. They therefore avoided either accepting or refusing the Dutch offer, and continued to order the establishment of new and unprotected posts or "factories" in different places.

Relations between the two companies grew steadily worse, until by 1618 they were at open war, and a hollow truce patched up between James I and the Dutch in 1619 did little more than add fresh fuel to the flames.

There is an incident in the records of the English company which gives an amusing idea of their methods at this time. One "Thomasine," the widow of a sailor who had lost his life in one of the company's ships off the Java coast, was given £20 in full compensation. This, Thomasine seems to have considered inadequate, and so (says the record) "she gathered other sorrowing widows and went to complain to the Lords of the Council." But on stating their case they were told that "unless they took themselves off forthwith they should be soundly whipped, whereupon they fled disconsolate back to their haunts at Wapping and Rotherhythe."

In 1623 the Dutch tortured and murdered a number of Englishmen at Amboyna, in the Spice Islands, on a charge of conspiring to seize the Dutch fortress there. This outrage put an end to all thought of co-operation between the two companies, and the Dutch redoubled their efforts both to prevent the English from gaining new stations, and to oust them from those they already held. Their severity to the natives made them feared wherever they went, and for this reason, as well as by virtue of the greater wealth at their command, they were able to prevail on native rulers to have no dealings with the English when they appeared. The London men, therefore, found the natives hostile at every Far Eastern point at which they attempted to settle.

In 1641 the Dutch took Malacca, in the Malay Peninsula, from the Portuguese, and there, entrenched in the great fortress built by their predecessors, they absolutely dominated all trade beyond India.

Meanwhile, however, the British company had established itself firmly in India, and had also first defeated and then made a treaty with the Portuguese, so that these two former adversaries now made common cause against the Dutch. The company suffered heavy losses under Charles I (who borrowed £50,000 and never repaid it), but its fortunes improved under Cromwell, who forced the Dutch to pay an indemnity for the Amboyna massacre, and under Charles II, too, it prospered greatly.

The Dutch, however, continued their hostility unabated, and at last succeeded in inducing the reigning Sultan of Jacatra to force the British to leave his country. They had no option but to obey, and went back to their old settlement at Bantam. But here, too, their rivals would leave them no peace. The Dutch made another "treaty" with the Sultan of Bantam, and he, too, ordered the Englishmen to quit his territory, emphasizing his instructions with a few particularly artistic murders.

A Chapter of Javanese History

When they were forced to abandon their trading stations in Java in 1684, it looked as though London's pepper trade was hopelessly lost. The English made an attempt to settle ashore at Acheen, off the coast of which the company's ships had anchored and traded years before. But news travels fast among native races, and although the ruler of Acheen, a native princess, was friendly, tales of Dutch retribution had reached her, and she was afraid of the consequences if she were to allow the English to build a settlement, especially an armed one, as, for once, they (not unnaturally) desired to do.

Another Malay ruler, however, agreed to a settlement at Bencoolan in 1685, and this was held by the English until it was traded to the Dutch for Malacca in 1824. During the whole period the settlers suffered every kind of disaster, disease, and privation; it was estimated that the settlement cost the company £100,000 a year, and only a few hundred tons of pepper ever came out of it.

Bencoolan, in short, was a tragic failure, which cost hundreds of lives and hundreds of thousands in money. And it was the need for a better headquarters for the British company that led to the treaty, made by Captain Light in 1786 with the Sultan of Kedah, by which the British gained Penang, an island off the Malay Peninsula, and later to the acquisition of Singapore by Raffles in 1819, and thus to the beginnings of British Malaya.

From the latter half of the seventeenth century to the close of the eighteenth the power of the Dutch East India Company was steadily declining. The drain on Holland's resources in the wars with France and England had seriously decreased the support available, and, moreover, the company's own policy was a potent factor in its downfall. Java and the other islands were regarded as a business undertaking, and shamelessly exploited so as to win from them the last possible florin's worth of labour and produce.

The result was an endless series of risings and revolts, which were crushed with ruthless determination; to accomplish which, lives and the company's wealth were recklessly expended. The history of those times is not a pretty one, for these wars were conducted with the most barbarous ferocity on both sides.

In addition to the desperately fighting native princes, the Dutch saw, or thought they saw, a fresh danger in the Chinese population, who, attracted as always by new business opportunities, had settled in great numbers about Batavia (as the town built on the site of the old native city of Jacatra was called, after the ancient name of Holland). So, in 1740, a wholesale massacre of these unfortunate people was carried out, the survivors of which took to the mountains and allied themselves with the hostile Javanese.

The corruption and dishonesty of the company's officials was another factor which contributed to its fall. And there was yet a third: during the whole of the company's existence the Eurasian population had been steadily growing. No white women came out with the pioneers, and marriage with the native women was general; it was, moreover, encouraged by the Dutch authorities, who thought in this way to establish a settled and contented community.

The Eurasian section of the population, however, although given European status, tended more and more during that period to be disloyal to the Dutch of pure European origin; whether from jealousy or for what complex racial reasons it is impossible to say. But whatever may have been the cause, the fact remains that they, too, plotted constantly against the company.

The worst of these uprisings was one organized by Peter Erberfeld, a rich half-caste, who plotted the massacre of all the Dutch in the Batavia settlement. A native girl betrayed the conspirators, and the leaders were beheaded. Erberfeld's skull was cemented over, and mounted on a wall in old Batavia, where it is to be seen to this day.

The Dutch company abandoned group after group of islands, and by 1795, when the British captured Malacca and the Moluccas from them, their Far Eastern territory had shrunk to Java and a few fortified stations in Sumatra, Borneo, and the Celebes. All the rest had been either abandoned or destroyed by the bitterly hostile natives. In the same year the company was declared bankrupt, the original charter issued in 1602 was annulled, and the Dutch East India Company had ceased to exist. Three years later a "Batavian Republic" was created, and took over the administration of Java and the remaining trading stations.

It seems extremely probable that, despite the decline of the Dutch company, the British might have confined their operations to India, where they were greatly prospering, and have delayed until too late the extension of their trade farther East, had it not been for those two great men, Francis Light and Stamford Raffles. It has, indeed, been authoritatively stated that but for them Malaya, as well as Java, would have been a Dutch colony to-day.

Light had to play his hand practically alone, and even against opposition, in establishing the station at Penang; and later on it was only through Raffles that Malacca was not abandoned, and that Singapore was ever acquired.

The histories of both places are intimately bound up with that of Java. When the British took over Malacca from the Dutch, the situation was so tangled that if it had occurred in these latter days an International Conference would certainly have picnicked at Geneva or Lausanne to discuss it. As it was, Malacca was held "in trust" by the British for the Stadholder of Holland, during the rebellion of his subjects, the English directors meanwhile considering in London (no doubt to the accompaniment of the usual banquets) how best to deal with the matter. They came to the conclusion that if Malacca ever had to be handed back to the Dutch, it would seriously affect the trade of their new station at Penang, of which, once acquired by Light, they had come fully to recognize the value.

They therefore, in 1807, decided to blow up the magnificent old fortifications built at Malacca by the Portuguese (of which, alas, only one splendid gateway remains), and did all they could to induce the population to migrate to Penang, hoping thus to fulfil their trust by handing Malacca back to Holland as a tract of uninhabited jungle.

The population, however, being unversed in the vagaries of high diplomacy, steadfastly declined to be evacuated; and when Raffles visited Malacca in 1808 he saw the absurdity of the attempt, and wrote a report pointing out that, even if the town could be emptied and the site abandoned, it would soon be reoccupied by a native ruler, and eventually reconquered by some other European Power.

Raffles succeeded in convincing Lord Minto, the Governor-General of India, that the old fort must be held. And it was at Malacca that the expedition which was sent from Madras to attack the Dutch and the French (who were using Java as a base against the English), refitted and finally set out in 1811. The British force landed near Batavia, and defeated the combined Dutch and French forces under Daendels, one of Napoleon's marshals, a few miles inland, on the site of the suburb now called Meester Cornelius.

Java was now at last a British colony, though it was not destined to remain so for long. From the very beginning it was uncertain whether it might not be handed back to Holland. But in the meantime Raffles was appointed Governor, and set himself at once to attempt the tremendous task of sweeping away the abuses of centuries first of native and then of Dutch misrule and oppression.

As with most Eastern potentates, the power of the Javanese princes over their people was absolute. Under the old native law, the land belonged to the prince and the crop to the cultivator, the latter paying rent for his land with a proportion of his crop and his labour. And as the Dutch defeated the native chiefs one by one, they took over the despotic native system as it stood, arguing that they had conquered the princes, not the people, and that they therefore logically came into the princes' rights.

These rights they exercised to the utmost—even more cruelly, according to Raffles, than had the native rulers themselves; they made hopeless serfs of the people, and left them not the slightest proprietary interest in the land they cultivated. Strange to say, however, in introducing the seven-day week to which they were accustomed, the Dutch did make one modification in the native's favour, for the "one day a week" free labour which the native princes had extorted was now one day in seven instead of one in five (the old Javanese "week" consisting of five days).

(It would be interesting to know, by the way, whether the rulers of Soviet Russia are aware that in substituting a five-day for the seven-day week as a stepping-stone towards the Ideal State, they are reverting to the ancient custom of an Eastern race in its days of barbarism?)

Raffles' first concern was to change this population of serfs into one of independent peasant proprietors; and among other reforms he established a system by which the dues payable from the farmer to the government were paid direct, instead of by a series of miscellaneous payments collected through so many hands (all of which retained "pickings" on the way), that in the end there was little left either for the government or for the luckless farmer.

But poor Raffles was not given long in which to carry out his reforms, for Java was handed back to Holland in 1816 by a treaty designed to secure Dutch goodwill in Europe. Yet although his scathing denunciation of the Dutch policy towards the natives brought down on him severe censure from the Home authorities, who "feared trouble with the Dutch on account of his language," he was everywhere acknowledged to be a great administrator. Like Francis Light, he had an extraordinary understanding of native points of view, which gave him superlative success in dealing with them. The Dutch, naturally, had no love for Raffles, but they paid him the compliment, nevertheless, of gradually adopting all his reforms, though it took them the best part of a century to carry them out.

Raffles' wife died in Java, and she lies buried under the great shady trees in the lovely garden of the Governor-General's palace at Buitenzorg. A clause in the treaty charged the Dutch with the care in perpetuity of her grave; an obligation which they have faithfully discharged to the present day.

When their Far Eastern possessions were restored to them, the government of Holland at once set to work to regain all that had been lost by the bankrupt East India

Company. They sent out strong forces and reoccupied all the abandoned settlements, revived all the old treaties excluding the British from trading, and made many new ones. Raffles made repeated attempts to convince the English company's directors that the Dutch were well on the way to establish a monopoly of trade in the Eastern archipelago, but it was not until 1818 that he was granted powers to establish a British station at Rhio (a group of islands near Singapore), and even then he was warned to "do nothing that could antagonize the Dutch."

However, he arrived at Rhio to find that, as in the old days, the Dutch had forestalled him, and had made a treaty with the Sultan of the group. So, acting on his own initiative, Raffles anchored, on 28th January 1819, off the island of Singapore, then inhabited only by the Dato Temmenggong of Johore, and about a hundred and fifty Malay fishermen and pirates.

Finding that the Temmenggong was willing to allow a settlement, and that the Dutch, for a wonder, had made no claims (though they made plenty later!), Raffles made a provisional agreement with him, which was ratified a few days later by treaty with the Sultan. So was founded the great port of Singapore.

An account of the place as they found it, written by a Malay protégé of Raffles, might make amusing reading for the tea-dancers and lounge-lizards of little more than a century later.

"At that time" (writes Abdullah) "no mortal dared to pass through the Straits. Jins and satans were even afraid, for that was the place the pirates made use of to sleep at and divide their booty; there also they put to death their captives and fought and killed each other in their quarrels over the spoil. All along the beach there were hundreds of human skulls, some of them old, some of them fresh with the hair still remaining, some with the teeth still sharp and some without teeth. Mr. Farquhar ordered them to be collected and thrown into the sea. They were all put in sacks and thrown in accordingly."[1]

[1] From the *Hikayat Abdullah*, translated by T. Braddell.

Java's "Conversions"

LIKE many another Eastern race, the Javanese have not so much attained religion as had religion thrust upon them. But happily for Java, by virtue, no doubt, of its comparatively isolated position, its successive "conversions" seem to have been effected with somewhat less violence than those of some other races.

Java has now been a Mohammedan country for nearly five hundred years. It would doubtless have been so far earlier if it had not been so well off the track, and present-day Java might have been a very different place; its richly cultivated hill-sides would perhaps still be clothed with trackless jungle, populated by a handful of primitive tribes, if the desert fanatics or the Turks had had their way with it, or if the Mongol conquerors who ravaged half Asia had chanced upon it and destroyed its ancient irrigation works, as they did those of Mesopotamia.

Happily, however, the people of Java and Malaya were not gathered into the fold of Islam until later, when the edge of the Prophet's sword had somewhat lost its keenness.

But the coming of the Fiery Crescent was by no means the first chapter in Java's religious history. Little is known of the island before the fifteenth century, but we should know even less if it were not for the ruins of the temples of various religions with which the country abounds.

Lying as it does on the natural sea route from India to

China, it is certain that Java and the adjacent islands must have been known to the very earliest Indian seafarers. As a source of food and fresh-water supplies these islands must have been invaluable to them, and they doubtless also learned before long that precious metals and the spices beloved of their Indian masters were to be had almost for the taking.

Chinese records prove that some time early in our Christian era there were Indian settlements in Java and some of the smaller islands. They were, naturally, in the most accessible places, and traces of many of them still remain. The native inhabitants were strongly influenced by the civilization of the colonizers from India, and to this day the people of outer islands in the eastern part of the archipelago are noticeably less cultured than those whose ancestors came in contact with the invaders.

Settlement increased as Java became the goal of the Indian navigators instead of merely a port of call, and by the sixth or seventh century A.D., at about the same period as that at which those other great migrants from India, the Khmers, were building their amazing temples in Cambodia, Indian architects and builders were doing the same in Java. And so, though the Indian conquerors have long vanished from the island, and their religion with them, they have left behind them the temples and images that they raised to their long-forgotten gods.

As in Cambodia, these relics are perplexing, in that some were evidently erected to the glory of one god and some to another. So that it is more than likely that the luckless Javanese were "converted" to each in turn, though with just what degree of religious zeal such conversions were effected in those far-off fanatic days there are happily no records to say.

Java's "Conversions"

Whether Brahma and all the strange array of terror-inspiring Hindu gods were replaced by the gentler Buddha, or vice versa, or whether they flourished side by side, no one can say. But the huge stone figures at Singosari and elsewhere are almost certainly not intended for images of the Buddha, whereas the wonderful temple of Boroboedoer, famous among Buddhist temples all over the world, is adorned with four hundred giant, smiling Buddhas, each in a miniature temple of his own, as though to prove that here, at least, no other gods need apply.

There is a widely accepted legend that this extraordinary temple, which is built in the form of an enormous cap over the top of a low hill, was covered with earth by its priests in the fourteenth or fifteenth century, to prevent its being found and destroyed by the Mohammedans. In any case, it was abandoned. And whether the story is true or not, the temple was certainly buried and hidden in soil and jungle-growth (though its existence was known) up to the time of Raffles, who ordered its excavation. The work was carried on after Raffles' departure by the Dutch, and to-day the temple stands much as it must have stood in the days when its builders left it.

Those days passed, and the waves of Islam engulfed Java at last, some time in the latter half of the fourteenth century. There was no means of keeping it out. Java was made up of a number of tiny kingdoms, each ruled by a cruel despot, who went to war periodically in the most barbarous way possible with all his neighbours. There was no Central Power to close the island to religious invaders as the Mikado closed Japan to Christian aggression later on. So when, after the conquest of Constantinople by the Turks in 1453, and the triumphant march of Islam along the remaining trade routes, Arab

A TYPICAL GALLERY OF THE TEMPLE AT BOROBOEDOER

THIS IS LINED WITH ELABORATE LOW-RELIEF CARVINGS. ONE OF THE 400 BUDDHAS OF THE TEMPLE PRESIDES FROM HIS NICHE ABOVE.

conquerors followed the missionaries who had first brought the Crescent to Java, the Javanese doubtless had little choice but to accept this latest new religion with a good grace (though possibly certain reservations), as they had accepted the religious foibles of all the earlier missionaries in their midst.

As time went on, and generation succeeded generation, the Javanese, in common with the people of Sumatra and Malaya, became devout Mohammedans. They are so still; but Islam has always adapted itself to, or perhaps been moulded by, the peoples it has conquered, and so the Javanese have evolved a sort of composite religion with characteristics all its own.

There is no question of their devotion to Islam. They learn and recite long passages from the Koran; they observe the ceremonies and keep the fasts—in their own way. They are particularly enthusiastic in their desire to become "Hadjis," and in consequence some ten thousand of the faithful make the pilgrimage to Mecca every year, providing a steady source of revenue for the shipping companies that take them there.

But underneath all this the people remain what they have always been at heart: animists, believers in spirits and "hantoes" (devils) and doekoens and "pawangs" (witch-doctors), in all kinds of magic, and in man-beasts, that are men by day and tigers by night—as they always have believed in them and always will.

You find evidences of it at every turn. Your gardener, perhaps, will tell you that his small son (who is the pride of his father's heart for his knowledge of the Koran) has a bad cough. The description suggests pneumonia, but he refuses to have a white doctor, and calls in the doekoen. After this worthy has tied a black string round the child's arm, made a decoction of herbs and poured it over him, muttering some weird incantation, the patient miraculously recovers.

"He is a very good doekoen, toean," the father gravely assures you. "I paid him five guilders" (which amounts to nearly half the poor old fellow's wages for a month).

It is worth quoting another instance to illustrate how ineradicable are the people's old beliefs, even after centuries of the simple faith of Mohammed, as well as long association with Western influences. The manager of a European company was transferred from Batavia to Soerabaya, and when he arrived, the previous manager's native chauffeur came to see him and asked to be taken on. The new manager, however, told him he had brought his own chauffeur with him, gave the native a small present, and, sending him away, thought no more about the matter.

But in a week or two he noticed that his own usually smiling old chauffeur was looking ill and miserable. Day by day he looked worse—his eyes were dull and his skin blotchy—until at last he said to his master: "Toean, I must leave you. I am ill, and so is my wife and my children also. My hair is coming out" (and he pulled some out to prove it!). "We shall all die. It is the hantoe that lives in the great tree in the courtyard who does this thing."

The poor fellow was sick with terror, and there was nothing for it but to let him go. He spoke the truth. He and his family were all wrecks, and there was no denying that his hair really was coming out in patches. And so, after twelve years' service, Ah Mat, an ardent Mohammedan, with high hopes of some day saving enough for a pilgrimage to Mecca, so that he might wear the green and white turban of the Hadji; an expert mechanic and driver, earning a good salary, and fully cognizant of the joys of town life (he was an ardent cinema fan), was driven by a hantoe to live in poverty among strangers in a distant village. But he cared not a jot if only it was out of the hantoe's range.

No sooner had Ah Mat gone than the other chauffeur came again to apply for the job. But the manager, who was beginning to feel suspicious, refused him, and engaged another instead.

That, however, was not the end of the story. After several months had passed, it happened that a big tree in the compound was found to be damaging the buildings, and was cut down. Within a few days Ah Mat, spick-and-span and smiling, was at the door waiting to see his old master. "News came to me that the tree was cut down and the hantoe had no place to live," he said joyfully. "Now I can come back to the toean."

Which he did, and they all lived happily ever after. There was no means of finding out exactly what had happened. But discreet inquiries yielded hints that the former manager's chauffeur had paid a witch-doctor to work the affair in the hope of scaring his rival away and securing his job. Whether or not there really was a hantoe in that tree (and you begin to believe that all sorts of things are possible after a few years among these people), at all events it certainly had the desired effect on poor Ah Mat's nerves!

As a final instance, I often wonder how many of the laughing, noisy tourists who discuss their first "rijst-tafel" at one of the finest hotels in Batavia know that the lofty, luxurious dining-room in which they are sitting is haunted at night by a terrible hantoe in the shape of a huge dog. And that not one of the smart, white-clad Javanese waiters who are serving them so deftly (some of them with quite a fair smattering of English) could be induced to put so much as his nose inside the place after the lights are out for a thousand guilders.

Yet, with their minds full of all these alarming beliefs, the Javanese are still devout Mohammedans. They admire and revere the Arabs, as the authors of their religion; and though there are only about three hundred thousand Arabs among more than forty million natives, they exercise great influence. The old port of Grissee, where the first Moslem missionary, Moelana Malik Ibrahim, lived and died, is still a place of pilgrimage. Many natives go there to visit his grave, and to perform their devotions at the mosque erected to his memory, where his sacred kris (sword) is preserved.

This same old town of Grissee is a link also with a later stage in Java's history. It was a busy and important place in the palmy days of the Dutch East India Company. But times have changed, and Grissee has now only about a hundred and fifty white inhabitants, though many of the stately old houses built for the rich merchants from Holland are still standing. They look deserted and forlorn but they are not empty. They are rented by Chinese, who use them as nesting places for the swallows that build edible nests, and the birds have proved most profitable and satisfactory tenants. So now those dark, lofty old rooms, once the home of the stout Dutch burghers, are encrusted with nests, and filled with the swooping flight of swallows—a queer fate for the stately buildings, but at least a happier and more dignified one than that of some other architectural derelicts, as, for instance, that noble church at Caen, in Normandy, which is occupied by a coal and coke merchant!

There is no doubt about the "official" religion of the Javanese when the month of Ramadhan comes round. It is the month which commemorates the period during which Mohammed received the revelation of the Koran, and for its whole duration the followers of the Prophet may neither eat, drink, smoke, nor use any perfumes between sunrise and sunset.

The natives appear to observe the rules most faithfully. There seems to be no question in their minds of evading them and, so far as it is possible for a European to judge, the law is as fixed and absolute to them as the rising and setting of the sun itself. But if they fast strictly by day, they certainly do their best to make up for it at night!

No sooner has the sun vanished below the horizon (he goes suddenly in Java, with none of the long-drawn-out twilight of colder regions) than the muffled tones of the "bedoek," the hollow tree trunk that hangs in every village as a drum to call the community together, sound faintly from each of the kampongs round about. They announce the glad tidings that the hours of fasting are over, and that the faithful may now eat—as much as ever the faithful please.

There is never much delay. For a little while the throb of the bedoeks goes pulsing on, and then soft beams of yellow lamplight shine out from all the scattered houses (or it may even be electric light, for Java's wealth of water power gives electricity to many a tiny country hamlet). The sound dies away. And you know that the hungry community has fallen to, and is doing its very best to make up for the past twelve hungry hours.

Feasting goes on for an hour or two, then gradually one by one the lights go out, and the kampongs sleep, but not for long. The native, being a simple soul, argues that if he fasts all day he must do what he can (allowing for the necessity to rest) to eat all night. He does his best; and if you happen to be awake in the small hours you will see all the kampong lights shining out again, for another meal will be in progress, and the people laying in supplies against the rigours of the coming day.

Java's "Conversions"

At the end of the month of Ramadhan the Javanese new year is celebrated. It is a great occasion for the giving of presents, and a general holiday; and every native walks abroad with his wife and family, all of them, if he can possibly afford it, arrayed in new garments from top to toe.

Sewing-machines have been humming in every kampong during the month of "poeasa" (fast); and now, with the whole community manifestly "dressed up," and looking as if it had just come out of the proverbial bandbox, the crowds that throng the roads are more than ever like a stage chorus. Every little native "nyonya" (lady) wears a brand-new muslin badjoe, not yet robbed by soap and water of its pristine brilliance, and carries a gay new sunshade; every sarong is stiff and fresh from the dyer's hands, and so is every Batik head-dress.

The children, for the most part, are dainty, flower-like miniatures of their elders, though sometimes, in the towns, a few, in dreadful little imported "sailor" suits and hats, show the taint of the West, and look like grotesque dolls. But happily there are only enough of these to supply a sort of comic relief—like clowns among the fairies at a pantomime.

The Javanese celebrate the coming in of our European new year with a graceful little ceremonial speech-making. In the morning, one by one, your own servants, or those personally known to you in a hotel if you live in one, will come before you, and with grave deference deliver a carefully rehearsed speech of "Salamatan," wishing you a "Salamat Tahoen Baroe," *i.e.* a safe and lucky new year.

The scoffer may say there is little difference between this Javanese greeting and that of the dustman in England, whose good wishes reach you in the form of: "Pleas'm, the dustman's called for his Christmas box!" It may be that the principle is the same, but the method is less crude and more pleasing. The Javanese makes his little speech, you return the compliment, he bows and departs. You may or may not give him a present later, but it would be in the worst of taste to offer it on the spot, though you feel far more disposed to it than you ever did to send down his half-crown to the man who demanded it, with no kindly camouflage of courtesy, via the housemaid, at the point of the gun.

There were just two places, strangely enough, that remained unaffected by Java's conversion to Islam. One is a small island off the eastern shore of Java, called Bali, which must have been an important Brahmin stronghold, for in it there are more Hindu temples and relics than there are in all Java. They are in perfect preservation, for they have never been abandoned. The Balinese, a distinct race, with a language of their own, still practise the Hindu religion with most of the rites observed in India, and it is only quite recently that "suttee" was abolished. But as for why they were never "converted" to Islam, there is no known explanation.

The other race that somehow or other escaped being drawn into the Mohammedan net is a very different one. They are the Badoejs, who live in a remote corner of Bantam, in the extreme western end of Java; an absolutely isolated, utterly primitive people, about whom very little is known. Their religion (according to Dr. van Tricht, one of the very few white men who has ever succeeded in penetrating into their hidden villages) is a curious and ancient one, which must have been theirs long before even the Hindus came to Java. They combine an animistic belief in spirits and magic with a very high sense of morality, and have no elaborate temples or monuments,

Java's "Conversions"

only a strange terraced stone sanctuary, to which they allow no approach.

Simple, primitive people though they are, they have yet managed to resist all successive attempts to "convert" or "civilize" them; and though an occasional member drifts away to the world outside, their little community of a few hundred souls still lives on in its jungle seclusion only a few miles away from modern Batavia, as it has done certainly for many centuries, and quite possibly for thousands of years.

CHAPTER ELEVEN

The Chinese in Java

OBSERVANT newcomers to Java, especially if they arrive by way of Singapore, often inquire why it is that the dapper Chinese "boys" who served them in hotels, and the Chinese coolies who had swarmed round them like ants on the wharves at the British port, are only conspicuous by their absence in the Dutch one.

The answer is, of course, that Java's native population is so abundant that there is an adequate labour supply even for all the island's ever-growing activities. But as to what is the reason why Java alone of all Malaya should be blessed with so large a population, well, no one knows.

Borneo, Sumatra, most of the other islands of the archipelago, and British Malaya are all covered with rich tropical vegetation, and repay cultivation just as generously as does Java. Yet in none of them is there a native population numerous enough to develop the land, except in this one specially fortunate island.

In the peninsula, when the first British settlements were established, each Malay state formed a small nucleus of life independent of all the others. Two primitive nomad races, the Sakais and Semangs (who were supposed to be indigenous peoples that had inhabited the country long before the coming of the Malays) roamed the jungles in bands, keeping entirely aloof from the other inhabitants;

and all around the coasts were villages whose inhabitants supported life by fishing and piracy, all the records of those times indicating that piracy was their true profession, and fishing (as with us) merely a sport, or a means, when all else failed, of feeding a hungry family.

Thus it was that when Malaya was "developed" by the Europeans, there was no indigenous hardworking population to offer, as in Java, a ready-made labour supply on the spot. The Malays, even what there were of them, had not, like the Javanese, been toilers and cultivators for generations. The only really active occupation they knew was piracy, and as that had been, to say the least of it, discouraged by these tiresome Europeans, the Malay was something like a modern business man who retires too early from business; he was bereft of his lifelong profession, and unfitted by it for anything else; he had, in short, "lost his punch."

He has taken kindly, however, to one or two nice light jobs provided by the white man. In the army he can dream pleasant dreams of killing all the people he particularly dislikes; as a traffic-policeman he can satisfy his love of "dressing-up," and with wicker "wings" fixed to his shoulders, to save him even the effort of holding up his arms, directing a stream of motor-cars at his own sweet will is quite a congenial amusement. He is in his element as a chauffeur, lolling at his ease on a comfortable seat, steering a delightful toy that goes as fast as he pleases, without the slightest effort on his part; to say nothing of all those happy hours when the master is in the office, and the chauffeur can sleep peacefully in the car parked outside, with his head on your best cushion and his bare feet hanging over the door!

But real hard work is something the Malay cannot and will not understand. He sees no sense in it. And that is why it is that the Chinese came in, and were brought in, in their thousands, and how it came about that (as Raffles put it) they "made Malaya."

Although they have not "made Java" in the same sense (the Javanese did that themselves), the Chinese nevertheless play a very important part in modern Javanese life. They most probably traded with the island from very early times; for, barbarous as those times undoubtedly were, silks and all kinds of ornaments were lavishly used at the various Sultans' Courts, as at those of all Oriental princes, great and small. And the raw silk for the hand-woven silken sarongs which the Javanese craftsmen, like the Malays, used to make in those happy, far-off pre-machine days, could have come from nowhere but China.

Things have not changed so very much in some ways, after all. There were "liners" as far back as the thirteenth century—and perhaps much earlier: huge Chinese junks, carrying several hundred passengers, and live stock and fowls to provide them with fresh food on the voyage, trading all round the south-eastern coasts of Asia, and calling at all the islands. So that Java must have been well known to the Chinese long before the establishment of the British and Dutch settlements encouraged some of the more enterprising spirits among them, with an eye to profitable business, to migrate from China and try their luck in a new country.

By early in the eighteenth century the Chinese had grown to be a sufficiently important part of the community to alarm the Dutch East India Company's officials, whose increasing nervousness made them see bogies everywhere. But even the barbarous massacre by which the Dutch sought to rid themselves of the danger did not discourage the ambitious Chinamen. The chance of making good money was worth a trifling risk like that. So, steadily, unobtrusively, the mercantile class Chinese drifted in, and the everyday retail trade, for which they have a genius, fell more and more into their able hands.

As the European communities grew, and their household and other needs with them, there was the Chinese tradesman to be found, in every department of commercial life, ready and waiting to supply them. As the island was opened up, and towns were built inland and in the cool hill regions, it was always the Chinese who occupied the shops; until to-day, throughout the length and breadth of Java (as in Malaya and the rest of the East Indies), the streets of every town are gay with their perpendicular ideographic signs in many colours, and European and all other shops are few in comparison.

The Javanese confine themselves, so far as business is concerned, to marketing their own produce, and to the sale of Batik and "curios" to visitors in the big towns. In these towns also there are a few fine Dutch stores and some particularly well-stocked book shops. A few "Bombay merchants" from India have established in Java, as elsewhere, their irresistible shops for the sale of Oriental silks, embroideries, and ornaments. A few Japanese are in trade here and there. But, broadly speaking, the retail trade in imported goods throughout Java is entirely in the hands of the Chinese.

They are equally important in the wholesale trade and in other departments of business. Almost all the rice mills are in Chinese hands, and naturally, in a country a quarter of whose area is planted with rice, their number is considerable; this fact alone gives them an impregnable position in commercial life. There are Chinese banks, shipping and insurance companies, and many other large undertakings; and Chinese are very generally employed as agents by European firms. In banks and business offices the clerks are almost invariably Chinese (though the Post Office, and other Government employees in subordinate positions, are generally Javanese natives).

The Chinese notably excel in three especially indispensable crafts: shoemaking, cabinet-making, and the making of woven rotan furniture; and in these they have established practically a monopoly. Chinese shoe shops are a feature of every street, a testimony to the ever-growing non-Javanese population, for the native still prefers to go barefoot. Hundreds of pairs of shoes, in lizard and crocodile and kid of every conceivable shade and of every imaginable pattern, adorn the shop windows and line the walls inside. You can have your foot measured with a strip of paper ribbon in the tapering, pale yellow fingers of a slender little Chinese lady the one afternoon and the next you can walk proudly away from the shop in your new shoes, made exactly according to your whim of the moment—and all for a few shillings.

The furniture made by Chinese cabinet-makers, mostly in the beautiful Javanese "djati," or teak, is always of admirable workmanship, and often delightful. Its pattern depends on the European influences to which the maker happened to be subject, and when these suffer from the taint of Tottenham Court Road (or the Dutch equivalent), the Chinese reproduction is correspondingly depressing. But given a pleasing model, or even left to his own devices, the Chinese craftsman produces furniture equal to any made in Europe, at about a tenth of the price.

As a weaver of rotan (a very tough jungle vine) the Chinese is unequalled. He makes baskets, perambulators, tables, lamp-stands, and all manner of other articles from it; and last, but not least—chairs. His chairs are chairs *in excelsis*. He knows to an inch the depth and the angle that will bring rest to the limbs of the weary, or the merely lazy, as no European chair-designer ever seems to know it. At the Chinese chair-maker's you "try on" chairs as though they were shoes, until you find one that fits you exactly. And when you have once acquired it, you sink into it for ever after with a sense of such utter comfort that you never think about the chair at all. The seat is just deep enough, the arms in the right place, and the back at the perfect angle. And it will live an honourable life for many years, having cost you only about seven and sixpence.

The Chinese are born shopkeepers. They are amazingly observant and adaptable, and have an unerring sense of fitness which enables them to cater equally well for all classes. A first-class Chinese grocer's shop, with its orderly pyramids and shelves full of shining tinned goods, and its polished glass-covered show-cases, tempts you to buy against your will, and is as attractive as the grocery department of any big London stores. Yet the very same shopkeeper knows exactly how to set out the open wooden stall at the corner of the next street, where the goods are sold in cent's worths, and where coolies and bullock drivers and all such humble folk come and bargain endlessly to get the full value for each of the grimy, hard-earned coppers they unroll from a little piece of cloth.

It is to these Chinese shopkeepers that a curious little item on the list of Java's imports owes its existence. To use new wrapping paper for his innumerable parcels would make too great a hole in his profits, so he uses newspaper, and uses it, moreover, in such great quantities that tons of "overprinted" journals are imported annually for his benefit.

The better-class Chinese in Java are very much

"Westernized." A considerable number of them are Catholics, for a great many Chinese children are sent to the Catholic schools. Many distinguish themselves at the State universities, and qualify in the various professions, notably engineering. The men wear European dress, and almost without exception they speak Dutch and English, and, of course, the inevitable Malay, which is the lingua franca of the island, as well as their own language.

Chinese ladies in Java have evolved a characteristic style of dress. They wear a sarong, never in the garish colours beloved of the native, but usually in blue and white; and a long "cutaway" coat of white "all-over" embroidery or some such material. Like the native women, they go bareheaded, and often carry sunshades. They are always neatly shod, and are particularly fond of wearing embroidered slippers, which set off admirably their slender, ivory-yellow bare ankles.

The less educated class, that of the small shopkeepers, wear Chinese dress. They all speak Malay, and not infrequently Dutch as well.

The Chinese in Java, as in Malaya, sometimes amass enormous fortunes, and it may be that their extreme care in obeying the old adage, to "look after the pence," has something to do with it. Driving with some Chinese friends in their imposing saloon car one day, one of the children asked his father for some ramboetan, of which he caught sight in the baskets of a fruit vendor. We pulled up to buy some, but the price asked was four cents (five Java cents are worth about a penny), whereas Mr. Goh Sieng refused to pay more than three. We tried several other vendors, but failed to come to terms—all for the sake of less than a farthing!

There are some enormous tombs of wealthy Chinese in some of the larger towns. One in Batavia, built all of

The Chinese in Java

black marble, cost hundreds of thousands of guilders, and is almost as imposing as Napoleon's tomb at Les Invalides. Ordinary Chinese graves are always if possible placed on a hill-side, and the coffin is pushed in endways. There are many of these cemeteries in Java, and they are a curious contrast to the modest resting places of the Javanese themselves, with their tiny headstones, and a "sembodja," or death tree, planted beside each grave.

The Chinese, being an ardent lover in his lifetime of a "show" of any kind, sees to it that his last journey to the grave shall provide a spectacle as good as any of them. Unlike the European, he sees no reason to make his obsequies an occasion for melancholy. A Chinese funeral is as merry an affair as a Bank Holiday on Hampstead Heath; it is accompanied by as many bands (each playing a different tune, for otherwise why waste money on more than one?) as the family of the departed can afford.

The procession is usually led by two men carrying enormous paper lanterns, followed by a long line of others carrying big silk or paper banners, each hung by the upper end from a long bamboo. On these are inscribed, in lovely ideographic characters, the good wishes of the relations for the soul of the deceased in the hereafter.

The catafalque is a magnificent affair—often an elaborate model of a Chinese house, mounted on wheels. The upturned corners of the roofs, which are super-imposed one upon another, are decorated with birds if the departed be a woman, and with lions if a man, the topmost pinnacle of all being crowned with an enormous specimen of whichever it may be. The bier is pulled by perhaps a dozen or more men, with ropes.

The eldest son of the deceased walks behind, holding the "soul guiding stick," and another bamboo stick wrapped round with joss paper, which latter is also

A FUNERAL CAR

THIS CHINESE HEARSE IS ADORNED WITH BLUE AND SILVER BIRDS, INDICATING THAT THE DEPARTED WAS OF THE GENTLER SEX. WHEN THE FUNERAL IS THAT OF A MAN, THE BIRDS ARE REPLACED BY LIONS.

carried by any other sons; the daughters follow empty-handed. All the relations wear sackcloth (or "sackdress," as a Chinese described it to me); and quite a becoming material it is when clean and new, as worn on these occasions. If there is a widow, she also wears "sack-dress," and so does a bereaved husband, unless (so arbitrary is custom in these matters) his departed wife's parents are still living, in which case sackcloth is not for him, and propriety demands that he must wear ordinary black clothes.

The family ancestral tablets follow, and food, paper money, and paper models of things likely to be useful to the spirit on its journey are carried behind, to be burned on arrival at the grave. A final lively touch is added by a "tin can" orchestra bringing up the rear, to frighten away any evil spirits that may be about.

The coffin is an enormously heavy one, usually of camphor wood, in which the body is sealed up, and often kept in the house for a long period—sometimes as much as three months in the case of a very rich man—before burial. Calling at the house of a Chinese business acquaintance one day, I saw a coffin in the hall, and was told that it contained the body of my friend's late aunt, the date of whose funeral was not yet arranged.

Burial must always take place an odd number of days after death, for the even numbers are regarded with great disfavour.

There are still some fine old Chinese houses in the less modern parts of many Java towns. But a great many of them have been turned into warehouses, and the sweeping lines of their beautiful upward-curving roofs are more than half concealed by the utilitarian severity of modern commercial architecture.

There are, however, some very fine temples, whose

myriad sharp-pointed eaves and flamboyant decoration, and the huge blue or yellow, blandly grinning lions that guard their doors, strike a strange note amid the simplicity of the buildings around them.

There are not many Japanese in Java, but those who are there have made a special niche of their own. As you pass along the streets of provincial towns, or through the less pretentious quarters of the larger ones, you will see here and there a sign-board on which is a crude painting of a gruesome anatomical specimen, vaguely suggestive of a newly split sheep's head on a butcher's block.

Closer inspection, however, will show you that it is not the butcher but a dentist who carries on business below, for the sign bears the legend "Toekang Gigi" (the maker of teeth), and more often than not he is a Japanese. The painting, moreover, is of no mere sheep. That one fiercely rolling blue eye, that strange rectangular jaw garnished with nightmare fangs, on a sanguinary background of crimson, make up a human head seen in section—presumably suffering from acute toothache. One would have thought it would frighten all business away. But the Toekang Gigi's must be a lucrative profession, for there are at least two in every village.

The Japanese are remarkably skilled photographers, and there is one to be found in most of the towns in Java. They are a boon and a blessing to amateurs, for most of them develop and print quite admirably, and at much lower prices than the European firms.

Yet it would almost be worth while to pay a little more, rather than less, to get your negatives and prints back in one of Mr. Oy Lan's envelopes, delicately inscribed in Japanese characters like a flight of birds, translated for English ignorance into "Washing negatives and every one page of print will good," than in an ordinary Kodak folder. (Though it must be admitted that when the films are valuable it is perhaps safer to send them to Kodak's, and take no chances!)

Japanese photographers, however, can give points to any European in the difficult art of retouching.

CHAPTER TWELVE

The Land & its Tenure

IN a country whose soil possesses such extraordinary fertility as does that of Java, and whose cultivation is one of the wonders of the world, the story of the land and its tenure have a special interest. That story dates back into very remote times indeed: to days long before the present landscape of placid rice fields and terraced hill-sides had come into being; days when mountains and valleys were clothed with dense forests like those of Sumatra and Borneo, and the people were only beginning to contest with wild Nature for the possession of the soil.

How many centuries ago those days may have been, no one can say. The Indians were already settled in Java in the fourth century, and native land laws must certainly have existed before that. The general principle on which they were based was that land was plentiful and people scarce. And although Java's population has probably increased at greater speed in recent than in earlier times (it has doubled in the last sixty-five years), there is every reason to believe that the island has been well populated for a very long time indeed.

The old native law held that ownership was established by clearing and cultivating a piece of land, on the principle that if a man could clear the jungle and make it fruitful he had earned it and could keep it. A sound idea, when the enormous labour involved is considered. Virgin forest, and all waste uncultivated land, was called "tanah mati" (dead land), and when cleared became "tanah hidoep" (live land); only, however, remaining "alive" so long as the owner occupied it, or it showed signs of cultivation. If it was abandoned, or allowed to go out of cultivation, the head man of the district had the right to put in another cultivator, to prevent the land being overrun and reclaimed by the jungle. If a rice field, it was forfeited if left untilled for three years, as it would be infested with rats and weeds and be a menace to neighbouring land; an abandoned fruit tree plantation, however, might be reclaimed after any number of years by the cultivator or his descendants, as long as signs of life could be found in one single tree.

The coming of the Indians brought innovations. They founded kingdoms and introduced monarchal laws, according to which the ruling prince was "Lord of the Soil"; but they did not interfere with the old law giving the cultivator the right to the land he had cleared. But he now had to pay taxes, in default of which his land and his crop could be seized; on the other hand, payment of the tax gave him a double right to his land, and he might not be dispossessed of it.

The law which was finally established, and which endured (subject, of course, to all sorts of minor variations) all through the long era of the Mohammedan princes, right up to the Dutch conquest, vested the land in the prince absolutely; but the crop was the property of the peasant, who had, however, to pay a fifth of it and of his labour as rent. Under a much later modification of this law the peasant who brought "dead land" into cultivation paid no dues for five years, after which he was taxed with the rest.

Great complications arose over the princes' practice of

giving away large tracts of land to their favourites, with "soerats," or title-deeds complete, regardless of the rights of the peasant cultivators. These unfortunate people were not allowed to leave the land, however much they wished to do so; they were regarded as mere appanages of the gift, and were forced to till the land for their masters, getting a living out of it for themselves as well if they could. And this although the prince had no lawful power to dispose of anything except his rights to produce and labour rent.

With the conquest of Java by the Dutch came changes so complicated in the laws of land tenure that it is difficult to unravel them from the records available. These changes came about gradually, as the reigning native princes were defeated one by one during the fighting which went on spasmodically for over a hundred and fifty years. In each case the Dutch East India Company regarded the conquered territory as its freehold, and often sold or granted land to private individuals in return for various services, thus creating a number of independent freeholds, apart from the tenure of the land by the company, which was the general rule.

There was, however, one prince, the Sultan of Soerakarta (or Solo, as it is often called, from the river that runs through the kingdom), whose opposition was so stubborn and prolonged that the Dutch found it expedient to make a treaty with him; it was an arrangement by which the European conquerors held all the real power, but allowed the prince to retain an outward semblance of it, as well as a large proportion of his revenues.

A similar agreement was made later with the Sultan of Djokjakarta, a State which is really part of the territory of Soerakarta, and which was virtually stolen from it by a series of anything but creditable intrigues.

Under these treaties the laws relating to land became extremely involved, for the agreements had been framed in such a way as to give a full appearance of sovereign rights to the Sultan, without in actual fact giving him any whatever. The land rents continued officially to be paid to him, thus giving him prestige in the eyes of his own subjects. But in practice, the Dutch Resident, or "Elder Brother" (as he was euphemistically named, by way of camouflaging the conqueror in a mask of brotherly love), was, and still is, always at the Sovereign's elbow to "advise" him, and had the real control of the funds, as of everything else (though the royal allowance has always been faithfully paid). And later, obscuring the situation still further, the Dutch arranged to "lease" the royal rights over the crops and over the free services of the native cultivators.

In general, with the exception of the two Sultanates, the Dutch appear to have taken over the land law very much as it stood, transferring the rights of the conquered princes to themselves. But in addition they forced the native farmers to sell their produce to them at a fixed price, and also to grow such crops as the company desired, of which they were obliged to supply a definite quantity without any recompense.

Before the conquest of the land itself, trade between the natives and the Dutch had been only in pepper and other spices. And heavy though the hand of the East India Company may have been on the native and his land, the immense variety of crops that came by degrees to be cultivated is undoubtedly due to the company's initiative.

By the introduction of the European seven-day week

the labour rent demanded from the natives was reduced from one day in five to one day in seven, being balanced, however, by an increase in the produce rent. This was paid in kind. And when, later on, the Dutch government took the place of the bankrupt East India Company, and leased land to private owners for sugar and other estates, the native occupiers of the land paid the produce and labour rents to their Chinese or European landlord, who in their turn paid a tax to the government on the capital value of the estate.

The labour rent due to the government was applied to the making of roads, building bridges and canals, and other public works. On private estates it was generally employed in cultivation, but a great deal of it also went into the construction and upkeep of the water channels serving the sugar factories, until about thirty years ago, when the whole system of "free labour" was finally abolished.

The labour rent was due only on "productive" land, that is, land that could be cultivated, and therefore, although every landholder was liable for it, any landless man, such as an artisan or craftsman, escaped it. There were many arguments and much jealousy, of course, and many attempts to evade the hated tax; above all, the villagers who duly paid it were determined to ensure that no one should escape it if they did not. So each village headman (who was elected by vote) kept a roster, and every one was given more or less fair treatment.

There was, however, a very weak spot in the law, and the village wise men could be trusted to put a finger on it. It was only the "householder"—the head of the family— who was liable for the day's labour, quite irrespective of the size of his family. And so long as the day's rent for the household was duly rendered, any member of the family could do it for their father. Out of this grew an ingenious scheme: a whole village would subscribe and employ between them several men to do the labour due as rent from all the village householders, and thus for a small sum rendered their legal dues, at the same time escaping the loss of the time and labour they needed to cultivate their own land.

When the administration of Java was taken over by the Netherlands government it proclaimed the land the "property" of each village community, but it was subject to the payment of rent to the government, and also to restrictions as to its use, and for a long time "compulsory cultivation" of certain crops for the government was carried on. The principle behind the system was a complete government monopoly of land, the understanding being that all native "owned" land was a grant to them from the government.

A restriction preventing the natives from selling their land to non-natives was imposed, and is still in force. It was designed to keep out foreigners and to strengthen the government's monopoly. On the one hand they gave the rights over the land to the natives only, but on the other they compelled the use of at least part of that land, with labour which, even though paid, was still compulsory, to grow such crops as the government might desire.

The payment of produce rent in kind, as can be imagined, is a somewhat tiresome business, and for reasons of convenience on both sides, the rent due is often determined by assessment. When this is decided upon, the landlord and the tenant together inspect the ripe rice crop before it is cut, and if they come to terms, well and good. The tenant cuts and sells his crop, and must pay the sum agreed within four months after the harvest.

But if they fail to agree, the whole village is called in. The crop is cut and tied up in bundles called "gedding," as big as can be held in the two arms, and put in heaps of five bundles each, of which the landlord takes one in every five.

There is no doubt, taking into consideration the native's love of argument, that most crops might have to be dealt with in this way, were it not that there are deterrent factors which restrain excessive demands on both sides; so that the method is comparatively rare. The villagers have to be paid (in rice) for cutting and stacking, so it is to the tenant's interest to agree to a slightly higher valuation by his landlord than he himself might otherwise bargain for. The landlord's greed, on the other hand, is curbed by the fact that when this system is resorted to, he has to remove his share himself. It is only when either party is especially stiff-necked, therefore, that they do not agree to a price, or to the one-fifth in kind of ancient custom. In the latter case the tenant must deliver it immediately it has been reaped.

Village rice lands belong to the whole village (for the rent due to the government is now paid in the form of tax), and every householder has a right in them. They are divided up every year by agreement according to the size of families and their ability to cultivate, though not without many arguments, of course. Many hitches also occur over a curious old law that permits an inheritor to hold a piece of land as "trustee for the dead," by which everything in regard to it must be done in accordance with the wishes of the departed.

In modern times, land may be leased, though it may not be bought, from the natives; and much of the land occupied by sugar, rubber, and other estates is so held, either from native landowners or from the Sultans of the two native States. There is also still some "private" land, whose ownership dates back to the time of the British occupation, and to that of the Dutch East India Company, when grants of land were made to natives as private estates. Nearly all these freeholds were eventually sold for arrears of land tax, due to the wild extravagances of the native "squireens." But the land remained out of government control, and is now still being gradually repurchased. Those areas planted as estates are leased back to the estate-holders who formerly owned them, and further complications are involved in old "manorial" rights over the peasants living on the land.

In the case of some of the land rented from native owners for estate cultivation there are interesting restrictions and reservations, allowing the owner to resume occupation of parts of the rented land at specified intervals during the lease, in order to secure rotation of crops and avoid exhaustion of the land. The area leased for a sugar estate, for example, is three times as large as the area annually planted; much the same applies to tobacco plantations, and sugar or tobacco is always planted on land from which rice, maize, or other native crop has previously been reaped.

The extraordinary wealth of Java's soil is well illustrated by a comparison of the relative prosperity of its enormous population with that of those in other countries. The population of this fertile island is estimated to average well over seven hundred to the square mile—the highest in the world—yet actual poverty is so rare as to be practically unknown. In Bengal, the next highest, where there are about five hundred and fifty people to the square mile, huge numbers live in squalor and on the verge of starvation. And even in Japan, with far fewer in proportion to its area—about sixty-six millions in a territory of some hundred and seventy-five thousand square miles—the struggle for existence, despite the great industry of the people, is a hard one, and there is urgent need for expansion.

The Story of Irrigation

NO one knows exactly when irrigation started in Java: whether the art of harnessing the mountain streams, of terracing the hill-sides and grading the valleys, was brought in by the settlers and conquerors who followed the Hindu traders from India a mere seventeen or eighteen centuries ago; or whether the natives of Java, like those of Mesopotamia, had known all there was to know about the art of irrigation, many thousands of years earlier.

The only thing in connection with it of which we can be quite certain is that the lofty mountains of Java, in common with those of Borneo and Sumatra, were once clothed with dense primeval jungle, and that every foot of the richly cultivated lands of to-day must have been laboriously cleared and levelled by the ancestors of those who now toil in them. How long ago, we know no more than they do, but at all events, rice has been grown on these intricately terraced and watered mountain-sides, just as it is now, for hundreds upon hundreds of years.

The most ancient waterworks on a large scale of which there is any trace were discovered a few years ago near Modjokerto, in East Java, near the site of Modjopahit, the ancient Hindu capital, which was destroyed by the Mohammedan conquerors. These waterworks consisted of a series of reservoirs, made by damming up narrow valleys, and also an elaborate system of dykes. There is, however, no clue to whether they were of Hindu origin or of even earlier date.

The irrigation of Java to-day is especially interesting because it is the world's finest example of native and modern methods in operation side by side and working in conjunction. According to the leading Dutch experts, the native is without a rival in the art of watering the steep mountain-sides and valleys, and there is no attempt by the Dutch, therefore, even to-day, to interfere with his methods.

The science of grading the land was evidently almost, if not quite, as perfectly known to the early irrigators of Java as it is to modern engineers to-day. And whereas nowadays delicate instruments are used, the experts of other days doubtless learned by simply using their eyes and noting how, and in what direction, water flowed. It is believed that among the natives there have always been these "experts": men of specially keen observation, looked up to by their fellows, who by a sort of sixth sense could tell lesser men how to grade their fields, and they were (and still are) always appealed to for advice.

On flat country, however, of which there are some surprisingly large tracts, even in mountainous Java, the native irrigator failed for lack of material. His earth-banked canals broke down, and were washed away in the heavy rains that he had counted on to fill them; and it was here that the Dutch engineers, equipped with modern science and, above all, with concrete, solved the problem. By means of permanent storages, concrete-lined canals, and pumping systems, they co-operated with the native farmers, and enabled immense areas of land to be watered and regularly cultivated, which formerly had been planted only in the wet monsoon, or not at all.

Irrigation is by no means merely incidental to Java, or

a thing to be mentioned in passing. To think of Java without irrigation is impossible. It is its lifeblood: the whole source and mainspring of its existence. Everything else in the island, its romance, its charm, its civilization, and its wealth, are all in the long run dependent upon it.

If Java had no irrigation it would not be Java as we know it at all. It would be just a beautiful, little-known tropic island, with perhaps a sprinkling of European settlement on the coast; and the rest, remote and mysterious, peopled only by a few primitive natives, as most of Borneo is to-day.

Thanks to irrigation, water is the dominant note of the Java landscape. It gleams and glitters everywhere. The island's area is about fifty thousand square miles, and more than a quarter of it is artificially watered. So it is scarcely surprising if the memories of Java that come first to mind, and remain the longest, are pictures of its irrigated rice fields, or "sawahs." For it was to grow his staple food that the Javanese first harnessed the streams, and became an irrigator. And though irrigation richly serves other crops also, in Java to-day, its principal mission is still the same.

In those districts where the Dutch have built irrigation works for the benefit of the native farmer the government constructs the necessary concrete main canals, dams, and sluices, and all the lesser subsidiary canals, down to those supplying areas of about two hundred and fifty to five hundred acres. For all smaller channels within those areas, the native farmers are held responsible, and construct themselves. They appoint their own native intermediary, and make him responsible both to them and to the government. The man chosen is always one that their experience has proved to be an expert: the "water-wise" man who seems to be found in every village. They expect him to look after their interests, and to water their land to the best advantage; and on the other hand, the government looks to him to keep the head canal that waters his area in good working order.

If the government engineer on his periodical inspections finds that this has not been done, his remedy is simple. He merely closes down the sluice, and refuses to supply any water until he is satisfied with the condition of the canal. And as any interruption of the water supply to their crops is a most vital matter to every member of the community, there is naturally not a moment's delay in carrying out the required repairs, and all is soon in order again.

On government irrigated land the native is charged a water-rate both on the area of the land he cultivates and on the value of the crop he harvests from it. A careful weekly record is kept in each area of the amount of water available, the crops and their various stages, and the water estimated to be required by each, water being released accordingly; a matter which inevitably gives rise to a certain amount of grumbling and dissension among those who consider that they have not been fairly treated.

Such arguments, however, are far more common on the village lands, where the natives carry out their own irrigation. Here, too, a local expert is placed in charge, but complaints of favouritism, and inequality in the supply of water, are constant. It is more than probable that many of the complaints are only too well founded, and that the well-to-do farmers, and those nearest to the source of the water supply, are pretty sure to be the best treated.

The Javanese handle their streams as easily as though they were so many pawns on a chessboard. There is nothing they cannot do with them, even to making them, to all appearance, run uphill. They harness and deflect and divide them with absurd little dams of stones and mud,

NATIVE IRRIGATION

THE PIPES IN THE FOREGROUND ARE MADE OF BAMBOO.   THERE MUST BE THOUSANDS OF MILES OF and lure them into channels dug across the faces of precipitous hills. They will split one stream into three or four, some of the branches watering different tiers of terraces, and others led down at steeper angles to carry off the water that has passed through them, to irrigate in their turn other series of terraces below.

Each terrace or shelf waters the one below it by an opening in the surrounding mud bank, which is scooped out by hand or with the bare toes. Sometimes a section of bamboo is pushed through the bank to act as a pipe, or a split piece may be used as a spout. All sorts of simple devices are used, but always with the same result; the water is always flowing, and yet remains always at exactly the same level.

Anyone who has ever tried the old experiment of adjusting the inflow and outflow of water between the bath tap and the waste-pipe knows that it is not by any means an easy matter. Yet I have seen a Javanese peasant woman come out of her little red-tiled house, with her baby tied on her back, look critically at a near-by terrace, and then stoop down (straight from the hips, with the babe sprawling head downward over her shoulders) and scrape away an inch or so of mud to increase the flow. It is second nature to these people, both men and women; they do it as unconsciously as they breathe, without realizing in the least that it is in effect a very delicate piece of practical engineering.

The streams are rearranged and divided up, over and over again, on their way down the mountain-sides, watering series after series of terraces as they go, and reinforced by other streams which appear as though by magic at every corner, led, from Heaven knows where, by a hundred and one ingenious inventions.

There are miles of bamboo piping, and rickety-looking

aqueducts made of hollow tree trunks resting upon lanky bamboo supports, and artificial channels innumerable, that appear to defy every possible rule of gravitation.

The valley floors have been dug level, and so skilfully graded in the course of centuries that they now fall in steps so slight as to be invisible to the eye, though it is enough to provide the necessary flow. The art has been handed on from generation to generation, and still to-day you may see the new contour coming into being when a village community decides to increase the cultivable area of some valley, by cutting away the steep sides and filling in the bottom. There will be stout bamboo revetments holding up the newly made terraces, and the stream that is to water them, evidently quite lately diverted from its original course, running as though somewhat puzzled and ill at ease in its new one.

And when you see such work in progress you know that you are looking on at a phase through which every one of the familiar flat-bottomed valleys of Java, with their shining sawahs, must have passed in their time; transformed from wild jungle gorges which had first to be cleared, and then planned out and graded with a mathematical precision that not even the most elaborate of modern scientific instruments can improve upon.

The history of modern irrigation in Java dates from the eighteenth century. The first canal (so far as is known) built by Europeans was the Kali Baroe, constructed by the Dutch East India company, with native labour, between 1739 and 1753. It ran from Katoelampa, above Buitenzorg, to Batavia. The first "Rules and Regulations" in connection with water supply were laid down in 1764, and an engineer of the company was placed in charge of the highland waterways above Batavia in 1777.

The Story of Irrigation

A system of compulsory cultivation, which was introduced by Governor-General van den Bosch, led to a great extension of the existing native canals, for sugar, indigo, and tobacco-growing. These waterworks were all built by the natives according to their own methods, but under the supervision of Dutch officials. A dam so built at Pasoeroean in 1846 was 470 metres long, and on it the natives supplied eight hundred thousand days' labour.

All these big native-built works failed to withstand the rush of flood waters. But expert engineers were few in Java in those days, and it was not until later in the century that really permanent works began to be constructed. With the creation of the Public Works Department, in 1854, a great development of irrigation on the plateaux and plains was begun. The "Irrigation Brigade" took over the control in 1885, and the present Department was formed five years later. The immense value of modern irrigation to native life in Java is proved by the fact that in the twenty-five years following the formation of the "Brigade" the irrigated area planted with rice, and consequently the rice production, actually increased by nearly twenty-five per cent.

The primary object of the Dutch in establishing irrigation works in Java, was the increase of rice production, to keep pace with the rapidly multiplying population. But its importance soon became apparent in other directions, particularly in connection with the growth of the sugar industry. It has come more and more to increase the wealth of the island by making possible the cultivation of many "secondary" crops, to nearly all of which it is now applied.

The infinite variety of European and other vegetables which the natives now grow so extensively for the markets, both in Java and Malaya, are almost always watered by irrigation channels, as are also the fields of flowers which flourish so well in the cool hill districts.

There are, of course, some industries in Java that are independent of irrigation, and some important ones too: tea, teak, and rubber among them. But teak is confined to very restricted areas; and neither tea nor rubber, big plantations of both though there are, provide the characteristic landscape, eternally shimmering with water. I doubt, moreover, whether there is a tea estate in all Java that does not look down over shining irrigated rice sawahs in the levels below; nor many rubber plantations from which you could not catch a glimpse of water gleaming through the trees in the distance.

CHAPTER FOURTEEN

Canals & their Queer Uses

IT is open to very reasonable doubt whether any other European people but the Dutch would ever have come within even measurable distance of succeeding, as they have, in reclaiming the marshy coastal regions of Java; and above all in laying out such beautiful towns as Soerabaya and Batavia on the muddy deltas of their respective rivers, the Brantas and the Tjiliwong.

To any other race of people the task might have seemed well-nigh hopeless, but to the Dutch, schooled in "generations of stubborn conflict with the angry elements" in the transformation of the marshy deltas of the Scheldt and Rhine into the green polders, and in maintaining the Low Countries' intricate canal system, from the fourteenth century onwards, it was mere child's play to drain the comparatively small areas of marsh that fringed the fertile inland of Java.

Old Batavia, of which there are many records extant, is described as "somewhat unhealthy and damp"; but, allowing for the difference in climate, it was probably little or no worse than quite a number of ancient towns in present-day Holland, Belgium, and northern France, in which the populations are still living and thriving.

Health in the tropics, however, is more vulnerable, and for this reason the new residential quarter of Weltevreden, two or three miles farther inland, was planned and built rather over a hundred years ago. Here, too, the principle of draining the soil by canals was applied, and the River Tjiliwong, harnessed with locks and sluices, was made to feed the canal system that serves such a diversity of purposes in the daily life of the town.

The Tjiliwong was formerly a disorderly stream, which straggled untidily all over the marshes in dry seasons, and flooded miles of valuable country higher up in wet ones; but now it was decently confined within concrete walls, to flow decorously through the town and across miles of wide flats, in its new and deeper bed, to the shore, where presently there was to come into being a busy, thriving, modern port.

The use in Java of canals as a means of transport is confined to the sections, half river, half canal, between the big towns and their ports, on which, by lighters and bamboo rafts, big loads of bricks and tiles, cement, "kajang" (palm-leaf) roofing, and many other materials, are conveyed at a trifling cost. Sugar, too, in huge quantities is conveyed by lighter to the port at Soerabaya.

But in addition there are other and far less orthodox uses to which the canals are put in modern times. Walk along the Nordwijk in Weltevreden—one of the Tjiliwong's canalized branches—any morning, and you will see dozens of busy "penatoes" (washermen and washer-women), some standing waist-deep in the brownish water, rinsing and squeezing out the garments and house-hold linen of the European community, and piling them on long bamboo frames or trestles beside them in the stream; others, engulfed in soapsuds, rubbing away at the "wash" on the shallow concrete steps that run down to the water at intervals along the banks; and others, again, spreading it out to dry in the sunshine on the grass slopes above the water, or along the wall beyond.

The water is brown, but it is cleaner than it looks. For

there is always a slight flow seaward, and twice a day the sluices above are opened and tons of water pour down through the canals, cleansing them of all impurities.

The Javanese penato lacks nothing in enthusiasm, and it seems a miracle that any linen should survive the vigorous scrubbings to which it is treated; and still more remarkable that the hundreds of white shirts and drill trousers and jackets, which daily hang like a sort of frieze along the canal-side, should ever be restored to their rightful owners. But by some mysterious means they are; losses are no more frequent than in the rest of the world's laundries, and the linen is quite as well washed—if not better.

These canal laundries must surely be the only ones in the world where the launderers can refresh themselves at any moment with a swim in the wash-tubs! The Javanese penato, having rinsed a few hundred sheets or towels or shirts, and loaded his bamboo stand ready for drying, "ducks" in just as he is, in his sarong, swims around to see how his friends and colleagues are getting on, and then makes for the steps, wrings out the tail of his sarong, and gets to work on the drying-ground.

Late afternoon and evening is the popular time for the natives' own laundry work, and for this the favourite venue is the main branch of the river, which flows in a canal called the Molenvliet, or Mill Stream, down the centre of the wide avenue leading from Weltevreden to Old Batavia. From four o'clock onwards it is a pretty sight to see. On every flight of steps leading down to the water and on every spare corner of the bamboo rafts (of which a whole fleet is always moored to the bank) are native women, garbed only in a sarong bound tightly round under the armpits and falling to just below the knees, leaving their almost invariably shapely arms and shoulders bare. They are soaked, of course, either standing in the water or squatting on the steps, and they too, in the intervals of their laundry work, and bathing a baby or so, have a swim with their companions and the children—all chattering and laughing as merry as magpies.

And when the work and the fun are over, and they are ready to go home, these little women slip on a dry sarong over their heads, drop the wet one off beneath it, and add a little muslin coat, effecting the change in the most charming and modest way in the world.

Both Batavia and Soerabaya are separated from the coast by a belt of flat country several miles across, now traversed in each case by a railway; and by a magnificent motor road, along which there races unceasingly, from morning till night, a stream of cars and lorries, all succumbing inevitably to the temptation to speed on the wide, straight, level track. Beside the road, for a great part of the way, runs the river canal, bearing its share of merchandise to and from the water front. Here there is a whole town of broad streets, laid out on the right-angle plan; and at the water's edge there stand in monotonous array rows of great "godowns," or warehouses, their blank white walls blinding you with the reflected glare of the sunshine and the sea. All day long the lorries bring their loads across the flats, to discharge them at the big sliding doors leading to the shadowy spaces within, where a hundred strange scents mingle in the gloom to make up the characteristic pot-pourri of a tropic port.

If you venture into this odoriferous cavern you are sure to see on one side the flat faces of a towering stack of

HARVESTING THE RICE CROP

EACH INDIVIDUAL HEAD OF GRAIN IS CUT BY HAND WITH A SMALL CURVED KNIFE.   THE
HARVESTERS ARE USUALLY WOMEN WHO ARE PAID FOR THEIR LABOUR IN RICE.

SOME BAMBOO RAFTS ON THE MOLENVLIET CANAL, WELTEVREDEN

ON THE LEFT IS A LOAD OF *Kajang* (PALM LEAF ROOFING).   ON THE RIGHT, NATIVE WOMEN ARE
WASHING CLOTHES.

three-ply cases, containing tea, looming high as the wall of an ordinary house. But the faint, delicious aroma that envelops it is drowned a few yards away (this more particularly at Soerabaya) by the strong, sweet, all-pervading smell of sugar in its stiff new bags, built up in symmetrical piles, between which you can walk on narrow pathways, giving the odd illusion that they have been hewn out of the living rock in some hot, heavy-scented mine.

Farther on, rubber also, in square, three-ply wooden cases, not unlike those in which the tea is packed, is piled up likewise—but with what a different aroma! Bales of kapok, tobacco, sisal, and tapioca; cases of quinine, coca, cocoa, and coffee; and sooner or later—most familiar of all to a nose attuned to the tropics—there rises the unforgettable smell of copra, stacked in a godown by itself.

On the farther side of the sheds the doors open on to the long lines of wharves, where the ships of all nations are loading and discharging, with their attendant swarms of brown coolies busy about them.

It is difficult to believe, as you look on at it all, that the whole wide belt of country, stretching to the city from where you stand, with its fields and gardens, and the roads and railways that run across it, as well as the busy port, with its godowns and wharves and offices, and even factories, were all built up on land that not so very long ago was nothing but salt and slimy marshes; and that where there now runs in and out every few minutes an electric train service far more up-to-date than the London "Tube," only a hundred years or so ago you could have gone a-fishing (if you were so inclined) in a sluggish, malodorous stream, twisting among the rank weeds and grasses of a tropic estuary.

Canals & their Queer Uses

One chapter in the history of the canals belongs to the days when Weltevreden had not long made its début as the residential quarter of Batavia; days when the dignified houses, with their high pillared porticoes, so many of which now survive only as hotels, or disfigured by shop fronts, were in the hey-day of their glory; days when mevrouw took the air on the broad, tree-shaded avenues bordering the canals formed by the Tjiliwong, in her barouche drawn by a spirited pair of Soembawa ponies; or (if mijnheer were a man of substance) by handsome, high-stepping, imported carriage horses. Then, when the heat of the day was over, mevrouw and mijnheer, refreshed by a dish of tea, would step from their cool, shady porch into the carriage, and be driven to the steps at the canal side, where their pleasure boat, in charge of two smart, uniformed natives, awaited them.

One by one the boats would take the water, to be rowed slowly to and fro, while friends and acquaintances greeted each other and discussed the latest local scandal, and the news from Europe. And the ample forms of the ladies, shaded with parasols of delicate hue, rose in tight bodices and fichus of flowered muslin from the billowing masses of their crinolines, which frothed over and almost hid the boats, so that they floated on the water like gigantic water-lilies.

Later in the evening the canals were the setting of a still gayer scene, for then every boat was lighted with lanterns, and the gently rippling water reflected a lazily drifting world of many-coloured glow-worms.

Drawings of the period represent the gentlemen arrayed in top hats and broadcloth, and in demeanour befitting a churchwarden. Whether they actually wore all these things, or whether it was merely so that the artist in Holland portrayed them, there seems to be no one living in Java to-day who can say with certainty. Nor has it been recorded how those good people who so disported themselves in that bygone canal carnival defended themselves against the mosquitoes, which must have been so much more numerous before modern, anti-malarial science had waged successful war against them.

Was "Obat Nyamok" (mosquito medicine), the Japanese smoke-wheel to which we now trust to keep the pest at bay, yet invented? Or did the broadclothed gentlemen wave evil-smelling Chinese joss-sticks before the noses of the fair to defend them from bites, or offer voluminous grass-lawn handkerchiefs, anointed with oil of citronella?

We shall never know. But I often wonder if their invisible ghosts are still rowed idly up and down the Molenvliet, shading their eyes from the powerful beams of the arc-lamps that shine through the trees, and etch the patterns of leaves and branches in silhouette on the tarred surface of the broad highway, where the "flying taxis" (as they are always called), and high-powered sedans and limousines, with shrieking horns, tear restlessly up and down, and scare away the frightened ghostly carriages, swaying noiselessly along on their high C-springs.

The genius of the Dutch in the reclamation of waste and marshy lands has not been confined in Java to the sites of their great ports, though it was in that connection that it was first employed. In comparatively recent years, following on the rapid expansion of the sugar industry at the eastern end of the island, Dutch engineers turned their attention once more to the valley of the River Brantas, which had already given them the site of Soerabaya's great seaport.

This river splits in two many miles from its mouth,

one branch flowing to Soerabaya, and the other to Porong, on the east coast, farther south, forming an immense delta. This area, after long years of patient toil, recalling the history of Holland itself, was at last transformed into an immensely valuable "polder," some eighty-three thousand acres of which are now irrigated by the waters of the very river which formerly made the land a worthless swamp.

Another rich polder has been reclaimed south of the delta from an area which previously was flooded and useless during the wet monsoon, and could only be planted by the natives in the dry season. And as it proved impossible to drain this land into the adjoining southern arm of the Brantas, a drain was actually carried underneath it, leading to the Soerabaya branch of the river. This polder also is watered profitably from the same source which in former times drowned its fertility, and it is now an important sugar-growing district.

The work of the Dutch in all their reclamation and other water schemes was lightened by having ready to hand on the spot the labour of natives to whom the handling of water was a natural heritage. And Fate was correspondingly kind to the Javanese (whatever criticism the Dutch may have earned by the harshness of their earlier dealings with them) when she gave them for rulers the one people best able, through their long experience, to appreciate the natives' skill in this respect.

As the Dutch had fought the elements in Holland for their low-lying plains, mastered the rivers, and driven back the jealous sea, so the Javanese had wrested from the mountains and the forests the land on which they lived, tamed the mountain streams, and trained them to do their bidding.

Unlike the Javanese and Dutch may be; two races with

fewer qualities in common it would probably be hard to find. But this one thing they chance to share, to their mutual advantage: a superlative skill, evolved through many centuries, in the handling of that most elusive and unstable of elements—water.

Twelve Thousand Square Miles of Rice

IF you can imagine an English West Country cornfield at midsummer, multiplied a million times or so, until it covered a good quarter of the whole surface of England, then you will have some idea of what rice means to the landscape of Java.

To visualize a series of small fields spreading over more than twelve thousand square miles (not acres) of mountainous country is not easy, but that is about the area planted with rice in Java in the irrigated fields and terraces known as sawahs, and in addition the "dry" fields, called "ladang," where no irrigation is practicable and the crop is grown under rainfall, make up another seven or eight hundred thousand acres.

Even with this immense area of land constantly producing its wealth of grain (for in Java there is no winter, and the pause between the crops is not a long one), the island cannot grow enough rice to feed its ever-increasing population. Since the year 1890 there has been a shortage, to reduce which the Dutch are constantly extending the operation of scientific irrigation on lands which it was impossible to water by native methods. As a result, the amount of rice produced has increased by about a quarter.

But in spite of this increase, large quantities have to be imported, amounting in some years to as much as twenty-five million guilders' worth; though as a partial offset to this, four or five million guilders' worth of specially high-quality grain is exported to other countries.

There may be (though I doubt it) other crops cultivated by man which are as beautiful as rice, but there is certainly none more so, nor any that can paint a landscape with so many varied scenes.

It might be reasonable to expect some monotony in the scenery of a country where thousands of square miles are planted with the selfsame crop. But, twist and turn through the Java rice lands as you will, mile after mile, and day after day, there are never two scenes quite alike, nor one that does not arrest you afresh with its beauty and with the ingenuity that planned it.

You will see rice growing on narrow, boldly curving shelves that form a green and gracious stairway up the steep slope of a mountain; you see it fringing the very edge of a deep ravine, into whose depths the water in which the crop is standing miraculously does not spill. It waves proudly in wide fields, or peeps shyly up from ridiculous little patches smaller than a child's garden.

The rice fields are beautiful and interesting in all their stages. They have an infinite diversity of shape and contour, due to the mountainous country and the engineering skill of the native farmers. Those awaiting the planter may be broad silver lakes, lying serene and smooth as mirrors, reflecting the distant mountains in their unruffled surface. They may be no more than twisted, glittering threads, piled one above the other on miniature precipices, climbing by laborious stages up the side of some tremendous gorge. Or they may be cut out in patches of all shapes and sizes, fitted into a pattern as crazy as that of our grandmothers' patchwork quilts.

All these are innocent as yet of rice, and their only "crop," if they have one, will be a crop of goldfish.

There are others, with the water drained off, where the good dark earth lies in symmetrical waves, where it has been turned up by the plough, as smooth and slippery as butter. In some you will see the plough at work, drawn by solemn, plodding, wide-horned water-buffaloes knee-deep in water, the ploughman toiling bare-legged beside them, coated with the rich mud; or else riding on the primitive wooden plough, which is exactly like all the ploughs that have been used by rice farmers for un-numbered generations, singing unceasingly his queer monotonous little song, beneath the spell of which the biggest and fiercest of buffaloes is as meek and docile as a chidden child.

Here and there, among the fields, you will see a smaller patch, looking like plush, of almost impossibly vivid emerald green. These are the "nursery" seed-beds, packed tight with the rice seedlings which will presently be planted in the sawahs all round about them.

Then you will see the planters—always women, for otherwise, so the Javanese believe, the rice will not be fruitful—standing in long rows, their sarongs well tucked up, ankle-deep in mud and water, with bundles of seed-lings lying half submerged beside them, as they bend straight from the hips, setting out the young, green shoots, leaving the smooth surface of the water pricked with battalions of slender spikes a few inches high. Rice grows fast; every day the strong green heads push their way higher and higher, and jostle each other more closely; the water glimmers more and more faintly, until at last its surface is hidden, the low banks between the sawahs are blotted out, and a sea of cool, pale green sweeps away unbroken across the valley and up the hill-sides.

Gradually its colour changes and deepens. It turns to a mellow gold. The water has been drained off, and the

"REVETTING" A NARROW AND OTHERWISE UNCULTIVABLE VALLEY IN ORDER TO MAKE TERRACES ON WHICH RICE CAN BE GROWN. THIS HAS BEEN A JAVANESE PRACTICE FOR CENTURIES.

DRYING AND STACKING RICE AT A JAVA MILL. THE STACKS ARE BUILT UP OF EXACTLY UNIFORM BUNCHES REAPED BY HAND IN THE FIELDS.

fields are dry and sweet-smelling as a sun-baked English cornfield at the harvest-time of our dreams. Then comes the last scene of all, when the harvesters—all the women of the village—descend upon the crop like a flight of gay butterflies (though they work as busily as bees), cutting every single head of grain by hand with a small curved knife.

In districts where plenty of water is available in the dry (east) monsoon, as well as in the wet, rice is planted twice in one year; in other less-favoured regions, three times in two years. It matures in four to six months after transplanting, according to which variety is used. The principal harvest is in May, but the planting time is irregular. Hence the curiously "patterned" appearance of some of the rice lands, where you may sometimes see spread out before you a series of sawahs in half a dozen or more different stages.

The reasons for this irregular planting are many. In the first place, a fixed time is not actually essential in a land of eternal spring and summer, and local conditions vary in every district. Buffaloes, for instance, are valuable property, owned only by the more prosperous, who hire them out to their humbler neighbours after their own fields are ploughed; ploughs are shared in the same way; each sawah in its turn is planted as though by magic with the willing hands of all the women of the village; and, most essential of all, the supply of water must always be adjusted, by natives as well as by European engineers, with most meticulous care.

If money is extra scarce, however, and he is in a hurry to get his sawah ready for planting, mere lack of buffaloes will not deter a native farmer from ploughing. I have seen two men in the Preanger Regency yoke themselves to the heavy wooden plough and toil up and down all day in the mud and water of the field—surely as terrible a slavery as could well be devised, and yet it was self-imposed.

Planting varies in every district. In some it is irregular, in others, where there is an extra large population, and many of them buffalo owners, you may see a whole region planted at the same time, and can watch from week to week the progress of one great crop from seed-time to harvest.

The method of culture is simple and laborious, and has probably changed but little, if at all, since the days when rice was first discovered in its native marshes, and artificially cultivated. No fertilizer of any kind is used in Java. The stubble is burned and ploughed in; otherwise the natives trust to the rich silt, brought in by the irrigation water, to provide all that is necessary.

As soon as there is water enough, it is let in to the sawahs to soften the earth and facilitate breaking up, which is done by hand in the small mountain terraces, where there is not room enough for a buffalo plough. Sometimes, if water is plentiful, the sawahs are filled, and goldfish are put in, to be sold six weeks or two months later at a good profit. The sawah, still flooded, is then ploughed and harrowed, and levelled with a sort of mould-board, and left to soak for another ten days before planting. The nursery beds are sown at the same time as that of the first soil-breaking, and after the seed is in they are kept covered with water during the daytime to protect them from birds, and drained at night.

The seed is soaked before planting, and very thickly sown, though sometimes a native will depart from the orthodox method and, instead, lay whole heads of rice, just as they are, side by side in the nursery beds, under water.

Whichever method is employed, forty-five to sixty days

after sowing, the nursery is deeply submerged for a day or two, to enable the young shoots (called "bibit") to be easily pulled out for transplanting. They are tied up in bundles, "topped," and dumped in rows in the wet mud of the sawahs in which they are to be replanted. The planters always put in three or four shoots together, in tiny squares, in case of any failures, and the superfluous ones are weeded out again by hand a month or six weeks later, as the young plants fill up the spaces.

The crop grows in water, the supply of which is gradually increased until the rice comes into bearing, and is then decreased so that the ground is nearly dry when the grain matures. After the last weeding, before the water is drained off, the embankments (made of mud, dead weeds, and straw) are chopped and pounded into a hard wall, and stripped of anything that might offer harbourage to rats, which constantly menace the crop, and cause great losses.

The harvesters are almost always paid in rice, the cost to the owner of the sawah amounting to about a tenth of his crop.

After cutting, the heads are tied in bundles and piled up to dry. Enough is set aside for the domestic needs of the owner, and the remainder is either sold to the local Chinese or Arab trader, or, if the grower can afford to wait for his money, it may be stored in a shed to await the most favourable market.

The sight of the golden bunches after harvest is one of the most familiar to travellers on the roads of Java. You can never go many miles without meeting miniature moving stacks of them, shining with a burnished sheen, like the neck of a well-groomed horse, loaded on grobaks drawn by bullocks or pairs of sturdy ponies. You will see small piles of them placed at the house doors of roadside kampongs to dry and at the first sign of a sudden shower of rain out come the owners, running, to carry them inside to shelter.

You will meet natives with heavy bouquets of bunches strung at each end of their pikoelans; or perhaps a woman carrying a solitary bunch (which is most likely the wages for her work in the harvest field). She will thresh it for family consumption with a stout bamboo in the great hollow tree trunk in the shade at the back of the kampong, after which she will winnow it, with graceful movements that many a dancer might envy, in a shallow, split-bamboo receptacle (one of the articles always carried round for sale by the kampong peddlers), and finally cook it by steam in a basket.

You will pass many rice mills, nearly all Chinese-owned (though there are some that belong to rich Arabs), where drying, in this moist climate, is eternally going on. The familiar bunches, exactly uniform all over Java, are laid out in concrete-floored yards, open to the sun, where they are constantly turned and moved before being built up into stacks like great golden beehives.

The rice grower has far to go before all his troubles are over and he can tuck the price of six months' toil and anxiety safely away into a fold of his sarong. He will have to pay land tax, the cost of planters and harvesters, and possibly also of buffaloes and plough. Rats and insects take a heavy toll, and no sooner is the grain set and beginning to ripen than the birds descend upon it in thousands. Against them he wages constant war. Often a bamboo platform, roofed with kajang, is built in the middle of the field, and cords, garnished with rags and bits of paper, are strung from its posts to others at the edges of the sawah.

All day long, and every day until the harvest, the

children of the kampong take it in turns to sit in the bamboo perch and twitch the cords in the hope of frightening off the greedy birds; and woe betide the watchers if they fall asleep or neglect their job! For, sure as ever the strings hang motionless, from somewhere or other unseen comes an angry voice, promising salutary punishment to the offender when it shall be his turn to come home to the kampong. Furiously then the cord begins to twitch again, the rags and papers dance a frenzied jig, and the birds, disturbed at their good rice feast, rise in a cloud, to descend again as soon as ever Ah Mat's vigilance relaxes, as of course it will the moment father's back is turned.

Sometimes a shelter is built in the corner of a field, whence there rises a wisp of blue smoke from a little fire lighted to keep off mosquitoes, and the watcher performs spasmodic prodigies, designed to scare all marauders, on an empty paraffin tin. Or a horribly deathlike scarecrow may startle you with the fear that you have chanced upon some tragic suicide.

Legends connected with the rice crop are naturally many in a land where its cultivation is so universal. Most interesting of these is the story, evidently of Hindu origin, of how the rice first came to the earth. It is found in its most elaborate form in Bali, where the Hindu religion and legends have never died, but it is well known also to the natives of Java. It has many variations, and is as full of vague irrelevancies as are all native stories; but it is perhaps worth quoting.

"There was once a great and wise prince called Pretoe, who was very much dissatisfied because the only food of his people was sugar-cane juice. So he asked the Goddess of the Earth, who was called Si Thi, to help him to find something better. She refused, but he persisted, and threatened and alarmed her so much that she turned herself into a cow in order to escape from him. He still pursued her, and at last caught her and made her promise that she would try to find another kind of food while she was wandering about the earth in the shape of a cow if, meanwhile, he would go to the god Indra and persuade him to make the soil grow the new food when she had found it. Pretoe went to the god, but he would have nothing to do with him, and a great war started between them.

"The god Indra wanted help to defeat the insolent Pretoe, so he applied to the god Vishnu; but he was away on the earth, and Indra saw only his spouse, the goddess Sri. She told him that her husband was on the earth in the shape of Prince Pretoe, whom she then followed to the earth.

"Meanwhile Brahma heard of the struggle, and to avoid being mixed up in it he decided to look after the matter himself, and to send the seeds of a new food to Pretoe. So he sent four different seeds by four birds. The seeds were black, red, white, and yellow. The bird carrying the yellow seed dropped it on the way, and they all went back to Brahma to tell him, and asked what to do. He was so angry that he cursed the yellow seed, and said it should never grow any food, but only a plant from which to make dye ; and so it is to this day.

"The other three birds he sent back again, and this time they overtook the goddess Sri, who was on her way to earth. She asked the birds to take her with them, and they did so. This time they all arrived quite safely, and Pretoe received his seeds; but having got them, he did not know what to do with them, as Indra had refused to teach him to prepare the soil. He asked Indra once more, and this time the god (who thought he was going to be beaten in his war with the prince) agreed, and sent a teacher to Pretoe to show him how to lay out the sawahs and the ladang. There he planted the three seeds, which were those of three different varieties of rice; and the goddess Sri remained on the earth as the Goddess of the Rice, which she has remained to this day."

These ancient legends have a tremendous hold over the simple minds of the people of Java. There is one, for instance, prohibiting the Tenggerese, who live in the mountain regions about Tosari, in East Java, from ever cultivating the rice plant, under pain of a most dreadful and devastating curse. Accordingly, not a single grain of rice is ever grown, nor has been within the memory of man, on the steep terraces of the range—terraces that from the native point of view must be otherwise perfect for the purpose.

But the fear of that ancient curse hangs over them, so maize is their staple crop; and, combining commercial sense with superstition, they also carry on a great and varied cultivation of European vegetables for sale in the markets down below.

"King Sugar"

TO find yourself in the sugar districts of Java is to understand very easily how the saying, "In Java Sugar is King," came to be coined.

Everything connected with the industry is on a scale that is nothing short of princely. Each of the great mills (and there are over a hundred and seventy of them) shining dazzlingly white in the brilliant sunshine, with its slender, lofty stack piercing far into the blue heavens like a colossal silver needle, dominates the scene as though it were a cathedral. And it does so in fact, as well as in appearance. It is no mere sugar mill, but the centre round which, set in encircling fields of cane, lies the model town that it has brought into being; a town of wide roads and shady avenues, and snug bungalows set in flowery gardens, with churches, schools, and shops complete: all established to accommodate the subjects and servants of the great King Sugar.

Sugar is hard hit, with the rest, by the slump (or the *malaise*, as the Dutch so much less hideously call it). But its immense importance as a factor in Java's life remains. For, apart from its own value as an industry, the water supply system it was obliged to create for its own needs has at the same time served those of rice cultivation, and by so doing has enormously increased the production of the natives' food supply.

When sugar was first planted in Java, about a hundred

years ago, it soon became apparent that the crop could not depend on natural rainfall. For, abundant though that rainfall may be, there are in Java, especially towards the east and north, where the land is best suited to sugar, marked wet and dry monsoons; and it is during the dry, east monsoon that sugar must be planted. It follows, therefore, that it needs most water just when there is least rain, and it is largely this fact that has made the story of sugar culture in Java a stormy as well as an interesting one.

Watering the crop did not appear at first to present any particular difficulties, as there was no reason why water-works designed to irrigate rice should not supply the sugar also. But it was not long before trouble began. Rain is very scarce during the east monsoon, and when the government went into business as a sugar-producer on a large scale, there was not nearly enough water to go round comfortably. The government—not unnaturally, for governments are only human—gave itself the preference, and by degrees there was devised a system by which the sugar-cane was watered in the daylight, and the native cultivators had to do the best they could with the water in the darkness.

From 1870 onwards, sugar culture was increasingly taken over by private enterprise, and the government estates changed hands. The land held by these sugar companies (as briefly mentioned elsewhere in connection with land tenure) is not their own property, but is rented or leased from the natives, under an arrangement by which only one-third of the rented area is planted with sugar, and the other two-thirds by the native owners with their own crops, three different crops being planted in rotation.

With the appearance of these private growers, disputes over water were multiplied. They were now not only between European and native, but between the rival companies themselves. Miniature wars broke out, over the precious streams that represented so many thousands of good silver guilders; and the native labour corps must have felt that the glorious days of their fathers had come back, as they stole out at dead of night from the mill which was the stronghold of some great white sugar chief, each armed with a "patjoel" (the heavy hoe with which all Javanese work in the fields, and a truly terrifying weapon), to divert an irrigation stream, and steal the water from the thirsty crop of a rival chieftain.

Armed guards patrolled any specially vulnerable channels or sluices; parties were sent out to attack them; battles, excursions, and alarms were the order of the day— or rather of the night; and plantation life in those days, in short, was anything but uneventful.

These squabbles were bad enough, and caused the government many heartburnings, but they were nothing compared with the situation between the sugar growers and the native cultivators, which presently grew to national importance.

The "day and night" system of watering had all along roused strong resentment. The native point of view is easily understood, for the disadvantage of watering by night is obvious; and the unfairness of the arrangement rankled, mingling with inevitable racial antagonism, to find expression in ever more bitter protests from native organizations, who, however, ignored the fact that as the cultivation of sugar increased, new irrigation systems were constantly being laid down, and native land watered which had never been watered before.

The sugar growers, moreover, argued in defence of the system that, whereas to water his rice crop all the native has to do is to let the water flow into his sawah, sugar has to be sprinkled by hand, from ditches running beside the plants—a process (known as "siraman") which could not possibly be done except in daylight. But this argument lost weight, because in many places rice was not planted at all during the dry monsoon, and the other crops cultivated by the natives instead needed just as careful watering as the European-owned sugar.

The protests grew, and were endorsed by the powerful "Sarekat Islam" party, a Mohammedan organization which has made itself increasingly felt in recent years, and by the " Sedio Moeli," or Federation of Regents. The matter became so serious that it was taken up by the government in Holland, who recommended that steps should be taken to abolish the hated system.

An alternative system was worked out by a government engineer named Cramer. He proposed that the water should be collected in artificial ponds, or "wadoeks," during the night, so that both the sugar and the natives' crops could be watered during the daytime. The system was approved, but many difficulties were encountered, and the old arrangement has so far only been partially replaced. Wadoeks have been constructed in places where the natives' protests seemed most reasonable, and in some other areas the regulation has been modified so that water is supplied to natives by two or three o'clock in the afternoon.

It would be difficult to over-estimate the extent of the sugar industry's influence in Java. It has built roads, railway tracks, bridges, canals, and sluices; it has distributed huge sums in rent to native landowners, in wages in its mills and plantations, and to carters and drivers of sugar trains. It has built whole towns and native kampongs, and maintains perfectly equipped modern hospitals, open to all the natives in the districts surrounding them, as well as to their own workers. It has built and equipped primary, technical, and agricultural schools; provides an admirable veterinary service; and enriches the land by the distribution of enormous quantities of cane manure, known as "ampas."

In certain districts the benefits due to "King Sugar" are even more remarkable, an outstanding example being at Goenong Sarie, in the region between the River Bondejoedo and the Kendong Hills, near Banjoewangi, which, before the advent of the sugar company, was almost entirely marshy forest and jungle. This land, which was quite useless to the community, was transformed by sugar into fertile soil, supporting many thousands of natives.

Few blessings can be set down to the credit of an active volcano. But in the region below Mount Keloed, the periodic eruptions of that ill-famed monster have created an area of land so rich and moisture-retaining that sugar can be successfully cultivated on it without irrigation—a very rare possibility.

Up to the beginning of the present century unpaid labour was employed on the construction and upkeep of the waterworks, which are the lifeblood of the sugar industry. The sugar companies supplied financial and technical assistance, and the work was done under the supervision of government engineers. Unpaid labour has now been abolished, but the smallest water-channels (which lead the water finally into the fields, after its journey through the network of larger channels from the main canal or storage) are made by unpaid labour on land which the natives cede for the purpose. They also keep these in repair, by their own free labour.

Every possible kind of device has been invented to increase the amount of water available in the dry monsoon.

Some immense reservoirs in which to impound the superfluous rainwater falling during the wet monsoon have been built by various companies at their own expense, their permits to do so from the government giving them preference in the use of the water for twenty-five years, after which it would be used for the benefit of the general community, the government reimbursing part of the cost of construction.

Once again, however, "preference" proved a burning question, and lengthy arguments, this time between the government and the sugar companies, ended in a decision to grant no more preferences to the builders of the reservoirs over the use of the water they themselves had impounded. It was a curious reversal of the old policy; but again native feeling had run high, and may well have influenced the decision.

The necessity for a plentiful water supply was so acute, however, that the sugar companies continued to build reservoirs, even though these passed on completion into government control, and the benefits of the water had to be shared with the general population.

Only about one-seventh of Java's irrigated lands are planted with cane, but the island is only second to Cuba in providing the world with cane sugar. In Cuba, nearly half the entire cultivated area of the island is devoted to the crop, and it produces nearly half the world's total supply. Java produces over one-fifth, and this proportion is not likely to be greatly increased, for the needs of the ever-growing native population make any reduction of rice cultivation in favour of sugar impossible, and therefore huge estates such as those in the West Indies can never be established.

Sugar-cane is planted (from cuttings) in Java between April and August, and harvested thirteen or fourteen months later. The plantations are almost all on the great alluvial plains of Central and East Java, in the neighbourhoods of Soerabaya, Kediri, Pasoeroean, Cheribon, Pekalongan, Samarang, Banjoemas, Kedoe, Djokjakarta, Soerakarta, Madioen, Rembang, and Modjokerto—the last of which, where the sugar-cane now flourishes, once saw the long-vanished splendours of the ancient Hindu stronghold at Modjopahit.

At Pasoeroean, on the coast of the Madoera strait, is a remarkable sugar experiment station, where cultural and chemical investigations in connection with the industry are constantly in progress, as a result of which the production per acre has immensely increased of late years. An interesting system of "chessboard" experiments is practised to determine the most productive varieties of cane.

The contrast between the landscape created by sugar and that of the familiar rice lands is remarkable, especially in the harvest season. The cane, ripe for cutting, rears its proud head fifteen to twenty feet into the hot, dry air, where the breeze passes through its stiff, withered, spiky leaves with a crackling rustle. It bounds the road on each side with a dense, impenetrable forest of slender, grey-green stems, close set as wheat, and to walk, or try to walk, amongst it is to experience something of what one may imagine to be the sensations of a prowling rat in an English cornfield.

By the sides of many roads in the sugar lands run narrow-gauge railway tracks, built by the sugar companies, and at any time during the hot, harvest months there crawl along them long, snakelike trains of open trucks, laden with towering loads of the curving cane, the light engine coughing its painful way wearily along, with sparks from the wood fuel blowing back in golden showers as it drags its heavy burden from the cane field to the factory.

Or you may meet endless processions of lumbering two-wheeled grobaks, with high sides but no ends, drawn by oxen. They are laden with cane, reaching from the horns of the bullocks that draw it, to project far behind the wagon until it almost touches the ground. These caravans are so long that you weary of trying to count the wagons as they creak slowly by, the noses of each pair of oxen touching the load of cane in front. And for the benefit of motorists it may be mentioned that these slow-moving convoys almost invariably travel on the wrong side of the road, presumably on the principle that it is preferable to be attacked by faster traffic in the front rather than in the rear!

CHAPTER SEVENTEEN

The Ubiquitous Bamboo—& Mountain Gardens

AS the kerosene tin is to the colonial, so is the bamboo to the Javanese, only much more so. You can do many things with a kerosene tin, but you cannot take a cutting and plant it in the back garden in the sure and certain hope that it will increase and multiply, and provide you with a lifelong supply of building, plumbing, and all sorts of other material.

That, however, is precisely what the bamboo does for the Javanese. In all the length and breadth of Java I doubt if there is a native house that has not its clump of bamboo growing in the garden wherefrom to cut for the thousand and one purposes for which it is used.

Next to the rice on which they live there is no one thing that could be named which is so utterly indispensable to the people of Java as this native of their jungle, which they now cultivate so universally.

It is no mean task to house forty million people—and comfortably and adequately at that. It is more, at all events, than all the builders and bricklayers of England have been able to accomplish. But, by providing an admirable building material, this is what the bamboo has done. Dotted about all over fifty thousand square miles of country are thousands upon thousands of neat little native houses, and every one of them is built of the stems of the great "bamboe petong," split and woven into

WOMEN SETTING OUT YOUNG RICE PLANTS
NATIVE CUSTOM INSISTS THIS WORK BE DONE BY WOMEN ONLY, AS OTHERWISE THE CROP
WOULD NOT BE FRUITFUL.

PLOUGHING A MOUNTAIN RICE FIELD WITH WATER BUFFALOES
THE PLOUGHMAN IS SINGING A LITTLE SONG WHICH KEEPS THE ANIMALS WORKING CONTENTEDLY
ALL DAY

sheets called "bilik." To the native, bamboo is actually synonymous with his habitation, as witness the fact that the literal meaning of the word bilik is a house, or room.

Having housed the native, the beneficent bamboo next provides him with transport, by means of the pikoelan, the familiar carrying pole. Its great strength and relative lightness, and, above all, its springiness, make it perfect for the purpose, and with it unbelievably heavy loads are carried for immense distances. Farmers carry their produce to market, household goods are brought to the kampongs, it brings their midday meal to the myriad workers in field and plantation, as well as the water they drink. And in this last case the bamboo serves them not only as a carrying pole, but provides the water vessels themselves, to make which, a section of big bamboo is cut off below the watertight joint, top and bottom; the result is a deep, narrow "bucket," which has the advantage of not easily spilling the water during the swaying trot of the carrier.

Of all the uses of bamboo, the part it plays in irrigation is the most interesting. There must be hundreds, if not thousands, of miles of bamboo pipes in the intricate pattern of Java's cultivated mountain-sides. A bamboo stem, of course, is hollow, but it is divided into sections by thick joints, and to make it into a serviceable pipe involves hours of patient labour characteristic of the Javanese. There are two methods. The more usual is to lash a sharp, curved, double-edged knife to the end of a bamboo of less diameter than the one to be pierced and force it down inside, cutting away the joints one by one. The other way is to cut off the stem on each side of the joints and then "telescope" the sections together again. Square openings are often cut in the upper side of very long pipes, to ensure a free flow and prevent choking.

Bamboo bridges are a feature of the Java landscape. In some parts of the island there are large and elaborate suspension bridges, built entirely of bamboo, which are triumphs of native skill. One of the most remarkable of these is near Bandjarnegara, in Mid Java. Smaller bridges, of which there must be countless thousands, for they cross every stream, are built of bamboo as a matter of course; and so are all fences, gates, stiles, seats, sheds, sheep-pens, stalls and mangers for ponies and cattle, tool handles, baskets, and other indispensable things too many to mention. The creaking of the great bamboo lever by which water is raised from innumerable wells, with the sort of "chanty" that accompanies it, is one of the familiar sounds of everyday life. Many Javanese musical instruments, too, are made of this universal material, among them the picturesque, faintly melodious "Ank-long," much favoured by strolling players, and familiar to all visitors to Java.

The one important native export industry, that of hat-plaiting, owes its existence to bamboo, and was formerly confined entirely to it. This industry is carried on chiefly at Tanggerang, on the border of Bantam. The bamboo is very finely split and woven, and was for long the only material used; but now the pandanus leaf, of which there is an indigenous variety, resembling that of Queensland, is also employed. Nearly a million guilders' worth of bamboo hats, and about the same of those made of pandanus, are exported annually. They go to all the European capitals, and are made in all the modern shapes, for which purpose models are imported and copied. It would be amusing to know how many expensive "Bang-kok" straws and other choice "named varieties" of millinery, purchased from fashionable modistes, were made by chattering Javanese or Soendanese girls in the obscure little town of Tanggerang.

The native police also wear locally made, broad-brimmed, shady hats, and they are growing in popularity among the peasants, who perch them precariously on the top of the inevitable kain kepala. Javanese women, however, have not yet succumbed to the charm of this local millinery.

When any sort of repair is needed about his house or farm, the Javanese does not have to measure it up and go off to town to buy materials, as we do. All he does is to go to his bamboo clump, hack out a stem with his "parang" (the big knife that every native carries), and set to work. I have seen a whole cottage garden neatly fenced with split bamboo that had been growing only a couple of hours earlier. Another day, passing a kampong, I came upon a householder about whose head a storm was raging. His wife, who was standing, rice-straw broom in hand, in the tiny garden, was reproaching him bitterly because the family buffalo, coming past the house to his stable the night before, had pushed the tip of his great horn through the wall of her house. Rain had come on, and had damaged the expensive kapok mattress they had bought from Ong Goe Tjeng's peddler only a week ago. How could she cook the food, and pound the rice, and keep the house and garden swept—how could she wash five children and their sarongs—to say nothing of those that he, Pioen, brought home plastered with mud after idling round the rice field behind the plough every day— if she had to waste her time carrying mattresses in and out every morning to dry? Why did he not repair the house instead of sitting there smoking?—a tirade, in short, that proved all angry housewives to be "sisters under their skins," whatever colour those skins might happen to be.

When I strolled past again, on my way home, poor old Pioen was hard at it, splitting up a newly cut green bamboo, and weaving it into a sheet about four feet square, which, by next morning (when curiosity took me back that way to see the end of the story), was so neatly fitted over the puncture made by the errant buffalo as to be quite invisible without careful inspection.

The climate of the Java highlands is greatly to the bamboo's liking, and it grows to an enormous size. Stems of eight or nine inches in diameter are quite usual, and a spar that would cost a yachtsman in Europe £5 or £6, if he could get it at all, he could buy in Java for thirty cents (about sixpence), having his choice of the whole clump. The only drawback would be that he would have to carry it away with him.

Big bamboo is transported from the hills to the plains lashed together in huge bundles like colossal asparagus, mounted on a two-wheeled bamboo frame, and pushed—or rather held back—by one man. And when one of these thirty- or forty-foot long obstacles negotiates a hairpin bend on its way down the mountain road, and meets an impatient motorist travelling upwards, the fun is often fast and furious.

Bamboo is planted in groves, or sometimes in clumps at regular intervals on steep hill-sides devoted to the cultivation of potatoes, where they serve a second useful purpose in preventing the soil from being washed away by heavy rain.

Huge quantities of potatoes are grown in the mountain regions, and supply not only Java's own European population, but contribute largely to the requirements of British Malaya. They possess the advantage of being always "new potatoes," and the large, thick-skinned tuber of our northern winters is unknown. In Java they mature very quickly, and are of oddly uniform size and shape—about that of an ordinary hen's egg.

A Java potato harvest is a pretty sight. The reapers are generally women, and, as often as not, hard pressed by a Chinese landlord or his agent, they sweep over the field like a multi-coloured wave, the smooth, pinkish potatoes fairly flying under their nimble fingers, until the field is dotted with small pyramids, which will be carried away to be stacked, sorted, and packed in a long, shady shed near by, where shafts of sunshine from the high ventilators paint the shapely piles with great splashes of orange.

The cultivation of European vegetables and flowers, so warmly encouraged by the Dutch in recent years, has entirely changed the landscape in some of the hill districts. Apart from the many acres of potato fields (which are usually the property of one large landholder), you can see in the course of one mountain tramp, where formerly there was only rice, native gardens with rows upon rows of cabbages, lettuce, carrots, leeks, onions, peas, beans, spinach, celery, tomatoes, marrows, and beetroot, as well as all the flowers that are familiar to English gardens. Most of them are watered by making a breach in the surrounding mud bank, letting sufficient water flow in from the stream alongside, and then letting it out again by the same method.

The native's ingenuity in making every inch of land productive is remarkable. You will see peas and marrows, or maize and onions, or any combination of tall and ground crops, planted together, and never a weed is ever allowed to show its head. The ubiquitous bamboo and banana appear in every odd corner, and for the banana the native gardener has found a most ingenious use.

When tender young seedlings are planted out, a banana is felled and the stem (which is really composed of leaves rolled tightly one over the other) is cut into six-inch "logs." These are split down the middle, allowing the stem to be pulled apart into curved sections, which are impaled on sharp bamboo spikes and stuck into the ground beside each young plant, to shelter it from the fierce rays of the sun.

Up among these mountain gardens, with no means of access except afoot by a steep path from the road far below, are the little kampongs where the farmers dwell. Not one of the tiny houses in them but has running water "laid on"; for the mountain householder simply "taps" a passing stream with a bamboo pipe and leads it to a small reservoir beside his home, whence an overflow pipe leads the water back again to the stream a little lower down, so that not a drop of the precious stuff is wasted. Many, too, have their own fresh fish supply in a little pond fed in the same way, and the housewife has only to show herself beside her "fish run," for a dozen snouts of greedy goldfish to appear above the water.

The produce of these gardens is carried down in baskets woven of bamboo or palm leaf, and the gay medley of colour in the loads makes them almost as attractive as flowers. All is trim and orderly; every unsightly leaf, and every speck of earth, is removed. In the early morning you may see, perhaps, a carrot grower and his wife, sitting by the side of the stream that waters their garden, dipping the carrots they have just pulled into the sparkling water, and scrubbing them with a small brush made of rice straw, before tying them up into flame-coloured nosegays, with feathery green tops diamonded by dew. You will meet whole families resting on their way down, with their varied loads beside them; and perhaps a toddler of three or so solemnly guarding his own—a slim bamboo with one cabbage in a grass basket hanging from either end.

Bamboo makes a public appearance on the grand scale every year at the "Pasar Gambar," the great native fair held in Batavia and every large town. It is a sort of Earl's Court exhibition, built entirely of bilik on frameworks of giant bamboo. Huge buildings of most elaborate design, with Moorish arches, or anything else that happens to occur to the builders of the moment, are erected each year, only to be torn down again as soon as the week or two's great show is over. The materials are offered for sale; the bilik is practically useless except for fuel, but the bamboo framework and the kajang roofing are in great demand at the low prices asked, and many loads, especially of kajang, are to be seen on the roads and canals at this time of the year.

The Pasar Gambar is a great annual event, and an interesting "shop window" of native arts and crafts. There is Batik, of course, of every kind; delicate basket work, mostly from Tasikmalaya; silver and brass work; buffalo horn ornaments; miniature Wayang figures; hand-woven sarongs; hats; and leather work in snake, lizard, and crocodile skin. But apart from all this, it is much like the fairs of other lands. The crowds—natives, Chinese, Eurasians, and the rest—surge in thousands through the entrance gates in the high bamboo walls; the roads round about the showground are blocked and traffic is diverted; the enclosure after nightfall is packed with a dense, slowly moving throng, through which it is almost impossible to edge your way.

The Ubiquitous Bamboo

There is nothing much, in short, to choose between the Pasar Gambar and the "Wembleys" of the world, were it not that the Pasar's buildings are unique. Nowhere else, I believe, except in Java, can you see a big annual exhibition housed in lofty halls, constructed of nothing more substantial than bamboo.

Model Dairies & Highland Settlements

ONE of the most surprising of Java's almost innumerable activities is its dairy industry. And here again, I am sorry to say, the English observer has to admit with chagrin a contrast between Java and Malaya that is by no means favourable to the British colony.

Inveterate tea drinkers from England or Australia who go to Malaya soon lose the taste for their national beverage, for the reason that no fresh milk accompanies it, except on the rarest occasions, from the Cold Storage, or at one of the very few homes where cows are kept. Generally speaking, the tea drinker must be content with condensed milk, or go without.

Such dairying—if it deserves the name—as there is in Malaya is in the hands of Indians, and is carried on in the indescribable conditions of filth and squalor habitual to those by no means hygienic people. To what extent the milk so produced acts as a propagator of disease among them has never been estimated, though such supervision as is possible is carried out. But certainly no European would ever dream of touching the product of the dens in which these miserable, under-nourished native cows are milked.

If, however, you cross over to Java, your very first cup of afternoon tea is accompanied by a jug of hot, fresh cow's milk, and there is not a town in the island in which a supply is not available.

You are quite as likely as not to see further evidence of how the miracle is worked before you have travelled many miles up country from the coast. Even on the road from Tandjong Priok, the port of Batavia, you may sometimes pass, looking absurdly gigantic by comparison with the small, slender, native draught-oxen and the diminutive ponies, two or three, or more, big, slow-moving Frisian cows, just landed from Holland or Australia, on their way to one of the many model dairy farms which Dutch enterprise has established in the cool Java uplands.

The importance of this industry is a great deal more far-reaching than the mere provision of a palatable cup of tea. It might not even be an altogether fantastic exaggeration to say that in it is bound up the fundamental difference between Java—where European settlement is as permanent as it is in our Dominions—and Malaya, where the white population is as shifting as the sands.

Reference has been made in another chapter to the contrast provided by the absence of white children in Malaya and the abundance of healthy young Hollanders in Java. And it does not seem unreasonable to connect the latter with an adequate fresh milk supply, without which a sturdy new generation of Europeans could not be reared.

Almost every high plateau in Java has a thriving European settlement, with its natural complement of schools. But though in Malaya there are mountains and plateaux galore, British enterprise has not yet disputed them with the jungle, save for two very limited exceptions. And even to those, for anything more than a day's visit, access is as hard (without a medical certificate of sickness) as for a Peri at the gate of Paradise.

The Dutch dairies in Java are run with the same punctilious care as are the model dairies of Holland. The stock is pure-bred, and confined to one breed, the Frisian, which has acclimatized most successfully, and is admirably suited to the purpose for which it was brought to Java, owing to the large quantity of milk given by the cows, though the cream content is rather less than that of some other breeds. The supply of fresh milk is the whole aim and object of the industry, and no butter-making on a large scale is attempted; it is, however, made in small quantities when there is a surplus of milk, and is either blended with imported butter, or sold in the vicinity of the dairies.

The cows are hand fed, and maize (which is cut green) and various other crops are grown for their benefit. Some dairies have small pastures on which the stock is grazed and exercised, but land as a rule is too intensively cultivated for much grazing to be possible, and these areas are necessarily limited. It may be mentioned in passing, however, that, apart from the grazing paddocks kept for dairy cattle, there are some rented by the racing fraternities in British Malaya, to which their imported blood stock is sent to be "toned up" by a bracing holiday. It is not only human invalids, but equine ones also, that find health in the highlands of Java.

Every dairy has electric light and power, an abundant water supply, and the most up-to-date of machinery and appliances; all are under the closest veterinary inspection, and many of the larger dairies have their own veterinary surgeon. All milk is "pasteurized," and delivered to the consumer in sealed bottles, exactly as it is in London; a fact that seldom fails to astonish strangers, whose previous experience has not led them to expect such compatibility between modern hygiene and the Far East.

The lot of the Frisian cow that emigrates to Java would

appear to be a happy one. She stands meditating for long, peaceful hours in her shady stall, which is washed out several times daily, and, being raised a foot or so from the ground, provides perfect drainage and cleanliness, as well as a refreshing draught. She herself has her personal attendant, in the shape of a small native boy, who stands by to gratify her lightest whim: to switch away annoying flies; to sponge her down from time to time (for no speck of dirt must ever be allowed to sully that flawless black-and-white hide); or polish her until his small, solemn, brown face is almost mirrored on her rounded sides.

The raised stalls are usually built round a quadrangle, and a wide concrete gutter running all round outside them enables the whole building to be kept clean and dry. In the case of outbreaks of "foot and mouth" disease—which do occur from time to time, despite all precautions, causing very heavy losses—these gutters are filled with a strong disinfectant, through which all the employees and anyone connected with the dairy are obliged to walk, to prevent a spread of the infection; no one else is allowed in at such times, on any pretext whatever.

The problem of whether Java's delightful "mountain resorts" grew up around the dairies, or whether it was the other way about, is rather like the problem of the hen and the egg; but, whichever way it may have been, they are almost always to be found close together.

Those admirable colonizers, the Dutch, have made such good use of the high plateaux with which Java abounds, to found European settlements, that one might almost imagine the whole island to have been systematically surveyed as though it were one huge estate, and the hill towns and mountain "resorts" to have been planted deliberately, like trees. At elevations of two thousand to two thousand five hundred feet above the sea, wherever a convenient situation offered, they seem to have planted a town; and running up from it towards the mountains, among whose foothills it lies, are almost always roads whose goal is a "Berg hotel," around which in its turn there has grown up yet another small community, with, never far away, the dairy farm.

These highland settlements of Java are unique. Like those of Switzerland, they were created for the dual purposes of health and pleasure, and they give even fuller measure of both gifts than is possible in the more austere atmosphere of the Alps.

The mountains that you see from your window at a Java Berg hotel are just as lovely as the peaks you see in Switzerland, but their beauty is kinder and more friendly. They do not glitter with the cold, hard magnificence of diamonds, like the Alpine giants; they lie dreaming drowsily in the sunshine, warm and breathing and alive. They are lofty and remote, but not inaccessible; splendid, but not terrible. Some of them, it is true, hold danger and even death pent up within them, but they hide it well; the iron fist is clothed in a rich green velvet glove.

They are crowned, not with snow, but with a glory of foliage, inviting you to come and rest in its shade. And you know that if you care to accept its invitation, and climb to the very summit, you will need no rope or axe; there will be no yawning crevasses to negotiate, no steps to cut in ice walls, no frostbite or bitter winds.

Your way will be long, for some of these mountains are as high as the Swiss peaks, but it is too varied ever to be wearisome; it will lead you up a winding path that runs sometimes in a deep lane between high hedges that might be in some corner of South Devon; sometimes across a gracious curve of short, sweet turf, where, if you sit down to rest and look back the way you have come, the slope falls sweeping away below you with nothing to intercept the view of the wide valley two thousand or more feet below, laid out with its chequer-board of rice fields like a living map, or a scene looked down upon from an aeroplane.

It will lead you through little copses of flowering bushes sweeter scented than dog roses, and through patches of fern rising shoulder high, that offer cool and springy resting places to the weary mountaineer.

It will wind on through groves of huge, smooth green bamboo, whose dry leaves crackle under your feet; it will skirt maize fields, and creep—now almost perpendicular—through gardens being laboriously terraced by some enterprising native on a strip of mountain lately won from the jungle, watered with streams newly tapped in bamboo pipes, not yet quite sure of their direction.

The path will bring you at last to the edge of the jungle itself, where you pass suddenly from the warmth of the sun-baked, open mountain-side to cool, dim shade, where the rich earth is soft under your feet, and every leaf in the massed foliage gleams with moisture; where every bend in the path is splashed by a shower of sparkling drops from a little stream, tumbling from higher levels into a clear basin, the very sight of which is an invitation to drink. Huge fallen mossy trunks block the way here and there, or bridge narrow deep ravines filled to the brink with tall tree ferns.

And in the very heart of the forest, when you think you must have reached a point far beyond human habitation, the sharp sound of an axe, or the rending crash of a falling tree, may strike upon your ear, and you will come upon a stalwart young native clearing a space in the jungle in which to make a garden and build a little bilik house—and found yet another happy little Javanese family. They can easily grow all that they will need, and water supply is never a baffling problem to a native of Java. For, as a leading Dutch engineer has said, these people can water a rice field on the very top of a mountain if they choose; there is always a higher point somewhere from which to "pipe" a stream, and they will bring it for miles if need be.

If, however, you go mountaineering in Java, thinking, like the Alpine climber, to reach a definite goal, you will be disappointed—unless you are one of those strange people who revel in sulphurous volcanic craters. There are plenty of those, but other goal there is none. Once in the forests that crown the heights, no other panoramas will be spread before you, and you can walk for hours along the crest of the ranges, climbing and descending alternately through the cool shadowy greenness, until inclination bids you turn homeward again.

You will meet all sorts of fellow-wayfarers on these mountain pathways, for there is never one that does not lead to some small kampong or other, tucked away in a crevice between the heights. They have no means of transport except their own tireless limbs and the sturdy mountain-bred ponies. You will often meet a whole caravan of these, loaded with panniers, scrambling gamely up the steep paths, digging in their small hoofs as though they were claws.

Sometimes—not often, for they are very sure-footed—a pony will slip, and then, heavy laden, there is little hope for him. He rolls helplessly over and over among the rocks and ferns, a slender leg snaps, and the driver climbs down to cut the poor, gallant little beast's throat, and end the life that has served his master so well. And his only requiem will be that master's weary grunts and groans as he drags the dead pony's load back to the path and shares it out among the others, already loaded though they are nearly to the utmost.

You will very likely meet a bevy of village lasses, dainty and smart in freshly washed sarongs and badjoes, walking in single file, bound perhaps for a wedding or some other celebration in the next village. They will probably stop, with the invariable query: "Dari mana?" (Where do you come from?); for these natives, like the Elephant's Child in Kipling's *Just So Stories*, are full of an insatiable curiosity; and when you have answered all their questions they will giggle like so many small children with an indulgent elder, and most likely ask for a little money to spend at the pasar.

A woodcutter from the forest above, resting, on his journey down, by the wayside, between his enormous twin loads, will greet you and perhaps invite you to try to lift them, and grin with delight when you fail even to make them budge.

Most of these "Bergplaats" are rather more than four thousand feet above the sea, and there are one or two as high as six thousand. Their climate is that of an English May or June as we would have them if we could, with warm, sunny days and cool, sometimes quite cold, nights, that brace both body and mind, and make the hot baths, that are always "on tap," a very welcome luxury.

The foliage of hedges, trees, and gardens has the clean, fresh growth of temperate climes, with an added quality of vigour all its own, which is yet quite different from that of the lush growth on lower levels. There are hedges of pale pink roses that transport you in memory to England, though the most common hedge is one of a strong-growing variety of sunflower, always covered with bloom, and, literally, a blaze of gold.

HOW BAMBOO FRAMEWORK IS USED IN JAVANESE BUILDINGS

NOTHING BUT BAMBOO IS USED IN MOST NATIVE BUILDINGS; OFTEN, AS IN THIS CASE, EVEN THE ENTIRE FRAMEWORK.

AN EXAMPLE OF ELABORATE BILIK BUILDING.   NOTE THE EFFECTIVE WOVEN PATTERN OF THE SPLIT BAMBOO

You can pick bunches of strong, clean-stemmed sweet peas or carnations, as cool and stiff as though they had grown in an English garden, or cut a delicately scented tea rose. And with no heat to wither them (although they are only a very few degrees from the Equator) they will remain fresh, and fill your rooms with fragrance for days. Maidenhair fern, to set off their beauty, you can pick on the shady banks of any of the small streams whose music is always in your ears.

It is to the Berg hotels that Dutch families in Java go for the school holidays, as in Europe they go to the seaside, and at these times the highlands are alive with children. One of the youngsters' chief amusements is riding, out of which the native pony-owners make a rich harvest. Every morning they appear, smartly dressed in their nattiest Batik, in twos and threes, leading fat, well-groomed ponies in roughly tanned, native-made saddles and bridles of an odd pinkish hue.

Then there starts the daily juvenile gymkhana. Sturdy, bare-headed young Hollanders, with blond hair standing on end from their sunburned foreheads, give dashing displays of horsemanship all over the hotel gardens, to the detriment of the turf and the flower beds, while admiring little sisters ride rather nervously, at a more subdued pace, along the gravel paths.

Bridge fiends lie low, for picnics are the order of the day. There is plenty of tennis, though it is hardly of Wimbledon standard; and volcano devotees can always find a crater or two in the neighbourhood if they wish. These devotees are usually English, seldom Dutch. I am inclined to think that the Dutch only "discovered" the volcanoes as an attraction for tourists, and are far from regarding them as an amenity of their own holiday life.

For swimmers the mountain bathing places are utterly delightful. The water is crystal-clear and very cold, and acts as a sharp tonic, but is not by any means to be recommended to those with weak hearts. The bathing pools are either natural basins, or are concreted in among the rocks, and fed by mountain streams, often falling from a height over an exquisite fern-shaded cliff, to provide a delicious natural shower-bath. There are neat changing rooms, and diving platforms and shady grottoes: everything, in short, that the heart of a bather can desire.

At most of the mountain settlements there is a colony of private bungalows, some of them set in the most beautiful flower gardens I have seen in any part of the world. A really first-class Dutch horticulturist, in conjunction with the climate of the Java uplands and Javanese labour, is a unique combination, which seems to be capable of achieving the otherwise impossible perfection of the gardens in an "Allingham" water-colour.

To attempt an enumeration of the flowers in these gardens would be foolish. They seem like the wildest flights of optimism in a seedsman's catalogue come to life. Every blossom that is familiar in temperate climes is represented, with the added glory that those of spring, summer, and autumn bloom all at once.

I have seen scores that were miracles of beauty. But one stands out in my memory, and always will—the garden of a house called "Nannij," at Lembang, in the Preanger. Who the owner is I have never inquired, but I cannot believe that as a flower gardener he can have a rival anywhere. And he and all the other gardening residents deserve the warm gratitude of every visitor for a free flower show that it would be hard to equal.

Strawberries ripen at all seasons, and a plateful eaten

with fresh cream from the neighbouring dairy adds the final touch to the delights of Java highland life.

Is it any wonder that the Dutch colonial, when he retires, turns with a shiver from the chilly memories of his northern homeland and settles, nine times out of ten, among the mountains of his adopted country?

CHAPTER NINETEEN

The Romance of Cinchona

THERE is nothing particularly romantic at first glance about that bitter and most distasteful drug, quinine. Yet of all the drugs in our pharmacopœia, the story of its origin is the most picturesque, and its production in Java, which has almost the world monopoly of its commercial supply, is one of the island's most interesting industries.

The tree from which quinine is obtained is a native of South America, growing on the slopes of the Andes at elevations from four thousand feet to twelve thousand feet above the sea. The medicinal powers of its bark were no doubt known to the very early inhabitants of those regions, and when the Spanish conquered the country in the sixteenth century, and the Jesuits followed them to bring culture and enlightenment and the blessings of Christianity to the poor, ignorant heathen, the heathen in their gratitude naturally passed on to the learned Fathers their primitive knowledge of simple native remedies.

Then one of the missionaries fell ill with fever at Malacastos, in Ecuador, and was cured of it by a devoted Indian convert with an extract of the bark. This seems to have convinced the good monks, for they thereupon adopted the medicine as their own, and renamed it, with becoming modesty, "Jesuit's Bark," commending it warmly to the use of the Spanish settlers, among whom fever was a constant menace.

After that it only remained for a high official, the Corregidor of Loxa Province, to be cured by means of the new drug, and the reputation of "Jesuit's Bark" was made.

But even then it might never have attained more than a local reputation, or might at any rate never have become available outside the best religious circles, had it not been that the Countess Cinchon, wife of the Spanish Viceroy of Peru in 1638, also fell desperately ill with the dreaded fever.

Her sickness baffled the skill of all the Spanish physicians, and her life was despaired of; but, on hearing of her desperate case, the Corregidor sent post-haste to advise that the Jesuits be asked for their wonderful remedy, with the result that the Countess was snatched from the jaws of death, and completely recovered.

The Jesuits, in their Christian beneficence, kept the nature of the drug a secret, and guarded it jealously. But the Countess, a famous beauty of her day, and a woman of high intelligence to boot, was resolved that the valuable medicine to which she owed her life must not be lost to a suffering world. Through her native servants she took infinite pains to find out all about the tree with the magic in its bark, and on her return to Spain, at the end of Count Cinchon's governorship of Peru, she took with her (though how she concealed it in her luggage the record does not say) specimens of the bark for the Court chemists to experiment upon.

The experiments were successful: the secret was out. More and more bark was brought over by the Spanish ships; and by degrees, under yet another and certainly the more appropriate name of "Peruvian Bark," the new drug became the standard remedy for fever that it remains to this day. The tree was christened "Cinchona," after

The Romance of Cinchona

the beautiful Countess who introduced it to the world; but as for what may have been the names of the vanished savage people who actually discovered it, no one knows, and no one cares.

At first, and until comparatively recently, the drug was taken in the form of the powdered bark, or in tinctures and extracts made directly from it. Now, however, modern science has made possible the separation of the active principles, or "alkaloids," of which quinine is the chief. The world's consumption of them is enormous, and ninety-five per cent. of that consumption is supplied by Java.

For over two hundred years the bark was brought to Europe from the Andes, where the trees, which grew deep in the forests, were cut down, and their bark stripped and carried with great difficulty to the coast for shipment. The method was extremely laborious and costly, and as the trees were destroyed for their bark, the drug became scarcer and dearer year by year, until it began to be feared that in time it would become unprocurable. It was so indispensable by this time that the scientists put their heads together. Dr. Royle, an English botanist, suggested to the British Government that an attempt should be made to cultivate the tree; but, characteristically, it was twenty years before they adopted his suggestion, and it was not till 1859, when Peruvian Bark supplies for India were costing the Government over £1200 a year, that seeds from South America were planted in the Sikkim Himalayas and the Nilgiris, and cinchona was so successfully established in India as to supply that country's needs.

At about the same time the Germans and Portuguese started cultivating the tree in their respective tropical possessions, but it was the Dutch who succeeded in doing so on the grand scale. In 1852 an expedition under Dr. Junghuhn brought a quantity of young trees of all varieties of cinchona to Java, and there began the experiments which were to result in placing this small island first among the quinine producers of the world.

The trees were first planted in the beautiful mountain garden at Tjibodas, near Sindanglaya, about five thousand feet above sea level. A few years later they were planted more extensively on the wide plateau at a slightly lower elevation, above Bandoeng, and it is there that the cultivation is now chiefly concentrated.

There are over a hundred estates, the most important of them being the government station "Tjintiroean," which supplies seeds and young trees to the other plantations, and at which cultural experiments of all kinds are constantly being made.

Dr. Junghuhn devoted his whole life to the establishment of the tree in Java, and when he died was buried at his own wish in the midst of the scene of his labours. He has been given a strikingly fitting memorial. His grave is on a gently sloping hill-side, surrounded by a shady plantation of different varieties of cinchona, each planted in a separate section and labelled with a name-plate for the information of the interested passer-by, who can learn from it that "Ledgeriana," the chief quinine producer, and the other principal varieties, except one, have narrow, slender leaves set in groups. The exception is "Cordifolia," which is of much more robust growth, with large rounded leaves, not unlike teak, in its early stages. As the result of Dr. Junghuhn's experiments, the delicate quinine-bearing variety is grafted on to the robust stock of Cordifolia, in which combination the tree most perfectly adapted to the local conditions has been evolved.

All round the mountain village where the old Dutch

botanist worked and rests there are groves of cinchona—small trees so uniform in height that from the hills above their tops look level as a field of wheat. They branch out freely from the stock on which they are grafted, a few inches above the ground, and these branches are thinned out in rotation when about one-and-a-half inches in diameter.

Among the streams of natives you will meet on the surrounding country roads, with every sort of burden swinging from their creaking pikoelan, there are always some laden with what appear to be bundles of small firewood. It is not until you meet them stepping over the bamboo stile that leads from a cinchona grove, and see in the plantation the many newly sawn stumps of uniform diameter, cut only from certain sections, that you realize that it is not firewood, but quinine in the first stage of manufacture, that they are carrying.

The next stage is absurdly simple in proportion to the importance of the industry. If you follow those seeming "firewood" carriers along the road between the high hedges gay with yellow sunflowers you will notice that a sound that has throbbed faintly in your ears all day long is growing stronger every moment, the sort of sound that, if you gave it a thought, you would probably have put down to an engine used for some purpose or other at a neighbouring dairy.

Certainly, until you come upon them, you would never guess that this rhythmical, monotonous sound is made by a bevy of comely young native girls, squatted on their heels in a big lofty barn, beating ceaselessly with small wooden mallets at cinchona branches on the ground. From the first to the last of the daylight the gentle, steady beating goes on, stripping the bark from the wood, which is stacked like a heap of slender, naked bones in a corner, while the ragged strips of precious bark are spread on round trays in the sun outside to dry, before being carried down the mountain road to the quinine factory at Bandoeng, two thousand feet below.

Cinchona trees are replanted in rotation year by year, for the alkaloid content of the bark begins to decrease after twenty-five years, and the trees are cut down. The cultivation is not highly profitable to the grower, and many of them are reducing their areas of cinchona, and interplanting it with tea. The total production of quinine in Java is about eighteen million pounds' weight per year.

The island is rich also in its own native medicines. Several hundred distinct drugs, derived from various herbs, grasses, bark, and fruits, are known and used by the natives as a matter of course in the treatment of different forms of illness, and the history of cinchona bids fair to repeat itself in the case of many of them. For they have proved so often to be the only cure for the diseases to which natives apply them as a remedy, that European belief in them is constantly growing.

A case of which the writer has personal knowledge was a particularly virulent one of dysentery, which, after yielding temporarily to the accepted European treatment, recurred again and again at ever shorter intervals, allowing the patient no time to regain strength. The case (like that of the Countess Cinchon) "baffled the skill of the European physicians," who began to despair of averting a fatal collapse from sheer exhaustion.

The sick man's Javanese servant, who had devotedly helped to nurse him, appeared one morning with a little bunch of faded herbs, and offered them gravely to the patient's nurse, with a speech which had evidently been carefully prepared. "The nyonya is good," he said, "and the toean also. We have been sad at heart these many weeks that the toean has been sick. The white man's toean doctors are very wise, but the toean does not get better. The people of Java are without learning, but the toean's sickness is a sickness of our people, and when this sickness comes upon us we make an 'obat' (medicine) with these plants, boiling them in water until the water falls half-way in the cooking-pot, and drinking a little of the medicine each hour. If the toean will but try this obat he will surely be well in two days."

It was more to please old Kromo than from any great faith in its merits that the patient consented to "try the stuff." It was duly boiled "until the water fell in the cooking-pot," under the solemn superintendence of the "boy," and a glass of the resultant faintly scented dark brown liquid duly swallowed. Next day a new supply was brought, and that evening, as he was quietly busying himself about the sickroom, Kromo remarked, half as though stating a fact, and half as a question, "The toean is better?"

He was. He recovered rapidly, although, rendered pessimistic by painful experience, he had little hope but that his enemy was in ambush, and would soon attack again. Under the gentle insistence of old Kromo, however, he continued to swallow his potion several times daily, in diminishing doses. A week passed, then another, then a month, with no sign of the foe; and after that—well, the reputation of the obat, whatever it was, was made.

The illness, however, recurred a month or two later, when the ex-patient, now recovered, was in Batavia on business. This time, it was no "white man's doctor" that he summoned, but a hotel "boy," through whom, from a native medicine-woman, well known (even to Europeans) in Batavia, he obtained a supply of the herbs, learning then for the first time their name—"seriawan oesoes." The obat was made, and quickly arrested the attack, and there was no further recurrence.

It is a custom of the natives to grow a number of the plants known to possess medicinal properties, in their kampongs. "Then," as one of them said to me one day, pointing to a row of insignificant-looking weeds growing along the fence in his tiny garden, "if a man does not feel well in the morning, here is medicine, ready to his hand." Which called up a pleasant vision of poor old Tanjong or Mat, after perhaps attending a birthday party over-night, pottering down the garden path and gathering the makings of a glass of "Eno's," all fresh with morning dew!

Members of the Research Institute say that in Java and the East Indies there are in all probability many hundreds, if not thousands, of these native drugs which would well repay proper study, and provide us with invaluable new remedies for disease. They have been investigated to the point of being roughly classified and their physiological action noted, but few, if any, have been exhaustively examined; and therefore, though their value is known to many, no European doctor (so far as I know) will pre-scribe them. Some of these drugs belong to the "alkaloid" group, the group to which cinchona also belongs. No doubt in the fullness of time they, too, will find their way into the lists of everyday drugs that we buy at our chemists, and we shall then, of course, be just about as grateful to the poor, ignorant Javanese who gave them to us as a malaria patient is to the South American Indians, to whom he owes quinine!

November Afternoon . . . Teak Forests . . . & Tea

THERE is a part of the Krawang-Poerwakarta road in West Java that can provide the traveller, especially in the month of August, with a rather curious experience.

Approached from the north, you will have been passing through flat country, between the endless miles of rice sawahs which feed the Chinese mills at Krawang. Or, coming from the south, you will have climbed the high range over which the road runs to Bandoeng, turning and twisting amid a bewildering variety of scenery, crossing rushing rivers and deep ravines veiled in tree ferns, past busy little kampongs, with their palms and cassava and bananas, and everywhere along the road, as part of every scene, rice, terraced up the steep hill-sides, or tucked into pockets of the valleys, each corner as you turn it revealing some new ingenuity in fitting a few odd square feet of rice-crop into an apparently impossible situation.

You round the last sharp curve, where the road crosses a narrow stream and enters a cutting, to whose farther side five or six variously shaped water stairs seem to be clinging precariously in defiance to all the laws of gravitation; then round another bend in the road, and, without warning, the scene is completely changed. You have left the green and smiling land of rice and tropic vegetation behind you; you seem not even to be in the East at all: you are home again in England, on one of those rare November days when the sun shines through a pale golden haze on to bare winter trees, and on the deep carpet of fallen leaves at their feet.

That is the unexpected scene that greets you here in the very heart of Java. As far as you can see, on either side of the road, stand the winter woods; ranks of tall, grey, solemn trees, leafless and dead-looking, with here and there a shrivelled leaf hanging from the naked branches. The weather is dry, and here, away from the watery rice fields, the air is filled with a fine dust, cheating the sun of his brilliance, faintly veiling the outlines of the great trees, and giving the forest a strange atmosphere of unreality.

Deep silence broods over the place. Not a bird's note disturbs the stillness. There is no sign of the familiar wealth of green vegetation; except for a carpet of grass along the roadsides all is bare, and with it has vanished the harbourage it gave to all bird and insect life.

These are some of the famous "djati" or teak forests of Java, and one more of its many sources of natural wealth. Djati is a native of the Java jungle, found mostly in the limestone of the north; and in immense areas in the lower mountain slopes, at altitudes between one thousand five hundred and two thousand feet, this proud tree so dominates its neighbours as almost to have the forest to itself. Its great value as timber was early discovered by the Dutch East India Company, who used to obtain huge quantities of jungle teak by forced labour, under a system known as the "belandong" service, as tribute from defeated native princes. As time went on, the tree was extensively planted and cultivated, and there are now more than a million and a half acres of teak forests and plantations under the control of the Forestry service.

Unlike most tropical trees, which change their leaves so

imperceptibly that they are always green, the djati sheds them all together, after the fashion of the trees of temperate climes, and it is thus that a Java teak forest is able to present the illusion of an English winter afternoon.

In no other particular, however, does the djati resemble our familiar trees. Tropic nature seems always to incline to the spectacular, and djati leaves are enormous—as big as dessert plates, or often even bigger, and nearly as round. One of these giant, withered derelicts, left alone high aloft on a bare branch, looks oddly like a piece of brown paper tied on as a scarecrow; and in the springy carpet that the fallen leaves spread below, the trunks stand three feet deep or more. It has also a big pale brown pod, covered with velvety fur and curiously like a hare's ear, which is a favourite plaything of the native children in the teak districts.

The forests are a government monopoly, and a valuable one, for djati timber is a hardwood of magnificent quality and very close grain. It is exported in great quantities, and is also in great demand locally, particularly by the Chinese for the manufacture of furniture.

The highways of Java abound in these contrasts and surprises, for the mountainous country creates such rapid alternations of climate that you may pass from tropic to temperate zones of vegetation in a quarter of an hour. Another strong contrast to the ubiquitous rice fields is provided by the tea plantations, of which there are about two hundred and fifty in the island, mostly in the Preanger Regencies, Mid Java. A few are on comparatively low levels, but most of the important estates are high in the mountains—at four thousand to five thousand feet above the sea. And though the total area (it is rather under two hundred thousand acres altogether) seems negligible compared with that given up to rice, Java is not far short of providing a tenth of the whole world's tea; rather a surprising total for one small island when the amounts grown in India, Ceylon, and China are considered.

The tea estates are places of outstanding beauty even in an island as lovely as Java. They are still more notably so in comparison with many plantations of the same crop in India and Ceylon, where on hill-sides bare but for the low tea bushes themselves the sun blazes pitilessly down on the baked soil; and where certainly no European would ever dream of spending a leisure hour, nor even so much as enter unless he were obliged.

In Java, the tea estates, on the other hand, are well named "tea gardens." They are cool and shady, and delightful places in which to walk, for almost invariably they are interplanted with shade trees; and the light, feathery foliage of the tree most used for this purpose, Albizzia Falfata, throws a delicate shade that adds greatly to the gardens' charm.

These shade trees are lopped back in the rainy season so as to give the tea the full benefit of the moisture, and grow again to shelter it in the hot, dry weather.

Like a glossy, dark green shawl, the tea covers the hill-sides, interwoven with the paler green of the Albizzia. It is crossed and recrossed in every direction by shady paths sunk deep between grassy banks shaven smooth as turf, whose crest, sometimes shoulder-high, borders the orderly battalions of sturdy tea bushes. Up and down and round about run these paths, sometimes level for a mile or more as they creep across the face of the mountain-sides and follow their contour, sometimes climbing steeply up on bamboo steps set into the soil, and every now and then, when the slope of the hill brings the path level with the plantation, yielding a glance of the rice sawahs gleaming silver far below, or, through a gap between the distant mountains, of a hazy blue smudge that is the sea.

On patches of level plateau, where the shade trees are older and have been left unlopped, the shade is deeper, and you have the sensation of being in a forest where the undergrowth that borders the grassy rides is strangely uniform; a forest that ends abruptly at the edge of the plateau, where the hill-side slopes steeply away again; and as often as not a "flamboyant" tree brandishes glowing masses of scarlet blossoms in the face of the sunny sky.

Sometimes the sweep of the estate is broken by gorges too steep for planting, and here the tea, on the verge of a slope almost perpendicular, rubs shoulders with the waving tree ferns and lush vegetation that cloak the inevitable mountain stream, chuckling and gurgling unseen down below; while the path, descending in easy zigzags, crosses sedately by a neat bamboo bridge.

Here and there, on some estates, where the paths meet, you will come to a little shelter, built of bamboo and roofed with kajang, for the benefit of all and sundry. These shelters do not encourage idling, for they seldom provide a seat (except perhaps one made of two parallel, polished bamboos, than which there are few resting places more unyielding); but they are a very welcome refuge in the sudden mountain storms. In them at such times you may meet all sorts and conditions of chattering estate workers, or any casual native passer-by taking this way home from the forest to his kampong.

The big European estates in Java are laid out with mathematical precision, and cared for thereafter as meticulously as the Dutch housewife cares for her home. A plantation is always divided off into sections, every one of which is numbered, and inspection and organization of labour are most rigorous.

The pickers are usually women, who gather the leaf into a big square of cotton cloth, and carry the bundle to the factory on their head or shoulder. The children, too, do their part. They are given tiny glass bottles, in which they collect insect pests from the trees, and are paid, on producing the "bag" to the overseer, at the rate of about a cent a score.

A very familiar sound in these tea gardens is the faint, bell-like note of a little bamboo gong, used by the workers to keep in touch with their children and with each other. The trees are dense and the people small, and they are completely hidden, except at the very edges of the plantation, until they slip out one by one, and file down the path, each greeting you as they pass with a "Tabek, toean" ("Good day, sir"). (Note: "toean" is a term of respect used to persons of either sex.)

Even tea pickers must eat, and as they cannot very well make portable sandwiches of the rice which is their staple food, demand, as usual, has created supply. So, just as the peddler brings the necessities of life to the kampongs, the "toekang makanan," or food merchant, brings food to the hungry tea workers; and any day towards midday, even on these remote mountain pathways, you will hear the familiar creak of the pikoelan, and along comes the travelling restaurateur with his two big square boxes, one containing the kitchen range, over which the rice is steaming, and the other, the dishes and pots and pans full of the queer dainties dear to the Javanese heart.

He has his regular pitches, known to the workers, at which he arrives punctually at the same hour every day; serves the little groups that come drifting along, chattering and laughing; then makes up his fire, replenishes the basket in which the rice is steaming, and trots off again with his heavy load to the next port of call.

The pruning of tea bushes is drastic, for upon it depends the growth of the tender immature tips, which are the only ones picked. Comparatively few of these are produced by each plant in a season. For that reason picking goes on constantly, as the shoots are always maturing, but do not do so all together.

On some estates the bushes are pruned every year; but when they are left, as is often the case in Java, for two years, the prunings are large enough to be in great demand by the natives for firewood. This simplifies matters all round; the tea bushes, cut back so mercilessly that not a leaf remains, making them look as though a plague of locusts had eaten them, are left standing, surrounded by piles of prunings a foot deep. But word has gone out to the district that firewood is to be had for the taking, and the whole population of the surrounding kampongs descend upon it in swarms, bind the prunings in neat bundles, and carry them off to a "dump," whence they can be taken home at leisure.

By the day after a section has been pruned not a stick is left on the ground, and all is as tidy as though it had been swept and garnished. Meanwhile, if you have passed that way, you will have met whole families laden with the spoil, in bundles of graduated sizes, perhaps down to the baby just able to walk, staggering along with a burden almost as big as his little brown naked body.

Tea has been grown in Java ever since 1690, when the Dutch East India Company first imported plants from Japan. Early in the following century they sent to China for seed; but cultivation on a large scale does not seem to have been undertaken until about 1824, when a fresh start was made with plants from both China and Japan. The beginning of tea growing on a really important scale dates from 1878, when seed from Assam was found to thrive better than the other varieties in the Java high-lands; and from that time it went steadily ahead, to be further increased by the "boom" of 1910. Many natives have also planted tea in the vicinity of the estates, and sell their freshly picked leaf, which is known as "kampong leaf," to the estate factories at prices up to about ten cents (twopence) a pound.

In a sheltered corner of every estate is the "nursery," where the baby plants, grown from seed, remain for two years, after which they are cut down and planted out as stumps. The factories are all extremely up-to-date, many having hydro-electric power; and much of the fuel for the drying rooms is supplied by the old tea trees them-selves, which are replaced by younger ones as their productiveness decreases, and which thus, even in their death, are able to perform a last valuable service.

London is the biggest buyer of Java tea, which is not surprising when it is remembered that Great Britain drinks more than half the tea produced in the whole world. Australia, too, is a good customer; and never a ship sails for the Commonwealth's ports but her holds are stacked high with the neat, uniform, plywood cases containing the tea that will be repacked and labelled with the names of the famous "Australian" brands of the national beverage.

Alas for that fond illusion! The only Australian pro-duct in a packet of Australian tea is the glue that sticks the wrapper. Even the paper that wrapper is made of is imported.

CHAPTER TWENTY-ONE

On a Rubber Estate

WE were sitting on the veranda of the manager's bungalow on a rather isolated rubber estate. It was a glorious night. The moon shone down serenely on the trim garden and etched the trees at the farther boundary of the shaven lawn, where garden and plantation met, as a black, sombre wall against the faintly luminous sky.

It was always quiet at night in this remote place, but to-night there seemed something not quite normal in the brooding silence. There was a tension, a sense of waiting: the piano stood open and neglected; there was no sound, as on other nights, of murmuring voices and laughter. The little house party sat silent, watchful . . . listening . . .

And then, suddenly, without warning, from the direction of the native labour quarters, pandemonium broke out: a deafening clatter of bangs and crashes, of fiendish, menacing shrieks and yells, of drums and rattling tins and howling blasts blown on buffalo horns; the unforgettable, terrifying tangle of sound that can only mean an outbreak of native excitement.

It had come—the thing we were waiting for; but though there were no heroes on that veranda, not one of the little party seemed much perturbed. Brown, the manager, took the pipe from his mouth, knocked it out, and pointed with the stem to the moon.

On a Rubber Estate

"It's started, you see, m'dear," he said to his wife. "Shall we stroll over for a bit?"

A faint shadow was just beginning to impinge on the edge of the moon's silver face. To the Europeans it was the start of a perfectly punctual, well-regulated, total eclipse, but to the natives it was an attempt by some evil spirit to put out the light of the moon—and they were not going to allow that if they could help it! They meant to frighten the intruder away by every means they could think of. Islam was all very well, of course; but there is a time for everything, and in a serious matter of this kind it was obviously better to leave nothing to chance!

Every tin, every drum, everything that could possibly be banged or rattled or blown, was pressed into service, and the chaotic symphony grew ever more deafening. But it was all, alas! of no avail. Little by little the shadow of the huge, ghostly "hantoe" (devil) of the heavens blotted out more and more of the vanquished moon, and the world was getting darker every moment. Groans and cries of horror went up on every side, until presently the medley of noise died away. Evidently it was all in vain. There remained nothing but to watch the progress of the battle.

But it seemed that no one must look directly at the mysterious enemy. A spirit who could thus extinguish the Lamp of Heaven must be a powerful one indeed; he might well punish any who should be presumptuous enough to stare at him, with sudden blindness. The wise men reported, however, that progress might be observed with perfect safety in a mirror; and accordingly deeply absorbed figures were to be seen squatting here and there in the dim light, gazing fixedly at the moon's reflection in polished tin lids or scraps of looking-glass. The passer-by, however, was solemnly warned by no means to interpose his shadow between the mirror and the spirit who was eating the moon. This was of all things to be avoided; it was a form of impertinence which the hantoe would never brook, and might bring down serious vengeance upon the whole community.

Meanwhile the situation was becoming desperate. It grew darker and darker, and the moon was now hidden but for a narrow rim of silver. The older men consulted together, and, after much whispering, decided to make one more effort. A procession was formed, led by the chief mandoer, with a boy close behind him carrying a shot-gun. It was a desperate cause, and needed a desperate remedy. If this fearsome phantom could eat the moon, who knew what he might not start next? He might even try to put out the sun—a horror not to be contemplated.

There was only one thing to be done. Shoot him!—and with a magic bullet. So, at the very moment of totality (which aroused suspicions that the old mandoer was not quite so simple as he pretended), the procession halted, and the gun was pointed at the now almost invisible moon.

A shot rang out—then another—and then, behold! Surely the shadow was retreating? The mandoer waved a reassuring hand. Wider and wider grew the thread of silver on the moon's side. Slowly but surely the dark curtain was withdrawn.

A tremendous sigh of relief went up from the watchers. All was well! The danger was over. The evil spirit was routed!

But, to make quite sure, it was better to let him know that brave men were on the watch. There was nothing to be feared from a retreating enemy, anyway, and he must be shown that we would stand no nonsense! So the awful clatter of tins and drums and blood-curdling screams broke out again—this time with success. For the monster, utterly cowed, made no further attempt on the moon. His shadow fell back as he crept away, doubtless mortally wounded by the mandoer's bullet; farther and farther, until at last the moon's white radiance flooded the world again as it had before the battle.

The eclipse was over, and utter silence fell again over the garden and over the dark entrance to the rubber plantation.

Whether it is make-believe, or superstition, or sheer love of dramatic effect born of the Wayang, or a mixture of all three, no one, certainly no European, will ever know. But whatever the cause, the Javanese reaction to an eclipse is certainly stimulating; and I am afraid that I should not have found a solemn pilgrimage with earnest persons to some uncomfortable mountain top, to take scientific notes of the phenomenon, half so entertaining as the spectacle of that procession shooting at the evil hantoe of the heavens with a magic bullet from a modern shot-gun.

The moon was saved. But perhaps the hantoe took his revenge. For the rubber industry, in common with so many others, is suffering a partial eclipse in the world slump. And many estates in all the rubber-producing countries, Java among the rest, which only such a few years ago were humming with activity, are now silent and deserted except for the skeleton "care and maintenance" staffs who remain to keep the jungle at bay, and prevent the rapid tropic growth from undoing the labour of years.

But every eclipse passes. The world may have slumped, but still it rushes faster and faster every day on its rubber tyres; and some day, unless civilization is extinguished altogether, the tappers will come back again to the trees that now are standing watching and waiting in the silent plantations for better times.

To England belongs the honour of having started, by means of a sensational smuggling feat, the cultivation of rubber in the East. The tree (Hevea) is a native of Brazil, whence seeds were sent to Kew by Sir H. Wickham in 1876. The Brazilian government thereupon, fearing to lose their trade in forest rubber, absolutely prohibited the export of seed; but Wickham, nothing daunted, managed to smuggle out some seventy thousand, of which two thousand were successfully germinated in the hot-houses at Kew Gardens.

The resultant seedlings were sent to Ceylon and Malaya, whence a few found their way to Java; and two of those original trees, hale and hearty, are still growing at Buitenzorg.

Although England pioneered the industry, Java possesses the oldest plantation in the world, at Sabang, in the Preanger. The trees, however, are not the Hevea, which became the recognized rubber of commerce, but Ficus Elastica, with which some early experiments were made.

Planting of Hevea on a large scale started in 1900, and, encouraged by several "booms," increased so rapidly that in 1929 five million acres of trees were being tapped in the East, British Malaya producing forty-three per cent. of the world's supply, and Java and the other East Indian islands thirty-five per cent., whereas in 1910 Brazil has. been meeting more than half the world's requirementd Which all goes to show that smuggling may be a highly profitable misdemeanour.

A rubber plantation, grown to maturity, has a characteristic beauty of its own, almost as great as the vanished glory of the jungle it replaces. The orderly ranks of the trees, and the cool, dappled shade they throw, have something of the charm of an English beech wood, especially on modern estates in Java, where the planting of a "cover crop" between the trees (to prevent the washing away of soil, and to encourage the formation of humus) hides the ground under a thick carpet of palest green.

The use of these "cover crops" is the result of one of many series of experiments undertaken by the Dutch in Java for the purpose of increasing the production of latex (the rubber-containing sap of the Hevea tree). Several different leguminous plants are used for the purpose. The favourite is Calopogonium, which grows very thickly, and only a few inches high; it is used in both newly planted and mature gardens. Mimosa is often planted with young trees on poor soils, or sometimes the Albizzia Falfata so familiar in tea estates: when this is used it is cut down as the Hevea approaches maturity.

The value of cover crops has been effectively proved by the poorer yield in old, clean-weeded plantations. The Dutch, always to the fore in scientific agriculture, have succeeded by this and other means in greatly increasing the production of rubber per acre; and, paradoxical though it seems, may well have contributed, by their very success, to the over-production which, it is to be hoped only temporarily, has crippled the industry.

There are now about a thousand rubber estates in Java, of which perhaps half are interplanted with tea or coffee. Most of them are about fifteen hundred feet above the sea, in various soils, for rubber is obliging enough to thrive in almost any except very heavy clay. The trees are usually planted as "stumps," grown from seed in seedbeds, in which they are left for about a year. Far more seedlings are planted out than it is intended to retain, for the rubber tree varies greatly in the amount of latex it produces, some giving ten times as much as others, and only the best are allowed to remain.

The trees are first tapped at five or six years old, after which they are thinned out for the first time. Thinning is then repeated from time to time, and a fifteen-year-old plantation often has half, or less, the original number of trees. The productiveness of the trees increases till the fifteenth year after they are first tapped, and then gradually falls.

Experiment has also proved that the latex vessels always run in a downward direction, from right to left, and consequently "tapping" (a cut in the bark at an angle of thirty degrees) is now usually done downwards from left to right, in order to sever the greatest number of them.

In normal times, on most estates, the trees are tapped every other day. The tappers, many of whom are women, start work at daybreak, and go on for about three hours. The cups, placed below each cut to catch the latex, are then collected, emptied into buckets, and taken to the estate "factory," where the latex (which contains about thirty-five per cent. of rubber) is poured into flat tanks with water containing formic or acetic acid—the sharp, pungent smell of either of which always calls up the whole scene for anyone to whom it is familiar.

By next morning the tanks appear to be covered with cream. But, unlike cream, the coagulated rubber can be lifted out in sheets, and is put through rolling machines, first grooved, and then smooth, some ten or twelve times. It is now *crêpe*; and after hanging up to dry for ten days or so, it is ready to be packed in the standard three-ply wooden cases, holding a hundred and fifty pounds *crêpe*, or two hundred and twenty pounds "smoked." "Smoked" rubber is poured into small sheet tanks, where the acid is added. It also is rolled, but passes in addition through a third machine with spiral grooves, called the "printer." It is hung up in the smoke house for ten days, which turns it brown and transparent.

Cheaper grades of rubber are made from the scraps left in buckets or in the rinsing water, which are all carefully collected and treated in the same way as *crêpe*.

By a more recent process the latex is pumped into receptacles at the top of a tower and sprayed on to a spinning disc, which separates the rubber from the water by centrifugal force. The moisture is evaporated by hot air, and the rubber falls in small particles on to trays below, whence it is collected, pressed, and packed in bales for shipment. There is, so far as I know, only one such plant in Java.

Much rubber is grown by the natives. This is roughly coagulated, and sold by weight in huge, evil-smelling lumps. It is customary to cut these through at the factory, as the native is not always able to resist the temptation to increase his earnings by embedding a large stone in the heart of the mass; and even an ancient axe-head has been known to be found on occasion!

CHAPTER TWENTY-TWO

A Diversity of Crops

THE tobacco growers of Java are inclined (though I believe they do it unintentionally) to play a mild joke on the unsuspecting visitor to their districts, who is naturally surprised to be told that an enormous shed in the middle of a very wet rice field is put there for the purpose of drying tobacco, though of tobacco there is none to be seen.

The visitor is apt to suspect a "leg-pull," but the shed is quite in its proper place, and is, moreover, a testimony to the thoroughness of Dutch agricultural methods.

Tobacco, as an eminent grower expressively remarked, is one of the most "pernickety" crops in the world; and certainly it is also one of the greediest. It is not difficult to grow, but it refuses stubbornly to yield a commercially valuable leaf in any but the particular climate, elevation, and soil that it prefers; and it robs the ground in which it grows so greedily that it has always to be planted in a new place.

In Java, after each crop of tobacco, which from first to last occupies about six months, at least two, or more often three, wet rice crops are grown in succession on the tobacco land, to allow the soil to recover the qualities of which the tobacco has depleted it, and to be fully replenished with the rich silt deposited by the irrigation water. This is the explanation of the tobacco shed in the rice fields, which puzzles so many.

A Diversity of Crops

The European tobacco growers rent their land from the natives on much the same plan as the sugar growers, under an agreement by which the tobacco is planted only once in every three or four crops on the same land, the native owners cultivating rice on it themselves in the interval. And even after that the soil has to be most carefully prepared, deeply cultivated, and aerated, before tobacco is planted again.

Java tobacco, which is used for the wrapping and filling of cigars, is of good quality, and commands a high price, but it is inferior to the famous wrapper tobacco grown at Belawan Deli, Sumatra. The superlative excellence of this leaf is a good example of the plant's particularity. It has chanced to find at Deli, out of the many districts in which it has been tried, the exact combination of soil, climate, and amount of moisture to bring it to perfection; and that precise combination is rare. Tobacco has been tried in many other parts of Java, Sumatra, and Dutch Borneo than those in which it is now grown, and also in British North Borneo, where it had only a very limited success. It is harvested from about twenty-five thousand acres in Java, distributed over nineteen estates, nearly all of which are in the Sultanates of Djokjakarta and Soerakarta. A quantity is also grown by natives, and sold by them to the European growers.

As an example of contrasts in methods of treating this most exigeant crop, two extremes may be worth quoting. At Deli, Sumatra, it is regarded with such respect that, after each crop has been harvested, the soil on which it grew is left fallow for no less a period than *seven* years.

But now note the airy attitude of the Queensland Department of Agriculture, in whose State a sudden outburst of enthusiasm for tobacco culture has occurred in the last few years. "Splendid Tobacco Land" was advertised, and taken up in areas of five and ten acres, whereon it was light-heartedly proposed to cultivate tobacco from that time forward for evermore, just as though it were turnips or cabbages.

It was only after the opinion of a Dutch expert had been given some publicity that the Department blandly issued the announcement that it "agreed with the Dutch contention that tobacco could not be grown continually on the same land," and advocated that in future it should be rotated with legumes and cotton!

The regions favoured by tobacco in Java are warm, moist areas between three hundred and nine hundred feet above the sea, and the crop is so "timed" that the maturity of the leaf shall coincide with the beginning of the wet (west) monsoon. The seed is sown in the nursery beds at the end of July, and planted out about six weeks later. It has to be regularly watered, and in addition to all this irrigation, rain, clouds, and a moisture-laden atmosphere are all necessary at the final stage if the leaf, especially if it is intended for "wrapper," is to come to perfection; and, finally, rain is absolutely essential before cutting.

The leaves are cut in pairs and hung on bamboo frames, and left in the sun to wither, which toughens the leaf, and prevents it from breaking when it is handled. The frames, with their loads of leaves, are then hung up from bars across the drying-house, which is usually built of bamboo and kajang, and so planned as to provide complete shelter from rain and the maximum circulation of air. The roof is high, sloping to within a few feet of the ground on each side, and the ends of the shed are provided with removable kajang shutters to keep out heavy storms.

Cutting is finished by the end of December. The leaves are left hanging up for periods varying from ten to twenty days, and are then piled up and fermented by their own heat. They are finally sorted into forty distinct grades, each of which is wrapped separately in mats and packed in bales of one hundred and seventy-six pounds, to be sent to Amsterdam and sold by auction.

The water used to irrigate tobacco is very often pumped back, so that it can also be used to water the neighbouring rice fields.

Cassava, probably better known to most Europeans through its familiar product, tapioca, is another important Java crop. It is cultivated entirely by the natives, but the manufacture of tapioca, and the other products of cassava root, is in European and Chinese hands. And the "Tapiok Fabriek," with its hundreds of pans of cassava pulp drying in the sun, is to be seen here and there from one end of Java to the other. These mills buy the native crop and, between them, export annually some two hundred and fifty million pounds' weight of tapioca, cassava flour, and starch.

Cassava needs less water than many other tropical crops, and is therefore much planted on non-irrigated land. It is a favourite extra crop with the Javanese, as its cultivation is extremely simple and inexpensive, and the returns from it are very large. It is said, in fact, to be one of the most profitable crops in the world, for an acre of cassava yields more than six times as much as an acre of wheat.

The areas planted with it in Java may be inconspicuous compared with the enormous stretches occupied by rice or sugar, but the small patches of cassava that appear here and there near to most native kampongs add up altogether into the respectable total of nearly eighteen hundred thousand acres, and the appearance of the plant soon becomes very familiar to the Java resident or traveller. It branches out from the root into a group of knotty stems from five to eight feet high, bearing bunches of long, slender, dark green leaves.

Its value is in its roots, and they, too, are a familiar sight on the busy Java roads, carried, as are all other kinds of produce, in baskets swung from the creaking bamboo shoulder yoke; or, in the neighbourhood of the factories, piled up in huge loads on the pony wagons.

The roots are anything but appetizing in appearance, for they are long, sprawling, shapeless, and dirty white in colour. They grow to a very large size, often up to two feet long, and are made by the natives into a sort of meal by grating and then drying the pulp, which is afterwards baked into thin, round cakes over the fire.

You will sometimes see a supply of meal from the family cassava patch being dried on the ground, in front of a house by the roadside, in round, split-bamboo trays as big as cartwheels.

No crop could well be easier to plant, for its woody stem is something like the earthworm, which, when you cut it in half with the spade, turns into two worms that wriggle away in opposite directions! All the native has to do to propagate cassava is to cut a full-grown stem in pieces and stick them in the ground on a slant. They begin to grow in a fortnight, and are well established in a month. The crop can be reaped any time from eight months to a year later; the only care that has to be taken is to get it quickly to the mill, as the root soon deteriorates after being taken out of the ground.

So full of life are the stems that they simply refuse to be killed. A fence made of them in lieu of bamboo will be a bushy hedge within a very few weeks.

There are two kinds of cassava—sweet and bitter. The bitter kind contains a considerable amount of prussic acid, but, in spite of its poisonous juice, it is the most

A TYPICAL JAVA HILLSIDE

THE TERRACES ARE WATERED BY MOUNTAIN STREAMS. ONE OF THE NEARER FIELDS IS BEING PLOUGHED WITH A WATER BUFFALO.

NEWLY PLANTED RICE ON A MOUNTAIN TERRACE

AS SPACE IS AN IMPORTANT CONSIDERATION, BANANAS ARE GROWN ON THE MUD BANKS BETWEEN THE TERRACES.

generally grown, as it gives a much larger return. It cannot, like the sweet variety, be used as a vegetable, but the poison is quite easily and safely dissipated by heat when the root is prepared as flour, or in the form of the familiar tapioca. This is made by hanging up the damp flour in cotton bags, where it forms different-sized balls, which are sorted and sifted into "Pearl" and "Flake," and stiffened on hot pans, greased with castor oil to prevent sticking.

Cassava starch is much in demand by natives for laundry work, for which they prefer it to any other. It is made by a very simple process, consisting merely of finely grating, sifting, and washing the cassava meal.

Another characteristic of the Java landscape is the kapok tree, always recognizable, when once it has been seen, by its complete unlikeness to all other trees. It is rather "scraggy," with meagre branches growing out almost perfectly horizontal, opposite each other, often on only two sides of the tree. Its foliage is pale green and scanty, and it always looks somewhat naked, even when it is in leaf; and when it is not, with its fat, bursting pods outlined against the sky, it is almost grotesque.

This unpromising tree, however, produces an extremely valuable crop of a soft, silky "tree cotton" of ever-increasing popularity, of whose production Java has nearly the world monopoly, though some of inferior quality comes from India and Ceylon.

Kapok is useless for spinning, as its staple is short and it contains little cellulose; but as stuffing for mattresses, pillows, and cushions it has no rival, and it is also, on account of its extreme lightness, used throughout the world in modern life-saving apparatus, for which purpose it is definitely specified by the Board of Trade.

The kapok tree is a native of the archipelago, and is

cultivated in small plantations as a "side line" by Europeans, natives, and Chinese, as well as being planted here, there, and everywhere on the borders of the rice fields, by the roadsides, and in odd corners of kampongs. Left to itself it grows to a considerable height, but when the crop is used commercially it is always lopped to a convenient size so as to facilitate picking the pods, or "bolls."

The tree begins to yield at about four years old. The cotton is so light that the entire crop of a mature tree (which may bear several thousand pods, nearly six inches long) will weigh only forty or fifty pounds, though in bulk it looks enormous.

Coffee was the first agricultural industry to be introduced into Java. A book of *Travels in Arabia*, published in 1573, had made the beverage known to Europe; and in the following century the famous "coffee houses" began to be established in London, Paris, Amsterdam, and the other European cities. The Arabian coffee plant, afterwards known as "Coffea Arabica," was procured from Mocha, and taken to Java by the East India Company early in the seventeenth century, and they established the industry so successfully that for a long time Java was the world's leading producer. The "Arabica," however, proved very susceptible to blight, insect pests, and disease; and eventually almost the whole crop was wiped out by them.

The industry was re-established with "Robusta" coffee, a native of the Congo, and Java now holds third place among the world's producers, with Brazil far in the lead, and Colombia second.

Very few estates in Java grow coffee only; it is almost always to be found interplanted with rubber, having originally been put in as a "catch crop" while waiting for the rubber trees to mature. So much so that when rubber was so extensively planted in East Java it was rare to find an estate without it. A shade tree called "Dadap," on which the pepper vine is trained, is also very often to be seen planted with coffee.

As in all tropical countries, there are in Java immense numbers of coconut palms. A "census" of them was taken some years ago, which gave the number of trees as about sixty-five millions; but it is estimated that there must now be very many more. They are almost all in quite small native-owned plantations. A large quantity of copra is exported, and the local native consumption of coconut oil is considerable.

"Citronella" is another interesting Java crop. It is cultivated on a much smaller scale than many of the others, but is yet of considerable value, and large quantities of the oil are exported both for use in the manufacture of perfumery and as the mosquito-bite preventive so familiar in all countries where the pest prevails.

The plant from which the oil is obtained is a tall, coarse grass, at first glance not at all unlike the hated pest "lalang." It is almost always planted as a "catch crop" in coconut, rubber, and other plantations. There is nothing to indicate its special qualities until, perhaps, a breath of heavy, sweet perfume is wafted towards you as you pass a distillery labelled "Citronella Fabriek," and see the pony grobaks that you have been passing all along the road discharging loads of the coarse grass at its door.

Citronella is a very easy crop to grow, as the grass thrives in almost any soil; all it asks is a bounteous rainfall. It is cut twice a year, and yields a fair but very variable return.

Coca, the shrub from whose leaves cocaine is obtained (not to be confused with "cacao" or "cocoa"), is cultivated in Java, and a large quantity of the valuable leaves are exported annually. The crop is of special interest in Java, in that coca is a native of the same regions of the South American Andes as the cinchona tree, which Java has made its own; and it is to those same Indians who gave us quinine that we also owe that other valuable alkaloid, cocaine.

When the Spaniards conquered Peru in the sixteenth century they found that coca leaves were valued so highly as to be used in place of money; for the natives then, as now, chewed the leaf when they had long or rapid journeys to perform, finding that it enabled them to do so, and to carry heavy loads, without rest or food. It is said that an Indian of to-day, if he has a "chew" of coca in his cheek, can go two or three days without food, and without feeling any necessity for sleep. And Sir Clement Markham, who visited South America in 1859 to collect cinchona seeds, wrote that he chewed coca leaves frequently, finding that they not only enabled him to endure long abstinence from food, but to climb precipitous mountains "with a feeling of lightness and elasticity," and without loss of breath.

The Indians sometimes mix lime with the coca leaf when chewing it, as the Malays and Javanese do with betel-nut.

Dutch cocoa is known all over the world for its excellence (it was a Dutch manufacturer, by the way, who originated the now generally used "soluble" cocoa, by treating it with an alkali), and that Dutch cocoa comes from Java, where the cacao tree, from whose pod cocoa is obtained, is much grown. The export, however, is of course not large compared with that of the Gold Coast, which is the world's unchallenged cocoa producer, exporting more than half of the thousand million pounds' weight that is consumed annually.

A Diversity of Crops

In Java the cacao seedlings are raised in split-bamboo pots or baskets, in shaded nurseries, and planted out at a few months old. They grow to a fair height, sometimes twenty or thirty feet—much bigger than coffee. The young trees are often interplanted with cassava as a "catch crop," as cacao does not come into bearing for about five years; and in other places kapok you may see planted with it as a permanent shade.

Cacao beans are fermented in a series of boxes, arranged in steps, so that the beans can be shovelled from the higher to the lower ones—a process taking some days—and are then very gradually dried off, after which they are ready for shipping.

Maize is largely grown by the natives and, after rice, it occupies the biggest area of cultivated land in Java— roughly about four million acres. Sweet potatoes, ground-nuts, and soya beans are all important crops, each of them covering the best part of half a million acres; and there are many others, including sisal hemp, the cultivation of which is increasing, vanilla, and a variety of other spices.

Many fruits are grown, but the banana is the only one exported. There are many varieties; "Pisang Raja" and "Pisang Ambon" are two of the best-known larger kinds, and the small, delicious "Pisang Mas," or "golden banana," is in a class by itself.

The mango, a native of the whole of the East Indies, abounds in Java as in all tropical countries, and it is said that over fifty distinct varieties of it are cultivated in the island.

The delicate-flavoured mangosteen is much grown, as is also the "ramboetan" (whose name means "the hairy one"), a curious-looking fruit rather bigger than a chestnut, whose flesh is a miniature edition of that of the mangosteen, but whose exterior is covered with coarse

229

red hair. A plantation of ramboetan, with masses of the crimson-haired fruit nestling among thick, dark green foliage, is a very beautiful sight indeed.

One of the most delicious Java fruits is the "sawoe" (known in Malaya as the "chiko"), a kind of sapodilla, whose modest exterior gives no indication of the delicate fruit within. It is about the size of a duck's egg, with a dark, dirty brown skin exactly like that of an old potato. Its flesh, in which are embedded the shiny black seeds, is sweet and fragrant, and so soft that it must be eaten with a spoon. The tree is a handsome one, growing to a height of sixty feet or more, with widespreading branches, thickly covered with rich, glossy foliage among which the fruit is hard to see.

The granadilla, an easily grown vine, is widely cultivated. So, of course, is the papaya (the "paw-paw" of the Pacific islands). And breadfruit, and jackfruit trees, with their enormous, deeply indented leaves and huge, rough, heavy fruit, are to be seen in the gardens of most native kampongs.

But of all the fruits of Java the most remarkable is the doerian, famous wherever its name is known for its strong, offensive flavour. It is shaped like a melon, is rather larger than a man's head, and has a very rough, prickly rind; and when it is in season the sight and smell of it are among the most characteristic of all those in the streets of Java. It is a cumbrous fruit, but the native, who loves it dearly, has neatly solved the problem of its transport. Two leaves from the frond of a "nieboeng" palm (a very tough variety) are crossed, and twisted together round each doerian to make a carrier; and in this way a number of the huge fruit can be "hawked" for sale in the streets, in gigantic bunches, hanging from the inevitable pikoelan, and can be equally easily carried away by the purchaser.

A Diversity of Crops

The peculiar pungent smell of the fruit is perpetually in your nostrils for weeks, and grows so familiar that you only notice it by its absence when the season is over.

The great size of the doerian makes an incident from a recent novel rather intriguing. In this romantic work a jealous native girl concealed a doerian "in the folds of her sarong," and later inserted poison on a knife through its "delicate rind" for the undoing of her faithless English lover. She must have had an extraordinarily voluminous sarong if she could hide a fruit as big as a large melon in it without showing a noticeable protuberance. And as for that delicate rind—it is at least three inches thick!

CHAPTER TWENTY-THREE

Of "Domestic" & Other Animals

THERE must surely be more Alsatian dogs in Java per head of European population than anywhere else in the world. The Dutch are keen dog fanciers, and their tastes seem to run to contrast, for the breeds in favour are at the two extremes of the scale in size, with nothing at all in between.

The Alsatian is especially popular. It is bred in the higher altitudes, where the cool climate suits it perfectly; and you can go to hardly any of the many mountain hotels without being greeted by two or three magnificent specimens, who promptly give the lie to the current tales of their breed's ferocity by lavishing upon the newcomer every sentimental blandishment known to the canine tribe, and subsequently taking upon themselves the duties of convoy on all the visitors' country walks.

There are some good kennels, and the dogs, which are in great demand as pets and guards for children, command high prices. Few Dutch youngsters, especially in the hill towns, go out for an airing without one of these aristocratic animals pacing sedately alongside as escort: not, as in England, ignominiously tied on to the perambulator by a lead. These tropic-bred Alsatians retain all their spirit and activity, and show no signs of degeneration as a result of the climate. One kennel has produced some giant specimens, which, for all their keenness and their ferocious appearance, are as harmless as kittens, and will take your hand in their alligator jaws and hold it as gently as though it were an egg.

Another big dog bred in Java, though not to the same extent as the Alsatian, is the Great Dane, which seems to find the climate and conditions equally to its taste. And at the other end of the scale is the Spaniel tribe, of which the Pekingese, Japanese, and King Charles are all very popular.

There are pariah dogs in plenty, of course, in the native villages, but fortunately their lot is a happy one compared with that of their kind in some other Eastern countries. The Java native often makes a companion of his dog, and it is rare to see one of the pitiful specimens so terribly common in India.

The Dutch have brought their taste for deer parks with them to the East. The beautiful green meadows surrounding the Governor-General's palace (sometimes called by the local Chinese the "King's Office") at Buitenzorg is full of deer; and in the grounds of country hotels and large private houses a miniature park is a very favourite feature.

Another popular "pet"—if a creature kept at the end of a chain can be so called—is the gibbon, or "Wah-wah," one of the tailless apes native to Malaya, whose plaintive cry, forlorn as that of a lost child, is a familiar sound wherever the virgin jungle is within earshot. You will often see one of these, chained to a pole with its house at the top, adorning the lawn in front of a Dutch home; and the visitor will be well advised to keep beyond its reach, for the Wah-wah lacks nothing of the exaggerated sense of humour peculiar to the monkey tribe.

The most highly developed example of this passion for pets I have ever come across was a charming, elderly Dutch bachelor, who bought a derelict "Zoo," lock, stock, and barrel, and set it up in his own, fortunately very large, garden. The period of its arrival and delivery, which lasted for a week or so, kept the whole native population (to say nothing of the European) on tiptoe from morning till night. Mysterious covered carts, from which there issued a variety of squeaks, grunts, or whistles; weird beasts or giant birds roped and blindfolded, each led by half a dozen rather nervous keepers, passed down the country road from time to time, invariably followed by an inquisitive crowd of natives, burning with curiosity to see what the unveiling would disclose.

It might be a cage of monkeys, fighting and chattering furiously; a terrified deer, with its feet tied together; a huge owl, blinking and shrinking in the bright sunshine; a disdainful eagle; a big brown bear or a small black one; three or four gawky emus, or a perchful of parrots or screaming cockatoos.

An extra big cage, so heavy that it had to be drawn by buffaloes, disclosed a pair of fine panthers, snarling furiously. And an elephant, the survivor of several which had to be shot because they firmly refused to leave their former home, was led in, and stood swinging his trunk unhappily in a shady corner of the garden, moored by a leg fore and aft to two coconut palms, churning the turf into mud, which he blew over all intruders in token of his displeasure at their presence, until a house with a concrete floor could be built around and beneath him.

Quarters for some giant turtles were provided, on their arrival, piled up in a grobak like so many huge stones, in an ornamental pond in the middle of the lawn, which was hastily cleared of goldfish in their favour. The turtles, however, made their opinion of this select situation clear by strolling away and taking cover elsewhere, some in the shrubberies and some in a neighbouring rice sawah, whence they were brought back after some trouble, and confined ignominiously under wire netting.

The climax came with the arrival of a full-grown crocodile in a coffin-shaped tank just big enough to hold him, with an iron grating let in over his head. Through this, at a respectful distance, a little group of natives was always to be found peering fearfully, almost falling over each other in their anxiety to get out of range whenever the brute's sleepy eyes opened to give them a greedy, malevolent glance. It was typical of the native attitude to all the great lords of the jungle and the rivers, that so long as they were close beside him their comments were respectful, not to say admiring. But once well out of earshot they let themselves go, and were anything but complimentary. And an infant specimen of the same charming species, about ten inches long, which was accommodated in a wash-hand basin on the grass, held no terrors, and was even more popular.

The building of quarters for his new and varied family, over which its new parent presided like a benevolent Mr. Cheeryble, occupied weeks, during which many small tragedies occurred, especially among the monkeys. When they were let into their spacious new quarters they held a sort of house-warming, in the course of which some of the bigger ones set deliberately upon their weaker guests and tore them limb from limb.

One small monkey, whom they chased into their bath, finding he was let alone as long as he stayed there, remained under water, with only his nose showing, for hours. He finally emerged, evidently petrified with cold, to shiver wretchedly in a corner until the others noticed him and chased him back again. He was rescued at last with some difficulty; but others, less fortunate, were horribly mangled.

However, there were other events more "interesting" and less distressing; so many baby monkeys were born in the early days of the new zoo that it might have been a maternity home. Every few days there were new arrivals: little wizened objects absurdly resembling human infants, which were exhibited with a comic mixture of pride and shamefacedness by each Mrs. Monkey, who, however, always showed a fine appreciation of the responsibilities of parenthood by putting her offspring across her knee in the approved fashion and spanking it soundly at a very early age indeed.

Sometimes one of the odd little mothers would carry on a murmured conversation, as she sat with the baby on her knee, with any passer-by, articulating queer sounds which, one can only suppose, described in monkey language all the beauties of her wonderful child. And the most amusing stage of all came when the babies, at a month or six weeks old, began, very feebly at first, to climb about the cage when mother's back was turned. She would suddenly notice the ambitious infant, drag it down, smack it, angrily chattering with maternal rage, and put it back in its proper corner—which, of course, it promptly left again at the first opportunity. After a day or two she would give a ridiculously human shrug, and let it go, only administering a little corporal punishment now and then, just to show who was really master of the situation.

The garden in which the zoo was installed bordered a rice sawah. And every day and all day long a trickle of natives crossed the narrow mud embankment in single file, to line up along the fence in the hope (so I gathered, from scraps of their conversation) that the first mortal monkey-combats might be continued indefinitely.

The native's idea of "pets" is expressed in terms of

cage-birds, and a very odd way he has of treating them. The cage (made of "rotan," or split bamboo) is fastened to the end of a long rope, and run up a pole or a coconut palm, like a flag, to a height of twenty or thirty feet, where, presumably, the inmate can enjoy to the full the spectacle of the wild birds' freedom as they fly past, or suffer their insulting chirps as they perch close by. What pleasure the native gets out of it is a mystery, but it is a very general custom.

The natives rear large numbers of cattle in Java for their own use as draught animals; their breeds have been much crossed, and they are of very mixed parentage. In Madoera and Bali, close by, however, there are indigenous breeds so good that they are kept pure, and extensively bred for export. The water buffaloes, so indispensable to the rice farmer, are, of course, bred in Java in great numbers, as are also ponies. But the local ponies are inferior to the "Sandalwood" ponies from the Timor archipelago, generally known as "Timor" ponies; and the powerful Sumbawa breed are much in demand for the heaviest draught work.

Pigs are much bred by the Chinese, and also, despite Mohammedan prohibitions, by many natives, for they are a very rich source of revenue. In Bali and Lombok the industry is in native hands, and great numbers are shipped to the Straits for Chinese consumption. The pigs are shipped alive, each in a torpedo-shaped basket made of split bamboo, in which he lies looking like an enormous larva in its cocoon. These giant cocoons are piled perhaps twenty feet deep on the decks, a sight that inevitably shocks Europeans. Yet the animals lie there to all appearance content, sunk deep in porcine repose. The springy baskets resist their weight, and it is extremely rare to hear a piggy voice raised in protest. At all events, there seems to be no alternative to this method of transport, and one can only hope for the best.

Goats and sheep, grotesquely resembling one another, of "leggy" and inextricably mixed varieties, are also bred (or it might be more correct to say, breed) throughout the island in large numbers.

The native-owned domestic fowl in Java, as all over the East, is a pathetic creature that gets its own living as best it can, and is a thoroughly unattractive bird. Unfortunately it does not share the placid temperament of its owners, but spends its whole time in rushing headlong out of the way of imaginary dangers, with the natural result that it has long, stringy legs out of all proportion to the rest of its miserable body. Still, the poor thing does its generous best to keep us supplied with diminutive eggs; and it is a staple of all European menus, though, as in life it is never fed, and for all the good it is as a table dish, it would really be much more seemly to give it decent burial.

Ducks are reared in enormous numbers everywhere, by both natives and Chinese. You will often see big flocks of them being herded homeward across the mud embankments between the rice sawahs, or driven along the roads, like flocks of sheep. These too, and also geese, figure largely on European tables.

Ducks' eggs are a noticeable feature in every native pasar, where you will always see great, pale green piles of them, with one or two hard-boiled and cut in halves, to show that they are fresh.

The lizard is not generally classed as a "domestic" animal, it is true, but its habits in Java are so homely that it really does deserve the name. It is impossible to imagine any home in all Java, whether it be native, Chinese, or European, without the "tjik-tjak," the friendly, miniature house-lizard, that sleeps all day and spends his waking life, from late afternoon onwards, on the walls and ceiling, and sometimes on the floor, busily killing and eating every insect that comes within his reach.

And the tjik-tjak's reach is a long one, for his movements are like greased lightning. You can never see them. One moment you are looking at him, motionless; the next, he is three feet away, motionless still, save for the tiny, powerful jaws, which are masticating their prey, a prey that may be anything from a mosquito to a moth as big as the lizard itself, a dragon-fly, or a "laron." And as you can often count a dozen or more tjik-tjaks on the ceiling of your room, the service they render in destroying insects can be imagined.

The name tjik-tjak is the native rendering of the sound made by the little creature—its hunting cry, most likely, as it goes about its useful business.

These lizards vary in size from an inch to about four inches long; they are most delicately modelled, the smallest looking exactly like an exquisite little Vienna bronze. Absurd though it sounds to say of a creature so tiny, the tjik-tjak can quite easily be tamed, and is evidently able to distinguish between one person and another. I once had one that came out at the same time every evening from the same corner underneath the seat of a big teak armchair, which he had adopted as his home; and so long as I was alone, reading or writing, he would spend the whole evening "hunting" within a few inches of my feet, and snapping up an odd mosquito that I killed and flicked to him now and then, as a puppy might a biscuit.

But if visitors arrived he was nowhere to be seen, and would always re-emerge, with bright eyes the size of pinheads peering eagerly to see if the coast was clear, directly they had departed. And some friends of mine had one that came on to their dinner-table and ate crumbs every evening for many months.

There is another less common house-lizard, called the "tokek," which is regarded by the natives as a luck-bringer. This one is much bigger: he is nine or ten inches long, and of stoutish figure, and often takes up his habitation in a secluded corner of the kitchen. He, too, is a valuable fly-catcher; but his chief claim to notice is his peculiar, reiterated cry—"Waak-aah" is as nearly as it can be written down—which he repeats, getting slower and slower towards the end, as though it tired him, usually about five or six times.

The moment a native hears one he starts to count—"Satoe, doea, tiga, ampat, lima"—and if by any chance the tally reaches seven, or more, his joy is great, for that means very good luck indeed. But almost always the call dies away, with a pathetic dying rattle in the lizard's throat, after the sixth, at latest.

Once, but once only, I heard one get as far as nine. He must have been a phenomenal vocalist—a very Sims Reeves among tokeks—but as for the equally phenomenal luck that the sound of his long aria was supposed to bring me—well—one can only keep on hoping!

"WHERE THE PAVEMENT ENDS"

A HUGE GAP, 200 FEET DEEP IN THE MOUNTAIN ROAD TO SINDANGLAYA, MADE BY THE ESCAPING
WATERS OF A LAKE WHICH WAS EMPTIED IN A VOLCANIC LANDSLIDE. THE GREY FOREGROUND
SHOWS THE TARRED ROAD SURFACE ENDING ABRUPTLY ON THIS SIDE OF THE CHASM, MATCHING
THAT ON THE FURTHER SIDE.

About Volcanoes

A VERY charming little guide-book, published in English (or perhaps, one should say, in approximate English), for the use of visitors to Java, issues a naïve invitation to travellers in these terms: "If you are fond of volcanoes, come to Java."

Now I cannot for the life of me imagine anyone feeling the slightest affection for volcanoes. There is nothing in the least lovable about the things. One would have thought that to admit to a volcano about the place was as bad as owning up to a skeleton in the cupboard, and that eruptions breaking out here and there all over the landscape were as unfortunate as the kind which break out on your skin. Yet the Java guide-books positively gloat over them. Every excursion seems to have a volcano for its goal; wherever you go you are told exactly how long it will take, by horse, foot, or car, to reach the local crater; in fact, with an odd perversity, you are invited to turn your back on all the delightful things around you, and to look only, as it were, on the dark side.

Certainly there is no lack of volcanoes in Java; there are somewhere about a hundred of them, altogether, which should be enough to satisfy the most ardent "fan"—if such persons there be. It seems as though the gods who dowered the island so richly with fruitfulness and beauty had dealt out these terrible fire-mountains with equal prodigality, just to show that the same hand which showered blessings could shower curses too: a true prerogative of the gods.

So, thanks to the guide-books, there are few visitors to Java (to Garoet especially, which is "blessed" with more of these attractions than most other places) who do not rise up early in the morning, and, mounting the sturdy island ponies, leave the gracious verdure of the lower levels behind them, and clamber up the stony pathways to the various craters that they "must not miss."

For the true volcano-lover doubtless the attractions are many. "Columns of smoke rise everywhere," says the little guide-book. "What one beholds is a large open space emitting gusts of sulphurous steam with a roaring and hissing noise from numerous fissures in the bottom. There are many steam-jets and furiously boiling cauldrons, mud volcanoes and other phenomena are found all around. The ground on which one walks is in some places so undermined by underground forces that a small volcano may be created" (what an ambition!) "by simply making a hole in the earth. It is strongly advised to follow the indications of the guide and not to leave the path pointed out. At the end of the path a large pool is to be seen, filled with a black-looking fluid which boils and bubbles, creating a thunderous noise forming such a thick vapour that the surface can only be seen at intervals when the wind drives away the fumes. The visitor will be surprised at the marvellous richness and brilliancy of colour at this spot, sulphur yellow, brick red, and pearl grey 'predominalting.' The colour of the clay varies everywhere as the soil is composed of layers of clay of different shades."

This "beautiful excursion," we are told, may be accomplished, if an early start is made, in time to be back for lunch. Which seems a judicious arrangement, for it is easy to imagine that after such a nerve-shattering series of beauties it would be hunger, rather than love of volcanoes, that would "predominalt" among the tourist's sensations.

The one redeeming feature about these hundred or so Javanese volcanoes is that they are so admirably camou-flaged. You can easily live in Java for years without ever realizing that any of the lovely mountains round about you are volcanoes at all. The desolate, sulphur-poisoned regions at their summits are well hidden by the thick jungle that swathes the mountain-sides almost to the top, and it is only if you deliberately climb them, or fly over them in an aeroplane, that these strange scars on Java's lovely face will show themselves.

To approach one from below is a strange experience, and perhaps worth doing—once. It is a study in contrasts. First you leave the soft greenness of the familiar rice sawahs for the deep silence and shade of the forest; then, little by little, the tropic growth seems to sicken as the path climbs upward, and the sulphur-charged air chokes the breath in your throat. At each turn of the road the jungle thins out more and more into a warped, stunted growth, recalling some of Australia's most drought-cursed regions; and then ends altogether, buried beneath the dried mud and stones of former eruptions. A horrid precipice yawns before you, and, far below, the lava is muttering to itself—calculating, perhaps, how long it must wait before the next display.

Krakatoe, the one volcano that the average person in England seems to associate with Java, is not actually in Java at all. It is itself a small island in the narrow Sunda Strait that separates Java from Sumatra, and lies about midway between the two. It is generally supposed that some long-ago eruption destroyed the strip of land that once joined them together, and left Krakatoe surrounded with water.

It is famous, or rather infamous, for the terrible eruption of just fifty years ago, which cost unnumbered thousands of native lives, and was one of the most phenomenal disturbances in seismic history. The "sound waves" generated by its frightful explosions travelled three thousand miles; waves fifty feet high swept along the shores of both islands, washing away hundreds of villages; the sky was filled with ashes five hundred miles away, and it was reported in the Press at the time that tidal waves attributable to it had reached Cape Horn, and affected the height of the tide in the Thames. The mountain itself was shattered, and lost a thousand feet of its former elevation.

Happily, serious eruptions are fairly rare in Java, but they have occurred from time to time. The most recent was that of Mount Merapi, not far from Soerakarta, in November 1929. A number of kampongs and their inhabitants, and the surrounding rice fields, were engulfed without warning in a river of boiling mud and stones, killing hundreds of humble, contented people as they were quietly going about their everyday affairs. Even some that were ploughing their rice fields were overtaken, and perished horribly, together with their water buffaloes. Several villages, spared by the capricious flow of the mud stream, were completely surrounded by it, and food was taken to the few survivors in them by air, until the mud cooled enough to allow passage across it.

Merapi has always had a rather bad name in Java's history, and the River Woro, which flows from it, is one of the most dangerous in the island. From time to time its bed fills up with sand and stones, and the river overflows, covering acres of the adjoining country inches deep with stones and rubbish. In one night, some twenty years ago, forty kampongs were destroyed in this way, and several thousands of acres of rich land ruined—possibly for generations.

Many of the rivers of Java have this dangerous tendency to flood, owing to volcanic disturbances and to frequent sudden and violent rainstorms. The floods rise very rapidly and are extremely violent, carrying down so much solid material with them in their wild career that in many places the rivers have had to be artificially diverted to prevent danger to the population. At Soerakarta the River Pepe has been led into a new channel to save the town from being flooded, and at several coastal towns the course of a river through its delta has been diverted to prevent the entrance to the port being silted up and closed to navigation.

Nature is very kind to Java, however, and the lakes that have formed in the craters of some of the extinct volcanoes are superlatively beautiful. Most lovely of these is at Pendjaloe, whose eruptive energies must have been exhausted very far back in the past history of the island— perhaps even before it was discovered by the Hindus. Here in the course of centuries the jungle has reclothed the summit of the mountain to the very edges of the lake so that its still waters mirror only the dark surrounding forest and the mountain range beyond.

A jungle-clad island, the result of what long-ago volcanic cataclysm no one knows, lies in the very centre of the lake-filled crater, and is the undisputed habitation of a mysterious colony of enormous bats, which are always to be seen rising in a dark cloud at sunset as they set out for their nightly hunting.

The Dutch, good folk, are prodigiously methodical; they leave nothing to chance if they can help it—not even

About Volcanoes

a proper appreciation of Nature's beauties. To them there is nothing inappropriate in directing you to this exquisite island by means of a board bearing the words: "To the Nature Monument." It is done out of sheer kindness of heart; they would simply hate you to miss it. And to make assurance doubly sure, a rhapsodical description of Pendjaloe and its surroundings is issued for the benefit of English-speaking visitors: a unique specimen of prose from which I cannot forbear making a few extracts.

"Snug and beautiful" (says this inspired writer) "is the lake of Pendjaloe that for the too large island resembles more the bend of a winding river than a mountain lake. If you hove not yet seen it, reader, then you hove missed one of Java's loveliest spots.

"The lake of Ngebel is also worth the trouble of a visit. It impresses one with its size, but creates a somewhat gloomy disposition. . . . The lake of Sarangan excels in beauty and graceful intimacy. The Lawoe misses the sharp contours of the Smeroe, Merapi, or Slamat. It has nothing threatening about it, notwithstanding that from one of its summits, the smoke of solfataras emits. It is the gentlest and calmest under the giants of this island, and it tolerates man right to the top of its green slopes. . . . In the easterly fold of its mantle, it shelters the opal lake, wherein the summits and the robust Sido Ramping coquettishly reflect, and that eagerly mirrors the laugh of the blue heavens. . . . It is here a jubilant luxury of light and sunshine and everlasting fascinating beauty. . . .

"The lake lies in unhallowed calmness, and on the undisturbed surface the summits of the mountains reflect with the vanishing light. Mirthful laughs of the boys returning home can be heard, but everywhere else there is repose. . . . Then only the language of Eternity is heard, the unhallowed silence.

About Volcanoes

"Only within the last few years has Sarangan become better known—the small hotel was gradually extended. Mr. ——, the affable and obliging owner, was in the meantime forced to oftenly turn away his visitors. At the present moment the building of cottages on the level lakeborder has been taken in hand, and after some years a row of villas will arise there."

At this point, however, there is a less cheerful note, for the description continues: "The Government bungalow is extremely uncomfortable and damp: I hear that the Controller intends to renovate the building, wich is urgently needed. When the hotel is crowded, visitors are compelled to hire furnished houses—among wich a few good ones and some abominable hovels—that are let out at exorbitant rates by their owners who reside elsewhere."

The writer goes on to describe a route by which, he says, "the distance will be considerably lesser"—the route "wich op to now, visitors have practically only taken," being, however, also very beautiful.

He concludes with the remark: "I believe I have sufficiently described this interesting mountain region to arouse the desire of my readers to wish to know this place. . . . The beaten path is too often taken to habitual and fashionable places; Java still offers innumerable beauties that are practically unknown outside the circle of own surroundings."

I quite agree with him. And what an example he sets in the proper exploitation of "beauty spots"! Now that the pound has fallen, and gold-standard tourists are coming to spend cheap holidays in England, what an opportunity to let ourselves go on such "nature monuments" as Ambleside, Snowdon, and the Scottish Highlands, in French, Dutch, or German! But I fear we never shall. The Dutchman's confidence in his linguistic ability is as serene as the waters of Pendjaloe, and we have it not. For us there remains, especially in a foreign tongue, nothing but our customary "unhallowed silence."

Another beautiful lake, which was formerly one of the great attractions at Sindanglaya, a mountain sanatorium near Buitenzorg, is now, thanks to a recent volcanic vagary, no more. A neighbouring volcano, Goenong Gedeh (which has not been guilty of an eruption, except for a few minor exhibitions of stone-throwing, for a hundred and fifty years), shrugged its shoulders ever so slightly one evening about two years ago. As a result, the basin of the lake cracked, and the thousands of tons of water that filled it poured out, washing the main road, which ran along one side of it, into the narrow valley below, leaving the lake empty; and the two ends of the tarred road, cut off as cleanly as though by a knife, were left to stand facing each other from the crests of perpendicular cliffs nearly two hundred feet high, across a gulf a hundred yards or so wide.

The road is, or rather was, a busy one, much used by motor-omnibuses; and although it collapsed without a moment's warning, at ten o'clock in the evening, by the grace of the gods who love Java, not a soul was on it, nor was a single life lost. But all the king's horses and all the king's men cannot fill up the lake again; and to bridge that hundred yards the road now has to go a good twelve miles round. And as for the landing-stage, from which visitors used to set out for a row on the lake in the cool of the evening, it now hangs forlorn, like a storm-struck tree, over a steep, rocky cliff, looking down on a tiny stream meandering along among the stones a couple of hundred feet below.

One must be fair—even to a volcano. And it seems they have just one point in their favour. The land that immediately surrounds them is even more fertile than all the other rich lands of Java, and for this reason these areas are invariably the most populated in the whole island.

It seems scarcely credible, as Stevenson observed, "that respectable married people, with umbrellas, should find appetite for a bit of supper within quite a long distance of a fiery mountain." But the Javanese are not one whit more impressed by the solemnity of mortal conditions on the slopes of their many volcanoes than were Stevenson's South Americans. The land is rich—and eruptions are rare. And the extra bunch or two of rice is worth the risk.

Dutch Life in Java To-day

ALTHOUGH Java and Malaya are next-door neighbours, and both are tropic colonies, the life that Europeans live in each of them is absolutely different.

The most notable difference of all has nothing whatever to do, so far as one can see, with the essential difference in nationality, for nationality does not explain why it is that Malaya, except for babies and tiny tots up to six or seven, is empty of European children, whereas in Java they abound. It is difficult to see why the fact of being born Dutch should render children immune to the tropic sun; or why, on the other hand, the British child should be more susceptible to it.

Both colonies are close to the Equator: on sea-level they have much the same climate; if anything, Singapore is rather cooler than Batavia. Yet it is the firm conviction of the British in Malaya that children cannot possibly be brought up there; and the equally firm conviction of the Dutch that their youngsters will be every bit as happy and healthy in Java as they would in Europe. And the fine healthy young Hollanders, sunburnt and sturdy and full of life, that you see on all sides as soon as you land in Java certainly give the lie conclusively to the theory that healthy children cannot be reared in the tropics.

In Malaya the sun is regarded as the child's most dangerous enemy. It is only in the early mornings and late afternoons that the Chinese "amahs" (nurses) are allowed to shepherd their charges out of doors. And even then the poor mites are made ridiculous as well as miserably uncomfortable by their fond parents' insistence on their wearing sun-helmets. The sight of a toddler of two or three years old, half extinguished by a pipeclayed "topee" big enough for its father, is a sight to make angels weep. Can it be that we conservative Britons have yet to discover that Malaya is not India, and that in its totally different climate sunstroke is unknown?

The pity of this sunless treatment is that it turns the children into pasty-faced, peevish, pathetic little creatures, who seem to grow pastier and more peevish every day, until the time comes when (to everybody's relief) their mothers take them off to England, to deposit them with accommodating grandparents, and come back without them.

One sometimes wonders (quite in a whisper!) whether this custom of "dumping" the children at home was really instituted for their benefit at all? It certainly does leave Mother so delightfully free for her busy life of bridge from ten till one, sleep from two to four, tea-dance, golf or more bridge, cocktails (known here as "pahits"), dinner, dance—and so to bed; which is roughly the routine of the average Malayan British matron.

Dutch parents, on the other hand, regard the sun as a friend, not as an enemy. Their children run about and ride their bicycles in the sunshine, bareheaded, bare-armed, and barelegged, not only in the hills, but in the towns on sea-level, and they thrive on it.

By way of demonstrating their confidence in the East Indies as a place in which to bring up children, the Dutch authorities have transported there the selfsame system of State education that is in operation in Holland. There are schools in every European town in Java, housed in admirably planned modern buildings, with spacious, lofty classrooms open to the air, and glorious gardens and playgrounds shaded by great jungle trees.

The curriculum is precisely the same as that in use in the Netherlands, with the addition of the necessary extra languages. There are primary, secondary, and technical schools, and several universities; and it is possible to qualify in most of the professions without leaving the East at all. It is noteworthy, however, that, in order to keep up the standard, it is considered desirable that all teachers and professors should be imported from Europe, rather than that they should qualify on the spot. They are very highly paid, and the cost to the government of the whole education system in Java is one of its heaviest commitments.

There are also a great many fine Roman Catholic schools and colleges, and all nationalities, including the Chinese, attend both these and the government schools.

The children's special festival among the Dutch—the day when Santa Claus arrives and there is a present for everybody—is not Christmas Day, but the feast of St. Nicholas, on the 5th of December; and in the schools in Java it is a very great day indeed.

For weeks beforehand the devoted teaching staffs have been scouring the local "tokos" (shops) for presents and prizes, which are laid out in impressive array in one of the classrooms, each having been chosen with due regard to the special tastes of the lucky recipient; and all heart-burnings being saved by a tactful arrangement according to which, though everybody cannot very well win a prize, every one at least has a present; and, after all, there is really very little difference, when we are very young.

The most entertaining part of it all is the immense

Dutch Life in Java To-day

earnestness with which the good Dutch enter into the "play-acting" part of the affair. They are the last sort of people of whom you would expect it, but perhaps even their matter-of-factness is infected by the native love of dressing up. So on the morning of the great day, Santa Claus, who is always an important local citizen, sets out, in full regalia of red robe and long white beard, in an open car, with almost the solemnity of an episcopal visitation, on a tour of the schools. He is accompanied by his black servant, "Piet," who carries a capacious sack, into which custom ordains that all really bad little boys and girls will certainly be thrust if their school record is beyond forgiveness, unless Santa's fatherly heart is touched, as, fortunately, it invariably is.

On arrival at the school, Santa Klaus (as he is here called) is met by the head master and led to his raised seat at one end of a lofty classroom, which is roofed in, but open to the air on all sides, letting in the sweet, heavy scents from the flowering trees in the garden. The children and their parents are all assembled: the Burgomeester's lady in front with her dazzlingly fair pigeon pair, a handful of other young Hollanders with their "moeders," a few Eurasians and Chinese, and the rest natives; all quiet and attentive, and as neat as new pins, especially about the feet, clad in the shoes and stockings demanded by the school regulations. These, in the case of the native scholars, it need hardly be said, are donned only just before coming into school, and pulled off again the moment after leaving it.

The bustle of Santa Klaus' arrival over, up gets the head master to make his speech, and it is no mere stereotyped speech of welcome, either, but a dreadfully detailed report of the scanty virtues and many misdemeanours of all the shivering youngsters before him.

Dutch Life in Java To-day

Young Jan, the Burgomeester's son, we learn, has earned the lamentable distinction of being the worst boy in the school. He is incorrigible! A truly awful list of sins is his. He comes late to school, plays truant on his new bicycle, has been caught smoking cigarettes, and never learns his lessons. But—well—he is a good boy at heart (and, after all, his father is the Burgomeester).

And when Jan grins a disarming grin you feel sure that all this has happened before, and that Piet's dreaded bag is certainly not for him.

But Cornelis, an awkward, overgrown young Eurasian, takes his indictment more to heart. He shuffles nervously, and looks wretchedly this way and that for a means of escape; and it is quite clear that the chief thing the matter with him is sheer stupidity.

Little Emma, another Eurasian, has also, states the head master solemnly, been a conspicuously naughty girl. Whereupon the graceless Emma sniffs, and stares straight in front of her without a ghost of expression on her rather wooden countenance. Obviously she thinks the whole thing rather silly.

So it goes on, until all the sinners have been pilloried, and all the saints given their due meed of praise. The master sits down, and Santa, not rising, but sitting back, with a benevolent, fatherly air, stroking his long beard, takes up the tale.

He is evidently well primed beforehand, and has an excellent memory, for he duly felicitates each saint, and admonishes each sinner, by name. And though Piet, grinning all over his well-blacked face, opens wide the yawning mouth of his sack for each in turn, there is always a reprieve, and the pious hope that "next year will be better."

There follow songs in Malay and Dutch, not much

better or much worse than school songs in other lands. And Santa, with a final gesture, departs to repeat the process at half a dozen other schools, memorizing, no doubt, the names of the next list of criminals as he goes.

After his departure the company left behind adjourns to see the presents; to drink "sirop," and eat sweet cakes; and to listen to sundry mothers holding forth, with extraordinary eloquence, on the striking qualities of their own children and the peculiarities of other people's.

Dutchwomen are wonderful housewives, as all the world knows, and happily they have brought their talent for home-making with them to the Far East. I have read (and chuckled over) novels about Java, in which the heroine (obviously "no better than she should be," but the authors assure us that we could scarcely expect anything else in that "awful climate") lived a limp, perspiring life, all languor and lovers, perpetually arrayed in a kimono.

I am sorry to disappoint you, but the Dutchwoman in Java isn't in the least like that. On the contrary, like the virtuous lady in the Bible, she looks well to the ways of her household; and if you should happen to catch sight of her in her kimono, she is pretty sure to be either on her way to a bath (we have several a day in Java) after some especially strenuous piece of activity in the kitchen, or else she has donned it for the afternoon siesta, which is the custom here, as in so many other hot countries.

I have never yet come across a Dutch housewife who had fallen into the fatal habit of leaving everything to the "boys," which is so dangerously easy to acquire where labour is plentiful and fairly efficient. She has one goal in Java as she has in Holland, and that is "Perfection." And because modern Dutch homes in the East Indies are very charming, and she has everything to hand to make them more so, it may be that her housepride is, if anything, even greater than it is in her home country.

The new Colonial Dutch style of architecture is designed on an altogether more modest scale than the old. But it is just as good of its kind. The rooms are lofty, the floors tiled, and the windows large; there are usually bathrooms to each bedroom, set-in basins, and all the most shining and up-to-date of electrical devices.

Every bride migrating to the East is quite certain to bring some old family china with her. Brass, Oriental pottery, Chinese embroidery, Batik, and all such decorative adjuncts are plentiful and by no means dear, on the spot; so that the Dutch matron's task of making the "Home Beautiful" in Java is a happy one.

Every house has its "voorgalerij," a wide front veranda, which is really a sitting-room open to the air on three sides. This voorgalerij is the pride, the shop window, as it were, of every house, large and small, for, having no front wall, except perhaps a stone railing and pillars, it is in full view from the road. The walls are hung with highly polished brass, and old blue plates and dishes. There are deep armchairs and lounges, covered with soft, inviting cushions; tall palms, and masses of maidenhair fern in pots, and jars of crimson and flame-coloured cannas (for whatever flowers there may or may not be in your garden, the canna is always in evidence all the year round).

At night the houses look even more alluring; and if you walk along the road in the European quarter of any town after sundown you will see every voorgalerij aglow with deep orange or rose-colour or gold, from lights shining softly through native-made silk lampshades.

Gates of any kind are the exception rather than the rule at the entrance to Dutch homes in Java, and the fences or hedges that enclose them are usually quite low. The gardens, like the houses, are their owners' pride. It is easy to make them beautiful, for labour is cheap, and the Javanese native, a descendant of countless generations of cultivators, is a gardener by instinct.

So the householder has no diffidence or shyness at all in exhibiting his garden, with the open voorgalerij of his house in the background, to the gaze of the passer-by. Nor has he any of our British exclusiveness in regard to himself or his family. You will be sure to see them sitting reading or sewing by the light of standard lamps (shaded like those in the veranda) in the garden after dinner. And when the sacred hours of the siesta (from two to four in the afternoon) are over, tea is usually carried out by the house-boys, and dispensed by mevrouw at a little table under the trees, or in the shade of a big, gaily striped umbrella.

As soon as mijnheer arrives home from business (for him, good man, there is no afternoon sleep) he has a bath, and dons pyjamas. And then, when he has finished a leisurely tea, he will stroll, as often as not, down the drive, and stand at the entrance smoking a large cigar, affording the populace ample opportunity to appraise his often very garish taste in "slumber wear," which, by the way, in deference to this little weakness of his for disporting himself in it in public, is invariably starched.

The Dutchman's tropical kit is not quite the same as that of the Englishman. He eschews the collar and tie of our convention, and the jacket of his white drill suit, instead of the usual turn-down collar and lapels, has a stiff, straight band fitting tight round the neck like a bandsman's uniform. It is known as a "badjoe toetoep" (literally, a "shut-up jacket"), or "toetoep," for short, and is fastened round the neck with two brass studs.

Dutch Life in Java To-day

That is to say, it is designed to be so fastened. But "India" (as Java is most often called by the Dutch, to the great puzzlement at first of the English visitor) is a warm country, and Dutch necks are seldom slender. So it is rare indeed to see a toetoep that does not gape widely apart at the neck, with two bright brass studs adorning one side, and two empty studholes on the other.

When a native (by virtue of a generous education system) has attained his heart's desire of "kredja toelis" (writing work, or, in other words, a clerk's job), he also adopts the toetoep, regarding it as the outward and visible sign of his clerkly attainments. Worn as he wears it, it is both smart and becoming, and I am afraid it must be admitted that his figure is a good deal better adapted to it than those for whom it was originally designed.

In post offices, and all municipal and government offices, these dapper young native clerks abound, cool, immaculate, and slender, in spotless starched white drill toetoep, Batik turban and sarong, and highly polished brown European shoes. Java is not hot to them. Why should it be? And at the end of the long day, which leaves the white man damp and crumpled, the "djeroe toelis" (clerk) is still as cool and starched, and his collar as neatly fastened, as ever.

I suppose that every one who has ever heard of Java has also heard of "rijst-tafel," the famous national dish of the country. It is really an adaptation—or perhaps it would be more correct to say an amplification—to Dutch tastes, of the native "nasi besar," or rice feast. Rice is the staple food of the people, and the foundation of every meal; and a feast, with them, is merely the addition of as many extra dishes as possible, to mix in the inevitable bowl of soft white grain.

But gradually it has come to be far more a Dutch than

a Javanese custom. For the native only feasts on rare and special occasions, whereas to the Java Dutch it has become the standard midday meal. No hotel in Java, large or small, would dare not to serve it, and in the bigger ones, especially those that cater for tourists, it is a kind of ceremony, and a sight well worth seeing.

A long procession of table "boys" is formed, led by the "mandoer" (head boy), who bears proudly, rather like a Scotsman with a haggis, an immense bowl of rice, served boiling hot, but flaky and dry, as you get rice nowhere else but in the East.

From this the "rijst-tafler," if one may so call him, lays a solid foundation in a deep soup plate, and the fun begins. The procession approaches in single file (there may be anything up to twenty or twenty-five "boys" in it), each carrying two dishes, from every one of which you are expected to help yourself. The first on the list is always vegetable curry; and after that, in bewildering array, come fried bananas, eggfruit, potato balls, curried chicken, fried chicken, fried duck, half a dozen varieties of dried fish (each more highly scented than the last), savoury rissoles, croquettes, pasties, sausages, fried eggs, baked eggs, liver, pancakes cut into strips, skewers full of scraps resembling cat's meat (but really delicious), cucumber, chopped onion, grated coconut, chillies, "zuurjes" (little pickles), and chutneys and peanuts, and a long list of other odds and ends. Last of all comes a dish of "kroepoek" (great crinkly biscuits as big as plates, made of rice flour and flavoured with prawns) which are eaten with the mixture in place of bread.

To the visitor it is merely an amusing experience, a joke. But to the habitué it is a serious affair, with a technique of its own, a technique which, I regret to say, I have never been able to learn. I only know (from

Dutch Life in Java To-day

constant observation of my neighbours) that the various
delicacies should be arranged on a definite plan, to which
end several smaller plates are set round the central soup
plate, like planets round the sun, so that each tit-bit may
go to its appointed place. The dry ingredients are put on
one plate, the liquid on another, and the greasy on a third,
while certain items seem always to go into the central
mixture direct.

The Dutchman's and Dutchwoman's capacity for this
gargantuan dish is truly impressive. It is not at all unusual
to see rijst-taflers of either sex summon the whole procession again when their plates are empty, and fall to a
second time with equal gusto. And finally, it must not
be forgotten that the correct beverage with which to
accompany the dish is beer, and in no niggardly spirit,
either.

There are other contrasts between Java and Malaya
beside the reaction of their respective children to the
tropic sunshine. The whole "atmosphere" is different.
There is a homeliness and simplicity about Dutch life in
Java that is entirely lacking in the British colony over the
way. The Dutch love their homes and really "live" in
them, not, as do so many English in the East, regarding
them merely as places to sleep in. This homeliness is
especially noticeable in the country towns; there is something pleasant and old-fashioned about life in them, despite
all their modern comforts, a restfulness sadly rare in these
days. The Dutch are "domesticated," as the English used
to be a generation or two ago. You will often see young
married couples out for walks in the cool of the evening,
with "Vader" pushing the baby's pram, and perhaps a
youngster, the next size larger, toddling at "Moeder's"
side.

The reason is that the Dutch really "settle" in Java as

we do (or used to do) in Australia and South Africa and New Zealand. They are not, like the English in Malaya, perpetually recovering from one "leave" or getting ready for the next, with always at the back of their minds the thought of retiring to England as soon as ever they have qualified for a pension.

It seems to me a strange ambition. And the problem of why anyone should ever want to leave the eternal summer of Malaya for the almost eternal winter of England remains unanswerable! Half of the unlucky optimists die of pneumonia before they have enjoyed that longed-for retirement for a year, but even that doesn't seem to teach the poor dears common sense! The Dutch have to serve a very much longer term of years before they are granted their first leave, so that from the beginning their roots strike deeper.

I am afraid that one could go on indefinitely with these rather invidious comparisons. They are certainly somewhat odious to our British *amour-propre*, but they are none the less intriguing. It would be so interesting to know, for instance, why the Dutchmen and Dutchwomen of Java use that most practical and economic steed, the "push bike," on every possible occasion, while we English would rather die (or leave the country, "broke") than be seen on one. It is painful to reflect that the only possible reason can be that the one community is sensible, and that the other is foolishly snobbish.

There is a marked contrast, too, in the accommodation available in the two colonies. If business or pleasure takes you to either Singapore or Penang, unless you are prepared to become a householder you have only two exorbitantly expensive hotels and a few indifferent boarding houses to choose from; whereas in Batavia or Soerabaya there are small, moderate-priced hotels in almost every street. There are these admirable hotels, too, in every country town in Java; in Malaya there are only the government resthouses, with their curious regulations restricting the length of your stay.

Hotels in Java are built on what is known as the "pavilion" plan. Your room includes a bedroom equipped with running water, a bathroom, and a voorgalerij furnished with writing-table, lamps, and easy chairs, so that you can work or play at your ease, or entertain your friends. In the country a number of these small pavilions are often built in the grounds surrounding the hotel itself, an arrangement that enables you to live in your own house and yet enjoy all the comforts of hotel life. The management provide you with a personal "boy," and you can eat at home or in the hotel as you please. What is most important, there are hotels of this kind to suit all purses. For life in Java (except, of course, in the big tourist hotels, and for those people to whom "club life" is a necessity) was, before the fall of sterling, as much cheaper than life in Malaya, as it was, and is, better and more enjoyable.

It is not only in contrasts between Java and Malaya that the student of international manners will find entertainment, but also in comparing the triangle of colonies, British, French, and Dutch, in this south-east corner of Asia.

Near neighbours as they are, they have developed on strikingly divergent lines, and national qualities in each case, mingling with local conditions, have combined to produce three strangely characteristic blends.

The French, passionately home-loving, regarding all absence from their beloved country as exile, have created, wherever it was possible, a little bit of *la belle France* in the Far East; and if a Frenchman could be dropped from some magic carpet straight into Saigon or Pnom-penh he might well rub his eyes and think himself at home again. There are the same wide boulevards, with patches of gracious shade thrown by avenues of tall trees. There are the same cafés, with their little tables in the open air. There are the same glass-fronted restaurants, with their creamy, lace-trimmed blinds and, best of all, inside are the savoury dishes and goodly wines of France. But there also, sad to say, too often, are the same small and stuffy rooms, the microscopic towels, and the bathroom almost as hard of access as Mount Everest. I have even been in hotels in Indo-China where the "boys" used it as a broom cupboard! France has done so many admirable things in this Asiatic colony of hers it does seem a thousand pities that she saw fit to import her peculiar notions of domestic hygiene with the rest.

Then the Dutch, those painstaking, orderly, methodical people—the race that a recent writer has described as sharing with the Scandinavian peoples the distinction of being the most civilized in present-day Europe—have made of Java, as nearly as may be, the perfect colony. It is a sort of tropical Holland, but a Holland modified and adapted to its new environment with all the skill that human brains could devise.

And the English. Well, being English, we never bothered to design our colony at all. It simply "growed." Singapore and Penang just straggled along the water fronts as occasion and commercial interests demanded, and there they stayed. Every now and then an imposing (and very costly) building is put up wherever there happens to be room for it, and the result is (especially at Singapore) a heterogeneous jumble of godowns, blocking out the sea for miles, along what might have been one of the most beautiful sea fronts in the Empire, and Chinese

Dutch Life in Java To-day

streets that are all tangled up with imposing European shops and banks and offices.

In the matter of language, too, the characteristics of the three nations clearly show themselves. The Dutch learn languages as a matter of course when they are young, and learn them fairly easily. The English learn them only when they must, and learn them painfully. But the French (except in rare cases) learn them not at all. Thus it is that the Dutchman in the East has always learnt English at school, and so is quite at his ease when he visits British Malaya; but it would be hard to find an Englishman in Malaya who could return the compliment. The English as well as the Dutch civil servants are compelled to pass examinations in the Malay language, so that members of the Malayan Civil Service all know it fairly well; the Dutch, both men and women, speak it fluently. But it has to be confessed that the Malay spoken by all English people, except those who have learned it compulsorily, is about on a par with our very worst schoolroom French; and I am sorry to say that there are few of my countrywomen who know more than a dozen or so words of the crudest "bazaar" Malay, picked up from their Chinese servants.

But we can take heart of grace. The French in Indo-China are even worse! They have not only refrained altogether from attempting to learn Annamese or Ton-kinese (the languages most in use), on account of their admittedly great difficulty (for both belong to the Chinese group of languages), but they went a step farther, and insisted upon the poor, despised, ignorant natives learning to speak French. The astonishing thing is, that though the natives of that part of the world are by no means to be classed as "quick at the uptake," many of them do speak it after a fashion, and quite as well on the whole as the average Englishman.

264

Dutch Life in Java To-day

The British population in Java mixes but little socially with the Dutch, and keeps very much to itself. It does its best to live exactly the same life as that lived in all British colonies throughout the East. It plays bridge and golf, meets at the English clubs, drinks pahits, and signs "chits," though this last practice it cannot indulge to quite the same airy extent as in a British colony. For the Dutch tend to look askance at the "chit" system, and the word "CONTANT" (cash) looms in large letters from the walls of most garages and many other establishments throughout Java.

It is not even unheard of for a large and imposing car, left for repair, to be detained by a garage proprietor until an account in arrears is paid; nor do his finer feelings prevent him from explaining the car's presence, doubtless by way of tactful warning, to other clients.

CHAPTER TWENTY-SIX

Some Matters of no Importance

IT was not to be expected that Java could produce a crop of any kind that was not a rich one, and the crop of generally accepted errors concerning it is almost as prolific as the rest.

The idea that seems to be most firmly ingrained of all in the minds of strangers is that the climate of a tropic island must necessarily be almost unbearably hot. So much so that I read lately in a guide-book issued by a firm of well-known travel-agents the statement that "in no part of Java is it cold, and only light tropical clothing is needed." So even they evidently accept the apparently obvious, and are blandly unaware that they are broadcasting what is really a rather dangerous piece of advice to the trustful visitor, for, tropic island though Java may be, it is so mountainous that it contains surprising variations in temperature. The roads run up hill and down dale, carrying you in effect from tropic to temperate zones and back again within a very short time indeed; and those roads are so gently graded that often, though you may have been perspiring freely when you set off on a journey, you will have nothing but a sudden shiver to warn you that you have climbed several thousand feet without noticing it, especially if evening is coming on when you chance to find yourself in those higher altitudes. If they only knew it, the warning that guide-book should have added was: never motor in Java without taking a coat, to put on over the light tropical clothing aforesaid.

It is harder still to realize that tropic nights can be not only cool, but actually cold, on occasion. A good thick blanket is more a necessity than a mere luxury at any point more than two thousand five hundred feet or so above sea-level (and there are a great many towns at that altitude in Java); and at another thousand feet higher up you may well want two. I have even known a hot-water bottle not to be despised; and at one mountain resort a fellow-traveller (who was neither old nor infirm), not content with the two thick blankets provided, must needs add the mat from the bedroom floor!

It is perhaps not surprising that a greatly exaggerated respect for the tropic sun is among the popular misconceptions about Java. Yet, in actual fact, where the climate is hottest, in such places for instance as Batavia and Soerabaya, the rays of the sun are so innocuous that it is perfectly safe to go about bareheaded, even at midday. In short, according to the highest authority on the spot, Dr. Braak, Director of the Royal Meteorological Observatory at Batavia, "The intensity of the tropic sun is often overestimated. In reality it is scarcely higher than at noon in temperate latitudes."

And, what is more, there is no fear of even ordinary sunburn until you reach altitudes several thousand feet above the sea. Red and painful necks and arms do not afflict the dwellers on sea-level in these regions. It is only on the high plateaux and among the mountains that the power of the sun makes itself felt in this way, and there your bare skin will burn just as badly as in England on a fine summer day.

As well as the different climates at varying altitudes Java also boasts two distinct seasons. There is no summer and winter as we know them, but there is a marked difference between the wet (west) and dry (east) monsoons. The wet one lasts, roughly, from October to March (though the "break" at each end is anything but punctual); and the dry for the remainder of the year. At the eastern end of Java, particularly, the difference between the two seasons is very marked, for in the dry monsoon there are long spells of brilliant cloudless weather, almost reminiscent of South Africa, when the rivers dry up, the ground cracks, and there is a haze of dust in the air. At the western end, however, such spells are more unusual, and the weather for the most part is moist and showery.

Batavia has its greatest rainfall in the months of December and January. But even then there is no set-in wet weather; heavy showers usually fall in the afternoons, yet anything but an exquisite morning is a rarity. After the heaviest storm in the evening or at night the dawn invariably breaks clear and fine.

There is a great deal of thunder in Java. Its dull, rumbling growl, no louder at times than the purr of some giant cat, muttering among the mountains, is one of the most familiar of everyday sounds, and is almost always to be heard in the afternoons, when the clouds gather along the mountain-sides. It occurs more rarely at other times of the day, and never in the early morning. At Buitenzorg, forty miles from Batavia, you can hear thunder on three hundred and twenty-two days out of the three hundred and sixty-five in the year, and every day during the wet monsoon.

With these daily storms, in a country so rich in timber, trees, naturally, are often struck; but, curiously enough, they do not succumb to the blow as they do in temperate climes. Their leaves all fall off, but the tree almost always

recovers, and the branches bud again as though it were
springtime.

The thunderstorms come up with dramatic suddenness,
and they have a terrible majesty that makes them a never-
to-be forgotten experience. One moment you may be
driving along in serene summer weather, whose beauty is
only enhanced by a dark, purplish cloud shadowing the
mountains ahead. The next, you are forced to stop, shut
in by walls of rain, sitting utterly isolated, alone in a
pitifully tiny shell on the floor of a terrifying ocean of
thrashing rain, whose roar is so deafening all about you
that even the terrific crashes of thunder are drowned, and
mingle with it in one magnificent, appalling maelstrom of
sound. The avenue of trees that stretched away in front
of you is blotted out, and the incessant lightning illumines
nothing but a brilliant, silver-grey blur of falling water.

Then, just as suddenly, it is all over. You start your
engine up again (if it is as faithful an engine as mine), and
drive on down the avenue of tall trees that has appeared
again by magic, the rain-black trunks reflected in the wet,
shining roadway. In a minute or two the sun comes out.
Every leaf is glittering with raindrops. A warm, sweet
scent of drenched earth and foliage is everywhere. Clouds
of steam rise from the tarred surface of the road, until soon
it is as dry again as ever, and the storm behind you unreal
as some strange dream.

Another firmly fixed belief that I have encountered on
all sides is that in Java we are "eaten alive" by insects.
There certainly are mosquitoes, and the net is always well
tucked in around every bed. But, owing to strenuous anti-
malarial measures, they are relatively few, and such as
there are react obediently to "obat nyamok" (literally,
"mosquito medicine"), a curly green smoke-stick made
by the Japanese and sold everywhere for a few cents. It is

safe to say, at all events, that no one who has ever passed a summer in Southern Europe or in Egypt will be at all disturbed by the mosquitoes of Java.

For some reason, that hypocritically virtuous, much overrated insect, the ant, is never mentioned among the insect pests of the island, but in reality it is by far the worst of them all, the only one that causes real inconvenience. Why it should be held up as a paragon of industry is an unanswerable problem, for it is stupid, greedy, and an incurable thief; and any sluggard who obeyed the Biblical injunction to "go to" it could scarcely be blamed if his indolence were augmented by smug complacency, for he could not fail to observe that the wretched insect he was bidden to emulate possesses countless vices and not one single virtue. You yourself need have no fear of being "eaten alive" by insects in Java, but any sugar or sweets you leave about most certainly will, and so may all manner of other less likely things.

I once left a portable gramophone unopened for a month or so on a table in my room, and then one evening, yielding to a sudden desire to hear some old favourites, I put on a record and started to turn the handle. It seemed stiff, and the record, too, was revolving sluggishly. "Wants oil, of course," I said to myself, and applied some, leaving the machine turning silently to "work it in." When I looked again the gramophone, the table, and the floor all around them were black with ants. They were pouring out of the screw-hole, as though I had disturbed an ant-hill, as no doubt in effect I had. I sprayed the whole thing with "Flit," and the moving mass of black pinheads thickened, and went on so long that it seemed like a conjuring trick; and when at last it was over, we swept the corpses up in millions!

Some Matters of no Importance

The black ant is bad enough, but the infinitesimally tiny brown sugar-ant is even worse. It is so small as to be almost invisible, but its staff-work is excellent, and in the mass it can do considerable harm. For instance, a watch in a folding leather case, used as a travelling-clock, a faithful companion that had never failed me before, suddenly stopped. It was fully wound, so it was opened, to reveal the whole of the works packed tight with myriads of the tiny brown wretches, which must have crept in down the stem of the winder, presumably for no better reason than to steal the half drop or so of oil inside.

Another odd pest, which luckily appears only very rarely, is the laron, an insect something like a small dragon-fly. Every now and then during the rainy season a huge flight of these will make its appearance, and the moment you turn on the light in the evening they surround it in a cloud. Within a few minutes, as though a curse had fallen upon the unhappy things, the floor is littered with countless thousands of papery wings and with ugly little grubs, that wriggle along as though they had never known what it was to have wings in their lives. Yet could there possibly be a more cruel reversal of Nature's usual processes? What must be the sensations of a grub that only a moment ago was a dragon-fly?

There are two more varieties of insects that cannot be passed by without mention. The first you seldom see but often hear—the cheery cricket, whose "whirr-r" sometimes fills the air till it vibrates all about you. His (I say "his" advisedly, for in the cricket family it is the male, not the female, that is the loquacious one) is a characteristic note of the Java countryside, especially in the hills, and to try to locate him, even when he is within only a few inches, probably making faces at you from the leaf of a tea-bush, is as hopeless as to find the proverbial needle in a stack of hay.

The other insect, or family of insects, is that of the moths and butterflies, in which Java is extraordinarily rich. The moths are some of the biggest in the world. I once measured one that settled on my window-pane in a mountain bungalow, and it was well over seven inches from tip to tip of the wings. I have seen even larger ones caught by native children, who use the unfortunate creatures as playthings, tying them to a string and "flying" them as living kites.

The ubiquitous cockroach, I am sorry to say, finds the climate of Java very much to his taste. He revels in damp places, and is quite unable to resist the attractions of the small drain through the bathroom wall, which carries away the water splashed on the floor. He has an annoying habit of appearing from this little tunnel, at the mouth of which he stands, twitching his long, sensitive antennæ at you while you bathe. But he is quite harmless, and as he hates to tear himself away from the neighbourhood of the water, you seldom meet him elsewhere.

A Java bathroom is quite unlike any other. It has a concrete floor, and a large bath (tiled or concrete, according to the sumptuousness or otherwise of the owner's quarters) in one corner. But the bath itself is a delusion and a snare; it is, in short, not a bath at all, but a tank, from which the bather, standing on the concrete floor, is expected to pour water over himself with the dipper provided for the purpose (which varies from a delightful utensil of highly polished brass, or brass-bound teak, down to mere aluminium, galvanized iron, or enamel). It is a method of bathing learned from the natives, and is a very much pleasanter one than it sounds, in a warm climate.

THE APPROACHING STORM

THUNDERSTORMS COME UP IN JAVA, USUALLY IN THE AFTERNOON, WITH DRAMATIC SUDDENNESS AND GLORIOUS COLOUR EFFECTS. FIVE MINUTES AFTER THIS PICTURE WAS TAKEN THE WHOLE WORLD WAS BLOTTED OUT.

It should be impressed upon strangers to the country that to try to get into this bath is extremely unwise. They will probably skid, they may possibly drown; and they will certainly be most unpopular if they ever happen to mention that total immersion is their chosen method of bathing in an hotel bathroom!

It seems a natural sequence from bath to breakfast, and a Dutch breakfast as served in Java is so unlike any other that it unquestionably deserves a place in any picture of life in the island. It is not, like the famous rijst-tafel, a recognized entertainment, but an entirely domestic affair, —so very Dutch that it is met with in its true form only at houses and hotels where no English are catered for, and where, if they do come, they must do as Holland does. It is, as I said, a family affair, and as such it must be served at a communal table, even though at the same hotel you may eat-your other meals as unsociably as you please in your own undiluted company.

Down the middle of a long table, side by side, are set a number of large dishes; on about one in every three there is a square loaf of white bread cut up into thick slices. The other dishes are filled with wafer-thin slices of cold delicacies, such as liver-, garlic-, and blood-sausage, ham, tongue, smoked fish, and (most important of all) cheese; all the peculiar edibles, in fact, that garnish the windows of German or Dutch "delikatessen" shops.

Like the rijst-tafel, a Dutch breakfast has its own technique. The correct procedure is first to help yourself (always with a knife and fork, for to use "fingers" would be considered most indelicate) to a slice of bread; then to dip (also with your own knife) into the deep dish into which the butter has been melted and allowed to set; and lastly, having buttered the bread, to pile on it a generous selection of the sliced dainties. The result is known as a

"Boterham," and is eaten with the knife and fork; and I am afraid it must be added that local custom appears to dictate that it should be consumed in mouthfuls whose generosity is not at all conducive to polite breakfast-table conversation.

A fried egg may also be placed on the Boterham, and eaten in the same way; and it is curious to note that although custom forbids bread to be taken in the fingers, it permits the finger and thumb to be dipped into the open "cellars" of salt and pepper (for which no spoons are ever provided), unless the point of a knife or the handle of a fork is preferred by the more fastidious.

It is only in recent years that Java has blossomed as a "tourist resort." The worthy Dutch seem to have been awakened to the possibilities of profitable exploitation of the island's beauties by the comments of an admiring visitor, published a few years before the War, and thereupon set out in their characteristically methodical way to develop the idea as though it were a new crop or industry. A meeting was called in Batavia to consider the best means of attracting foreign tourists to the island, the outcome of which was the founding of the Official Tourist Bureau, a government institution of admirable efficiency, which smooths the path of the visitor, and supplies him with all the maps and literature that the heart of the traveller could possibly desire.

Unfortunately, however, the jam contains a large and extremely unpalatable powder. With the coming of the "slump," the regulation demanding a landing tax of a hundred guilders, which hitherto as often as not had been ignored, was not only strictly enforced but raised to a hundred and fifty, a sum which at the present exchange is not far short of £20. And the luckless visitor who obeys the summons of the official guide to "Come to

Java!" not only discovers to his chagrin that before he is allowed to land the money must be handed to the purser, but that, on landing, a "Toelatingskaart" (a sort of local passport, for which two photographs and all the usual intimate family and personal history are required) must be secured. Nor is the official undertaking to repay the money if the traveller leaves Java within six months much consolation, for he has nearly £20 less to spend, and is irritated by the flat refusal of the authorities to disgorge until the last moment on the wharf before he re-embarks, so that he sails away with a bundle of guilders which he has no means of exchanging.

It is rather difficult to account for so paradoxical a policy at a time when common sense suggests that tourist traffic would be a welcome source of revenue. But perhaps it is merely a question of temperament. It is no more unreasonable, after all, for the Dutch government to fine the traveller for coming in, and pay him to go out, than it is for the Australian authorities to subject him to rigorous cross-examination and taxation before they will allow him to take ship for another country. We English escape income tax by living abroad; but the Australian, if he dares to do the same thing, is charged a heavy "absentee tax!" Is it any wonder, in a world made up of such conflicting ideas, that the Economic Conference was such a ludicrous failure?

CHAPTER TWENTY-SEVEN

Disturbing Elements & Defensive Measures

THERE is a tendency among the Nordic races to class together all the people of any coloured Eastern race as "natives," and leave it at that. It is an error especially easy to fall into in the case of a simple-seeming people such as the Javanese, with their colourful dress and their childlike ways and beliefs. But these "quaint" people, in their gay Batik head-dresses and sarongs, no more belong all to one class than do the people of England, and there are many conflicting elements mixed up beneath that picturesque surface.

The rank and file of Java's huge population, gentle, good-natured, and tractable, are probably as contented as any in the world; as well they may be, for never in their history have they been so well off as they are to-day. It is a very long time since their ancestors fought in barbarous battles against the European interlopers; the old hatred is forgotten, and so long as they are allowed to pursue their everyday round without undue interference, and to earn enough for their simple needs, the peasants care little or not at all whether Java belongs to the Javanese or to the Dutch, or anyone else. But these very easy-going, amiable qualities of his make the Javanese highly susceptible to any influence that may come his way; and disturbing influences are not lacking, even in Java, in these latter days.

It was scarcely to be expected that so world-wide a

movement as that of Communism should ignore the possibilities of a fabulously wealthy island of over forty million inhabitants, and the emissaries of the Moscow International have long been busy in Java. There have been several rather startling disturbances within the last few years; one in Batavia itself, where a conspiracy very reminiscent of that two centuries earlier, was brought to light. There were a few casualties, and the ringleaders were arrested. They were not, however, beheaded, like their predecessors, but banished instead to New Guinea, there to build up ideal communities to their hearts' content—an enterprise which evidently failed to satisfy them, for a moving appeal was recently sent by the deportees to the government, imploring permission to return to Java.

Another tremendously potent force that is undoubtedly working beneath the surface is the ever-spreading "New Islamic Movement," with its resistless power of religious appeal; and there are many students who regard the faint stirrings of Javanese unrest as part of the gigantic re-awakening of Islamic fervour which is going on throughout the Near East, India, and Mohammedan Africa—everywhere, in fact, that the faith of the Prophet holds sway.

A third element has arisen inevitably out of the access of the Javanese to Western education. In Java, as in the rest of the modern world, there has come into being among the "intelligentsia" a nervous, restless generation, influenced by every new revolutionary idea in turn, and forming itself into groups for "discussions," in which they lash themselves into fury over all sorts of real and imaginary grievances. This same tendency to form groups and secret societies has spread downward from the upper to the lower classes, and this kind of unrest, therefore, has a very long arm.

There is also to be reckoned with, garlanded though it may be on both sides with a show of brotherhood, the spirit of the old Javanese aristocracy. The glories of the old Sultanates have vanished, all save two, whose splendours ring pitifully hollow, and whose Sultans have lost their power. But the descendants of that old nobility still possess the pride of their ancient ancestry and some, at least, of the spirit of their conquered forebears. And that spirit is still inevitably resentful; it remembers that it was the Dutch who robbed their forefathers of their royal power, and who hold it still. And this spirit, moreover, is the stronger that it has never been weakened by inter-marriage, for the early Dutch settlers had to be content with women of the humbler class. Those of noble blood would have none of them.

The old fables and beliefs of the common people, too, harmless enough in themselves, might well serve as fuel to a fire once started. There is, for instance, no Javanese but believes that if ever the two mysterious old cannon, one of which is now in Batavia, should be found lying side by side, it will mark the end of Dutch power in Java. Fortunately, native opinion veers between an old gun at Serang, in Bantam, and another at Soerakarta, as the true mate; otherwise, no doubt, some inspired agitator would have tried to unite them long before now. The Batavia gun is regarded by the natives with great reverence, and is believed to possess the power of conferring fertility. It is always half buried in pathetic, heat-faded posies of flowers; and native women are daily to be seen enlisting its aid by bringing it little offerings of cakes and incense.

So, much as though by its own volcanic mountains, the peaceful surface of Java's life is disturbed now and again by spasmodic mutterings, by murderous attacks on Europeans by plantation coolies, or by an incident such as the recent capture of a Dutch warship by its native crew, who steamed away at top speed in their stolen ship among the islands, with the rest of the colonial navy tearing after them, threatening vengeance by wireless unless the ship was surrendered. The mutineers were protesting against what they regarded as injustices in the navy pay and regulations, and offered to surrender on arrival at Soerabaya if these were amended.

But the pursuers, coming within range, dropped shells on the truant ship, killing several of the loyal Dutch officers as well as the mutineers who had overpowered them. Had it not been for this grim finale, the episode of a perfectly good warship—playing hide-and-seek round the cannibal islands, saying, in effect, "Peep Bo!" to the rest of the navy—would have been irresistibly comic; and it is more than likely that the native crew entered into the exploit as a huge joke, more out of their characteristic, childish love of showing off, than with any serious idea of mutiny. But they paid dearly for their bit of swagger, and the outcome was a clear proof that the Dutch do not feel that they can afford to regard such incidents lightly.

Quite a large army, of between thirty thousand and forty thousand mixed European and native troops, is maintained in the Dutch East Indies, distributed between Java and the other islands; and at Tjimahi, near Bandoeng, in Mid Java, there is a very charming army town, a kind of miniature tropical Aldershot, without any of its ugly features. It has shady avenues, commodious barracks, and picturesque bungalows set in pretty gardens; it is true that the Dutch colonial army and its officers may not be very generously paid, but they certainly have most attractive quarters.

I am afraid that by no possible stretch of imagination

can either the European or native "rankers" of the army in Java be called smart or soldierly in appearance. But then neither can their officers. The men are unshaven; their uniforms are baggy and shapeless; harness and equipment are dirty and uncared for; and the "army," as it straggles past on its morning exercise, the native ranks shuffling painfully in huge, unaccustomed boots, is anything but an impressive sight, except, perhaps, by virtue of numbers.

However, the native soldier, though his boots are purgatory, finds consolation in the excitement of wearing uniform in which to "cut a dash" in the eyes of his lady friends, and is obviously a very happy fellow off duty. And those to whom falls the important duty of taking the officers' chargers for their daily airing are happier men still. These horses are imported from Australia, and their turnout is somewhat of an exception to the general army average. They may not be groomed quite up to British army standards, but at least they are considerably smarter than the soldiers themselves. They pass a peaceful existence in being led proudly up and down under the shady trees by their grooms, to the manifest admiration of the populace, with only occasional short interludes of carrying a very heavyweight Dutch officer.

The second, perhaps even more important, branch of Java's defences is the Field Police, which is in effect a highly mobile army mounted on nearly a thousand motor-bicycles (which, it is gratifying to note, are nearly all of British manufacture) and ten thousand push-bicycles. They perambulate every nook and cranny of the island, and are a means of keeping the scattered population under very close observation, besides giving them a good impression of widespread organized control. This service is very popular, and native recruits are plentiful.

Disturbing Elements

It is hard to describe the native traffic police in Java. They are simply too good to be true! They would look far more at home in the *Pirates of Penzance* than they do on point-duty in real life, even in Java. No one could possibly take them seriously, and apparently nobody tries; no European, that is. You will occasionally see one of them holding up a native pony driver or cyclist, but motorists seem to ignore them completely.

They are, however, very pleased with themselves, and their equipment is certainly impressive. They carry a large and intimidating truncheon, which they flourish in their more wakeful moments, and wear a short sword slung behind them. What does it matter that it is far too rusty and dirty ever to be drawn? Their uniform is of thick dark cloth, and they slump unceasingly from one foot to the other to ease the discomfort of heavy boots on feet accustomed to go bare. The picture is completed by a wide-brimmed, shady, brown straw hat, coquettishly turned up at one side, a product of the native industry at Tanggerang. Whether these brave fellows contribute at all to the keeping of the island's peace I cannot say. But they are unquestionably a most diverting addition to the variety show of the streets.

Whatever may be said about the army and police, there is certainly no hint at all of "playacting" where the Java Air Force is concerned. Both military and civil aviation have been brought to a very high pitch of perfection indeed, and the Dutch are doubtless right in believing that this arm of their colonial defences is well worth the very large sums that are spent upon it.

At the military aerodrome at Andir, near Bandoeng, punctually at six o'clock every morning, flying practice begins, continuing for several hours; and the inhabitants of the neighbourhood are treated to a display of "stunting" equal to any that crowds elsewhere have to pay good gate money to see.

Ten or twelve 'planes in the air at a time, flying in perfect formation which never seems to vary by a hair's breadth, are so everyday a sight that not even the native population seem to think them worth the trouble of a glance skyward; nor do twists and spirals and "looping the loop," nor that horrifying manœuvre, the "falling leaf," seem to impress them in the very least.

The European residents look upon the morning aerial exercises variously, according to temperament, either as a mild entertainment or an unmitigated nuisance. It certainly is a little disconcerting to have half a dozen or more aeroplanes swooping one after the other with a deafening roar to within a few yards of your roof, leaving the coconut palms swirling and rustling behind them as though in a heavy storm. And you never feel quite sure that one fine morning one of these light-hearted young flying men may not take it into his head to land in the garden among your very best cannas; or that you will not see a 'plane fluttering just outside your bathroom window. I heard lately that the tenants of houses near the aerodrome had applied for reductions in rent, on the ground that it was just as bad as living near a railway line.

So much for the marvels of science—and the Conquest of the Air!

In civil aviation the Dutch are extremely advanced. There are daily air services all over Java, others to Singapore and Sumatra, and a weekly service between Java and Holland. They all run with the regularity of express trains; and a chart, with an arrow marking the progress of the outward and inward Batavia-Holland air mail, is published daily in the Press, so that you know exactly when letters for Europe reach their destination.

Disturbing Elements

The 'plane (Fokker three-engined monoplanes are used in this service) leaves Batavia to the minute every Friday morning at six o'clock, and on the record trip reached Holland the following Thursday afternoon at half-past four, letters for London being delivered the next morning. The scheduled time for the trip, however, is ten days. It is a little tantalizing for residents of British Malaya, whose letters take nearly three weeks, at best, to reach England; but I believe that a British service is at last to be started. Better late than never.

With the one exception of the terrible disaster to the "Olivaar" at Christmas, 1931, when five of the seven persons on board were killed, this service has been run without a hitch ever since it started three or four years ago, and its departure on its long flight is as casual as though it were a country motor-bus leaving Oxford Circus or Victoria. The passengers settle themselves, the pilots jump in, the door is slammed, a few handkerchiefs wave, and amid farewell calls of "Da-ag," "Totziens," "Goede Reis," off they roar, to shiver a week later in the chilly winds and rain of Amsterdam.

CHAPTER TWENTY-EIGHT

Modern Java—Roads, Railways & Electric Power

IT is the fashion nowadays, whenever Java is mentioned, to criticize adversely the whole administration of the island by the Dutch.

Possibly the custom has its roots in the ancient strife between the British and Dutch East India companies, but in any case I take leave to doubt whether even Raffles himself could have desired for Java a better administration than the one it enjoys at the present day.

The smooth efficiency of the public services—the roads, bridges, railways, telephone—the ordered perfection of life generally, are a never-failing source of wonder to strangers, especially to those whose conception of a tropic island and its ways is based on acquaintance with (for instance) those of the South Pacific.

Enormous sums have been spent by the Dutch in the development of the colony, as was only fitting in an island which is in itself such an inexhaustible source of wealth. The decade just before the Great War especially was one of tremendous activity, when extensions of the road, railway, and harbour systems on an immense scale were put in hand, as well as a great expansion of the government's industries and monopolies. Despite this huge expenditure, however, the even larger income derived from the colony's rich resources enabled the government to balance its budget consistently up to the War period; but the execution of their great undertakings was still in course of being carried out after the giddy rise in the prices of all imported materials, and for the first time expenditure could not be met by the revenue, and loans were floated to meet the emergency.

Although Java (with the rest of the Dutch East Indies) is politically part of the kingdom of Holland, it is autonomous so far as finance is concerned. It derives its revenue from the monopolies, which include the Madoera salt industry, opium, and pawnshops; government industries such as quinine; from its teak, rubber, and other estates; the public services—post, telegraph, telephone, railways, and harbours; and last, but by no means least, from the taxes, which gather everything and every one into their net, from the humble "push-bike" to the tennis lawn.

The roads of Java must surely be some of the most delightful highways in the world; at all events, I know of none in any country to compare with them. There are (Heaven be praised!) none of those bare, characterless racing tracks with which we have defaced the fair countryside of England; but the surface of Java's main roads is as perfect as that of any "arterial" horror, and even that of the by-roads is so excellent that if it could be reproduced on the main highways of Australia it would transcend the Commonwealth motorists' wildest dreams.

The main road from Batavia to Soerabaya, which was built in the ruthless days of Governor-General Daendels, at the cost of many thousands of native lives, is the backbone of a magnificent system that has been gradually developed, especially during the last twenty-five years, by the Dutch Works Department. There are more than two thousand miles of main motor roads, and considerably more than as much again of by-roads; the mileage is always increasing, and such gaps as there are in the system are being rapidly filled. The making of these roads in so mountainous a country has called for great engineering skill, and the grades are so easy that often it is only a pleasant freshness in the air which tells you that your car has climbed a couple of thousand feet.

From one end of the island to the other you pass through panorama after panorama of unsurpassable beauty and extraordinary interest, a living chart of varied production and industry.

Rice fields, thousands upon thousands of them, yet never two alike, spreading far across the flats, and climbing the hill-sides on watery stairways; shady plantations of rubber trees, their feet in the soft green cover crops; modestly small cassava (tapioca) fields; acres of ground-nuts; solemn, gloomy teak forests; miles of sugar-cane; kapok trees, with their queer, horizontal branches, wasting drifts of snow-white cotton on the ground; fields of sweet-scented citronella; tobacco; maize; and, high in the hills, tea, and the invaluable, insignificant-looking cinchona.

You can see all these things, and many more, from the Queen's highway, without ever leaving your car. You will pass an exquisite lake now and then, and cross bridges over rivers innumerable, hurrying down in their rocky beds, brown with the rich silt they are bringing to the rice fields. And ever in the background are the mountains, without which no Java landscape is complete.

Motorists owe much to the vigilance of the Java Motor Club, familiar to all who use the roads as the "J.M.C." This most efficient body not only sees that the roads are kept in perfect repair by the various local authorities, but surrounds the motorist with a care that is almost fatherly. There is not a sharp bend, nor a zigzag, nor a steep or dangerous hill in all those miles of mountainous country but is clearly indicated on a warning board at the road-side; there are so many of them that there is not a stretch of road of any length without one. And sometimes, when the occasion seems to call for it—when more than ordinary dangers lurk round the corner—these signs wax almost hysterical in their kindly anxiety for your safety, pouring out their whole vocabulary of hieroglyphics indicating hairpin bends and up and down hills, reminding one rather of an excited Frenchman. One of these signboards that I specially remember, on a particularly steep and tortuous road in West Java, seemed to have abandoned all attempt to specify the dangers ahead; and simply announced: "To Tjawi, many——!" followed by a whole row of terrifying exclamatory warnings.

Another invaluable service rendered by the "J.M.C." is the provision of a board bearing the name of each town or village, hung across the road from tree to tree, so that you always know, as in other countries so often you do not, exactly where you are.

On the country roads the traffic consists almost entirely of motors, and when you begin to meet pony sadoes and wagons it is a sure sign that you are approaching a town. There are many motor-bus services between all the towns, to which both the native and Chinese populations have taken very kindly. The buses are always crowded, and considering the great distances that can be travelled for a few cents, it is not surprising.

A very practical addition to the bus services is the use of "trailers" nearly as big as the buses themselves, in which vegetables, flowers, and all kinds of country produce are brought in to town to market every morning, towed behind the bus in which their growers are riding. These ungainly, heavily laden two-wheeled monsters, swaying perilously from side to side as the buses race along the quiet country roads at forty miles or so an hour, are among the most familiar sights to early morning travellers, on the outskirts of any large town.

The motor is so general a means of transport in Java, owing to the excellence of the roads, that one might be tempted to ignore its even more remarkable railway system, were it not that this adds to rather than detracts from the interest of the landscape.

The tremendously mountainous nature of the country demanded more than ordinary skill in providing it with railways, but fortunately Holland is favoured in the possession of some of the greatest of modern bridge designers. Many of the lofty viaducts that span the tremendous gorges, and sweep in splendid curves across the winding valleys, are not only miracles of skill, but, strange to say, also things of beauty. The huge pillars of metal framework that rise to giddy heights from the deep green valleys below are dwarfed by their stupendous background of mountain and forest to a fragile-seeming tracery of delicate lacework, and each of the long, curving bridges that crown them seems to rest as lightly on its slim supports as the skeleton of a great snake cleaned to the bones by a nest of ants.

There are some magnificent bridges, too, across the wide rivers of the lowlands, and some mountain climbs and scenic routes that can have few rivals in the world. There are places where the line twists upwards like a snake through narrow cuttings in the rocks, crossing gorge after gorge, each with a river shining silver among the foliage far below. Or it creeps along a narrow shelf, cut at the crest of a mountain wall, looking sheer down, more than a thousand feet, to the plain, with its chequer-board of rice fields.

There are about three thousand five hundred miles of

railways in Java altogether, some owned by the State and some by private companies. The services are well run, punctual and comfortable; and the stations have a quality that is rare among railway stations: that of being invariably ornamental, with charming little formal gardens. And what is more practical, they display the name of the station in preference to advertisements: no stranger in Java will ever have to inquire, as it is easy to believe a foreigner in England pathetically did, why all the places had the same name: "Bovril"!

There are some express trains, though not many, and for them the natives have coined the neatest of names. An express to them is a very Raja of a train: a thing of aloof magnificence, that rushes through stations, looking neither to the right hand nor to the left, royally ignoring their desire to stop it and get in. So they call it the "kereta sombong," the "proud" or "haughty" train; and in tribute to their aptness the term is in general use among Europeans.

Electricity has been developed to an astonishing extent in Java through the abundant supply of water power provided by Nature. Huge mains run straight down the mountain-sides in many places, conducting water to great turbines and power stations, and there is a network of electric cables conveying power and light all over the island.

As a result there is electric light everywhere, even in the most unexpected places—in remote mountain hotels, and humble mountain villages; and all the many sugar, tea, rubber, and other factories have electric power.

It is claimed that Malabar, the wireless station in the mountains above Bandeong, is the most powerful installation in the world. It lies snugly tucked in among the dark foliage, a big white building with a reservoir or two, and a neat little settlement of staff quarters and gardens clustered about it, in a deep narrow valley between two peaks, and its great aerial is suspended high above it across the valley, not from poles, but with its attachments embedded in the living rock.

Malabar is utterly baffling to the mind unversed in the meaning of its high technicalities; it leaves only the impression of Power: Power pent up and enormous; omnipotent to bridge time and space. The air that hums oppressively, though not loudly, all about you is charged with it; Power is latent in the very track across the floor over which you gingerly pick your way, from which a spark can be touched anywhere, as when you test the ignition of your car. The whole place is alive with Power, devastating and tremendous; even your watch you leave outside, lest its very vitals be torn from it. You can telephone home to London if you wish, but why or how I do not pretend to know; and a technical description of Malabar I cannot write. I shall not try.

The administration of Java, with that of the whole of the Dutch East Indies, is in the hands of a Governor-General, appointed by the Queen of Holland. He is supported by the "Council of the East Indies," consisting of five members; by another Council, formed of the heads of all the State Departments; and by the Secretariat.

The island is divided up into "Residencies," each of which is administered by a Dutch Resident, under whom there is a whole catalogue of native officials, including the native magistrates who preside over the native courts. The head of all these native officials is the "Regent," who is always a member of one of the old native noble families, and thus a person of great importance in native society. In the two Sultanates the Sultans retain a full outward semblance of power, but the Resident really holds the reins in his guise of "Elder Brother."

There has been some native representation since 1916, in which year the "Volksraad," or People's Council, was formed. It consists of forty-nine members, twenty of whom are natives, and is partly appointed by the government and partly elected by local assemblies. It has, however, no legislative power whatever, and is only an "advisory" body.

There is complete freedom for all religions in modern Java, a freedom that has put an end to much tiresome dissension which was formerly rife, not, as might have been expected, between Mohammedans and Christians, or natives and Chinese, but between two Christian sects, the Catholics and Protestants!

Eurasians have full European status, and there is nothing to prevent them from filling the very highest posts in the island. It is estimated that over seventy-five per cent. of the so-called European population has some admixture of native blood.

As regards the law, there is equality for all nationalities, except in so far as matters relating entirely to native life are concerned, to deal with which the old native law has been retained.

The lingua franca of Java, as of British Malaya, is "Malay," quite differently spelt from that used in the British colony, and with its vocabulary somewhat affected by the local Javanese and Soendanese languages, but fundamentally the same. Malay was the first East Indian language known to the early navigators. It was originally spoken in Sumatra, and thence was taken across the Strait by the migrating inhabitants to Malacca, where it attained considerable literary importance. There is constant mention of the Malay language in the records of very early travellers, and by the sixteenth century it was known to be in use all over the Malay archipelago. A "vocabulary" was published by the Dutch in 1603, and a dictionary for the use of missionaries was issued in Rome during the same century.

The import and export trade of Java is immense, and this small island has "contacts" with almost every part of the world. More than eighty per cent. of its trade passes through Singapore, so that the link between the British and Dutch colonies is a close one, and England and Holland are almost exactly equally large purchasers of the island's products. Neither of them, however, ranks among its best customers. These are Japan, India, and the United States of America.

CHAPTER TWENTY-NINE

A Cameo—& Cavalcade

I PULLED up one morning outside the "Telefoon Kantoor" of a small country town and sat idly waiting in the car while a friend put a call through to a house several hundred miles away, a matter which, in this exemplary island, you may accomplish at your ease in ten minutes or so, sitting in a spotless whitewashed office, in even the smallest town.

The Dutch are justly proud of their perfect wireless telephone system, and of the fact that you can speak, if you are so minded, to any place in Europe, getting through with automatic ease. A Dutch business man of my acquaintance rings up his wife in Amsterdam every Saturday evening, and never fails to emphasize the ease of the proceeding compared with the impossibility even of speaking from Singapore to Penang: an unkind cut indeed!

I really should not have minded very much that morning if a trunk call had taken ten times as long. For to sit in drowsy comfort in the shade of a great "flamboyant" tree and watch the world go by is as pleasant a way as any I know to see a true moving picture of Javanese native life.

It was the very middle of the morning, and all the world and his wife were abroad on their lawful occasions. But for all that, the street, in its setting of deep green shade from the over-arching trees, with their scarlet blossoms, was very quiet. From the school just round the corner came the drone of children's voices, no louder than the hum of bees round a hive; the busy crowds of passers-by were all afoot, and barefoot at that, or else in rubber-tyred sadoes; and the only noise to be heard was made by the patter of small, swift-trotting hoofs and the jingling bells on the ponies' harness, for in this fortunate street cars are few and far between.

The roadway is alive with people, and their noiseless movements and bright array make them seem curiously unreal; they might be the players in a coloured Pathé film. Every woman, and four out of every five men, wears a coloured sarong, in every imaginable shade and design of blue, red, green, brown, and yellow. The women's badjoes, of muslin or silk, are of brighter colours still, fastened with ornate gold and silver brooches; their scarves echo the patterned sarongs; and brilliant-hued, oil-paper Chinese sunshades throw luminous shadows on the wearers' sleekly dressed black hair and smiling brown faces.

There is slightly more variety in the men's fashions, for Western ways are reversed in Java, and here it is the woman who is the more conservative of the two. Men of the upper class pass by in sarongs of deepest red or purple silk, starched white coats buttoned round the throat, leather sandals, and the inevitable Batik head-dress. Others are in sarong and vest, in vest and shorts, in shorts or sarong only, in loose striped cotton suits like pyjamas, or in European coat and flamboyant Batik trousers; but despite the exceptions, at least nine out of every ten wear the universal native dress of badjoe and sarong. And all the Javanese men, of course, wear some kind of head-covering, their shapes varying as much as those of a Western woman's spring millinery.

Yet in spite of their delightfully theatrical "get-up," how little difference there is, when all is said and done, between these good people and ourselves! You might find just the same types, only of a different colour and in different clothes, doing exactly the same things in the street of any English country town. Coming towards me, erect and dignified, is a Javanese lady, of complexion no darker than an Italian, with a mass of glossy hair swept smoothly back into a great knot low on her neck. Her coat, of flowered muslin, is draped about with a Batik scarf, which tones harmoniously with her sarong of blue and a soft shade of brown, which in turn matches her slender bare ankles. Her sunshade is a kaleidoscopic medley of colours which has the happy knack of "going" with anything and everything, and in her free hand she carries a bunch of golden bananas.

Just as you might in the High Street at home, she meets some friends: a grey-headed old lady in red and yellow flowered sarong and black silk badjoe, and her daughter, a slender wisp of a thing, in lilac and rose. Greetings are exchanged, and eager hands dive into the recesses of long scarves to exhibit their owners' purchases, while the ladies rest their sunshades head-downward in the roadway beside the bunch of bananas. Something in the younger woman's collection greatly excites the older lady—so much so that she says she really must run back and get one too! But she has spent all her money, so, amid much chatter and laughter, the other gropes beneath her draperies, and from some safe hiding-place produces a coin, with which her friend trots gleefully back in the direction of the pasar. Probably it is "Bargain Day" at one of the local emporiums.

Next come a pathetic pair of poorer folk: a wizened little woman in sober browns, old and faded, but neat and clean, padding along at a half trot, followed by an old man, whose trot, though it keeps pace with hers, has a sort of hesitancy; and you notice that, while she avoids the sharp stones that might hurt bare feet, he never does. The reason is plain, for each of them holds the end of a short, slender piece of bamboo: the old man is blind, and she is guiding him.

A fish merchant comes up the hill, intoning "Ika-a-n" as he passes, and is stopped by a small, flower-like lady, who chooses a shining two-pound goerame from among its fellows in their bed of cool banana leaf, and stuffs it away in her already bulging selendang.

A tall Arab, probably a man of substance and of considerable local repute, is made way for respectfully by lesser folk. Wealthy he may be, but he has evidently not acquired the Javanese habit of soap and water.

An odd figure follows. He wears a starched white coat, a pair of pyjama trousers cut off at the knee, his sarong draped over one shoulder, and a white solar topee perched on the top of his Batik head-dress. A thick gold chain and fob complete his toilet, and he carries a smart Malacca cane, with which he occasionally smites his shapely bare calves. A gay dog, evidently, and as confident that he is irresistible as any gay Parisian.

An earnest-looking youth, his costume faultlessly European to the waist except for his head-dress, but adorned from the waist downward in a gorgeous pair of baggy Batik trousers patterned with crimson roses, rides slowly past on an obviously brand-new bicycle, followed by admiring glances from every side. A bullock-cart comes creaking slowly past, drawn by two cream-coloured oxen with dark, dreaming eyes, the driver's sarong twisted up to show nondescript trousers, reaching half-way to his ankles, as he walks alongside.

A sturdy fellow, with three skinny chickens in each of the baskets that hang from his pikoelan, stops and asks me to buy one, assuring me that it is really very fat! He seems surprised and a little hurt that I should refuse. And a neatly dressed old man, with black coat above his dark sarong, asks me for money (more, I think, by way of being polite to a stranger than anything else, for beggars are rare in Java), and overwhelms me with gratitude for a few copper cents.

It was all like a scene in some Eastern play, a restful, pleasant play, with no disturbingly dramatic action. And it set one idly wondering just how much the scene and the players in it might have changed in, say, the last thousand years or so; and whether very much the same types as these that had been unconsciously entertaining me might not have been drifting up and down, perhaps along this very lane, across the stage of everyday Javanese life, for many hundreds of years.

Changes there had been, of course: changes wrought by the various conquerors who had come, been gradually absorbed, and then vanished off the stage again, to be replaced by others who in their turn ruled, mingled, and fell; while all the time the same native type persisted (with always a few bold spirits adopting the modern innovations and fashions of the time), but little affected in the main by the adventurers who one after another had come seeking the wealth of this treasure island.

First the Indians, bringing with them architecture and literature, the faiths both of Brahma and the gentle Buddha, the tricks of trading, and the splendour and the evil of courts; intermarrying with the natives and producing a mixed race which (for all we know) was regarded in its time much as the Eurasians are to-day. But most things settle down in a thousand years: the Indians ruled in Java for far longer than that, and it is certain that every one had long forgotten that the race had ever been "mixed" at all, and had accepted the established order of things as permanent and static, centuries before the coming of the Arab missionaries and conquerors put an end to Indian rule.

Then once again the Javanese watched the setting of the stage being changed about them: saw mosques appearing in every town, and the great temples of Brahma and Buddha falling into ruin; the splendours of new courts rising from the ashes of the old; and accepted and absorbed it all, including its new God, until, in the course of a few generations, this new regime too seemed fixed and unalterable.

Then came the white man, and though the mosques and all that they stood for remained, the reign of the Mohammedan conquerors, short compared with that of the Indian Hindus and Buddhists, was over. For though it is just possible that the immediate entourage of the "reigning" Sultans of Solo and Djokjakarta may believe in their royal masters' power, to the rest of the native population the Dutch are as much "kings" as were ever the other conquerors that came before them. And this new scene that they have set for the island's life, with its concrete buildings, and roads and railways and motor-buses, has now in its turn become the established and apparently unchangeable order of things.

But that through it all the native is still practically the same as he has always been is proven by his close resemblance to the Badoejs of Bantam, the remnant of the oldest known race in the island, whose religion and customs date back to pre-Hindu times—perhaps two thousand years—and who have avoided contact with the rest of the Javanese world for centuries. The few who have succeeded in visiting them (there are said to be only fifteen living persons who have done so, although their jungle stronghold is not far from Batavia) say, and the photographs that they have taken prove, that in physical appearance and dress and manner these people differ little from the simplest type of modern Javanese peasant (such, for instance, as the old blind man who passed just now). They wear a knotted head-cloth, and badjoe and sarong of roughly handwoven cotton cloth, exactly as their ancestors must have done for thousands of years (for they came in contact with no other fashions), and very much as the poorest native does still.

And if all the successive influences of these different mighty invaders have altered the Javanese race so little, there seems no reason why the descendants of the people I had been watching should not continue to go about their affairs in the centuries to come very much as they do to-day in this neat Dutch town, and very much as their ancestors did in the days of the Indians and the Arabs, whatever new scene may be set for them, and whatever the turn of Fortune's wheel may bring.

It was so pleasant a subject for speculation that when my passenger reappeared I was almost sorry. I had been looking at a perfect little cameo of native life, and it had reminded me for the hundredth time that when your home is in Java, be your business or personal anxieties what they may, life can never be dull or monotonous. You need no theatres or cinema shows to distract your mind from tiresome preoccupations, for the show, a non-stop variety of infinite charm and interest, is all around you as you go about the ordinary avocations of the day. Entertainment is yours on every hand for the mere trouble of looking at it, if you have eyes to see.

A hundred varied types come on the stage and play

their brief parts before you, passing too swiftly to be noted down, arousing your interest, piquing your curiosity. The whole history of the East, with its ancient beliefs, its strifes and conquests, is written there for you to decipher if you will.

Javanese, Soedanese, Madoerese, Malay, Chinese, Arabs, Armenians, Japanese, with Heaven only knows what racial and religious fusions behind them; the Dutch, whose master-hand, beneficent in the present as it was cruel in the past, has moulded Java into the world's model colony; British, Germans, Danes, Swiss, and Americans, with their commercial enterprises that are the very soul and spirit of modern history. There they all go, yourself among them, urged forward by the Moving Finger towards an unknown destiny; all part of the cavalcade that travels tirelessly through the green and lovely transformation scenes of the Java Pageant.

I N D E X

301

Index

Index

Index

Index

J. AND J GRAY, PRINTERS, EDINBURGH. 1934

Some other Oxford Paperbacks for readers interested in Central Asia,
China and South-East Asia, past and present

CAMBODIA

GEORGE COEDÈS
Angkor

MALCOLM MacDONALD
Angkor and the Khmers*

CENTRAL ASIA

PETER FLEMING
Bayonets to Lhasa

ANDRÉ GUIBAUT
Tibetan Venture

LADY MACARTNEY
An English Lady in Chinese
Turkestan

DIANA SHIPTON
The Antique Land

C.P. SKRINE AND
PAMELA NIGHTINGALE
Macartney at Kashgar*

ERIC TEICHMAN
Journey to Turkistan

ALBERT VON LE COQ
Buried Treasures of Chinese
Turkestan

AITCHEN K. WU
Turkistan Tumult

CHINA

All About Shanghai: A Standard
Guide

HAROLD ACTON
Peonies and Ponies

VICKI BAUM
Shanghai '37

ERNEST BRAMAH
Kai Lung's Golden Hours*

ERNEST BRAMAH
The Wallet of Kai Lung*

ANN BRIDGE
The Ginger Griffin

CHANG HSIN-HAI
The Fabulous Concubine*

CARL CROW
Handbook for China

PETER FLEMING
The Siege at Peking

MARY HOOKER
Behind the Scenes in Peking

NEALE HUNTER
Shanghai Journal*

GEORGE N. KATES
The Years that Were Fat

CORRINNE LAMB
The Chinese Festive Board

W. SOMERSET
MAUGHAM
On a Chinese Screen*

G.E. MORRISON
An Australian in China

DESMOND NEILL
Elegant Flower

PETER QUENNELL
Superficial Journey through
Tokyo and Peking

OSBERT SITWELL
Escape with Me! An Oriental
Sketch-book

J.A. TURNER
Kwang Tung or Five Years in
South China

HONG KONG AND MACAU

AUSTIN COATES
City of Broken Promises

AUSTIN COATES
A Macao Narrative

AUSTIN COATES
Myself a Mandarin

AUSTIN COATES
The Road

The Hong Kong Guide 1893

INDONESIA

DAVID ATTENBOROUGH
Zoo Quest for a Dragon*

VICKI BAUM
A Tale from Bali*

'BENGAL CIVILIAN'
Rambles in Java and the Straits
in 1852

MIGUEL COVARRUBIAS
Island of Bali*

AUGUSTA DE WIT
Java: Facts and Fancies

JACQUES DUMARÇAY
Borobudur

JACQUES DUMARÇAY
The Temples of Java

ANNA FORBES
Unbeaten Tracks in Islands of the
Far East

GEOFFREY GORER
Bali and Angkor

JENNIFER LINDSAY
Javanese Gamelan

EDWIN M. LOEB
Sumatra: Its History and People

MOCHTAR LUBIS
The Outlaw and Other Stories

MOCHTAR LUBIS
Twilight in Djakarta

MADELON H. LULOFS
Coolie*

MADELON H. LULOFS
Rubber

COLIN McPHEE
A House in Bali*

ERIC MJÖBERG
Forest Life and Adventures in the
Malay Archipelago

HICKMAN POWELL
The Last Paradise

E.R. SCIDMORE
Java, The Garden of the East

MICHAEL SMITHIES
Yogyakarta: Cultural Heart of
Indonesia

F.M. SCHNITGER
Forgotten Kingdoms in Sumatra

LADISLAO SZÉKELY
Tropic Fever: The Adventures of
a Planter in Sumatra

EDWARD C. VAN NESS
AND SHITA
PRAWIROHARDJO
Javanese Wayang Kulit

MALAYSIA

ISABELLA L. BIRD
The Golden Chersonese: Travels
in Malaya in 1879

MARGARET BROOKE
THE RANEE OF
SARAWAK
My Life in Sarawak

HENRI FAUCONNIER
The Soul of Malaya

W.R. GEDDES
Nine Dayak Nights

C.W. HARRISON
Illustrated Guide to the Federated
Malay States (1923)

BARBARA HARRISSON
Orang-Utan

TOM HARRISSON
Borneo Jungle

TOM HARRISSON
World Within: A Borneo Story

CHARLES HOSE
The Field-Book of a Jungle-Wallah

CHARLES HOSE
Natural Man

W. SOMERSET
MAUGHAM
Ah King and Other Stories*

W. SOMERSET
MAUGHAM
The Casuarina Tree*

MARY McMINNIES
The Flying Fox*

ROBERT PAYNE
The White Rajahs of Sarawak

OWEN RUTTER
The Pagans of North Borneo

OWEN RUTTER
The Pirate Wind

ROBERT W. SHELFORD
A Naturalist in Borneo

CARVETH WELLS
Six Years in the Malay Jungle

SINGAPORE

RUSSELL GRENFELL
Main Fleet to Singapore

R.W.E. HARPER AND
HARRY MILLER
Singapore Mutiny

MASANOBU TSUJI
Singapore 1941–1942

G.M. REITH
Handbook to Singapore (1907)

C.E. WURTZBURG
Raffles of the Eastern Isles

THAILAND

CARL BOCK
Temples and Elephants

REGINALD CAMPBELL
Teak-Wallah

ANNA LEONOWENS
The English Governess at the
Siamese Court

MALCOLM SMITH
A Physician at the Court of Siam

ERNEST YOUNG
The Kingdom of the Yellow Robe

* Titles marked with an asterisk have restricted rights.